# THE

# LIVELY

# IMAGE:

4 Myths in Literature

Richard E. Hughes

Winthrop Publishers, Inc.
Cambridge, Massachusetts

*Library of Congress Cataloging in Publication Data*

Hughes, Richard E
  The lively image.

  Includes bibliographical references.
  1.  American literature—20th century—History and
criticism. 2.  English literature—20th century—History
and criticism. 3.  Mythology in literature.
4.  American literature. 5.  English literature.
I.  Title.
PS228.M9H8    820′.9′37    74–22190
ISBN 0–87626–500–X

Illustrations and cover design by Roger Stearns

*Copyright © 1975 by Winthrop Publishers, Inc.*
17 Dunster Street, Cambridge, Massachusetts 02138

# CONTENTS

# PROLOGUE

Over the past several years, there have been two cultural developments that have especially jostled my curiosity. One of these phenomena has been the abounding interest in "getting in touch with one's self." It is as if our interest has turned away from that world *out there*, and become more fascinated by the world *in here*, to put this inner space into a better condition and to live there more comfortably. This interiorness of ours has brought about significant alterations in our social behavior (greater stress on intimacy and on human relationships as means of self-discovery), in our spiritual interests (less institutionalized, more personalistic), in our literature (increasingly self-conscious and confessional), in the reasons we have for our various side-interests ("I want to find the real me"). Unfortunately, much of the phenomenon has become "trendy," commercialized by the exploiters who market everything from tooth-paste to religious movements with promises of Self-Realization. But for all the cheapening, the phenomenon exists, and must be counted as one of the characteristics of this generation.

The second development has been the renewal of interest in myth and mythology. "Myth" has become one of our code words, signifying a particular value or interest or eccentricity. New novels are touted as having "mythic significance," a film director is credited with fashioning "a new myth," diplomatic strategies are hailed as being of "mythic dimensions." Courses in mythology permeate our universities, and the publishing industry seems to have found an insatiable market, greedy for everything from anthologies of classical myths to re-organizations of traditional literary material into mythological categories. The current fascination with occultism, with the para-rationality of magic, astrology, witchcraft and the like, could not be completely cataloged without including the present preoccupation with myth.

In a sense, this book is devoted to suggesting that these two cultural developments, the stress on self-awareness and the strong interest in mythology, have something to do with each other. The central theme of the book is: if you study myth, you study yourself. A proper apprehension of myth ultimately requires that you look within yourself. Myth comes from and leads back to the interior.

Out of the near-infinity of myths that might have been chosen to demonstrate the point, I have selected four: the myths of Narcissus, Dionysos, Orpheus and Christ. There are two reasons I have for such a choice. In the first place, to read these particular myths in succession is to see the gradual unfolding of *selfhood*, for each myth presents a different stage of personality development, from the psychologically infantile to the totally fulfilled. In the second place, these four myths are strikingly rich in literary possibilities. Their themes are wonderfully amenable to literary treatment; and since I believe that literature is the most satisfying revelation of the whole human experience, I naturally opted for those myths having a rich literature to support them.

A special comment might be made on my choice of the Gospel of St. Matthew as the fourth "myth" in the series. My identification of Christ as the apex of the pattern that sequentially reveals itself in these myths is not doctrinal, it ought not be taken to mean that I offer traditional Christianity as the necessary termination of the search for self. My own tradition is Western and Christian, and I prefer to deal with a representative of wholeness and complete self-realization with whom I am familiar. Were I a Hindu, I should write of Brahman, a Buddhist I should write of Buddha. Beyond this, I find myself mightily impressed by the literary values of St. Matthew's narrative of Christ.

As to the Interludes that follow on each of the chapters: they are what their name implies, a playing-between-times. They are a chance for the mind to play with each of the myths in a new costume, to see how the myths take on new shapes. A myth is supposed to edge the imagination over into new perceptions and I hope these interludes will do just that.

# Introduction

# APPROACHING

# MYTH

For something that has been with us for so long—it is probably not much younger than language itself—myth is surrounded by an amazing disarray of opinions and theories. To most people, "myth" is synonymous with "superstition," "falsehood" or "connivance." So we hear "the myth of Victorian prudery," "the myth of the complete soybean diet," "the myth of the Miami Dolphins' invincibility," and the like; and always the intimation is that *myth* equals *deception* or, at the very least, *misapprehension.*

Those who take myth more seriously and try to define it sound like the blind men describing an elephant: it's very like a tree, much like a wall, like a snake. One sympathetic definer has commented (with, perhaps, a touch of desperation), "Looking at the matter coldly, unintoxicated and unentranced, I am willing to prophesy that fifty theobotanists working for fifty years would make the current theories concerning the origins of much mythology . . . as out of date as pre-Copernican astronomy. I am the more willing to prophesy, since I am, alas, so unlikely to be proved wrong."[1] There is apparently no end to man's ingenuity in assembling definitions to deal with that mercurial mass, myth. So, we are told that myth is the mind at play; that myth is a form of primitive science; myth is a disease of language; a way of maintaining tribal identity; a transformation of dull reality into a glowing super-reality; a defense mechanism against the confusions of existence; a way of making contact with our origins; an utterance of the unconscious; a preparation for life.[2] Beginnings, middles and ends—origins, structures and functions—have all been examined.[3] The role of myth in serious and pop literature, in contemporary advertising and politics, and in religion has been scrutinized.[4] It's altogether likely that new approaches, new assessments and even new histories of myth will be written in the wake of the women's liberation movement, since the chief myths that have been preserved are strangely male-dominated.[5]

The state of the art of comprehending myth is, to put it simply, fluid and contradictory. There is no way to reduce myth to a single system, whether it be cultic, anthropological, psychological, or whatever. Myths are engendered in the same place that dreams and poems are born, and that place has never been completely charted by any analytical explorer. The best we can do is annotate the suburbs, marking the inner territories as the medieval cartographers did those unexplored land masses on their maps: *Here there be tygers.*

From the little we can tell about that place where there be tygers, a singular discipline is in effect there. Bits and parts of experience that don't seem to have much to do with one another in the ordinary way of things come together and merge. Identities and offices change, times and places shift. A stallion in an open field might turn into Death; a flower might become a woman's face; nouns might become verbs and verbs become adjectives. Such happenings are unthinkable in stable geographies, where objects and events remain fixed long enough for us to classify and define them; but not so in a dream or a poem (or a myth). In *that* place, there are far more identities, interconnections and interpenetrations. When the poet John Donne described the love between a man and a woman as a phoenix (as he did in "The Canonization"), he perceived an identity between a self-renewing, bisexual legendary creature who regularly arose from the fire of its own destruction, and the mutually sustaining and continuing passion of true lovers. In his dream of liberation, Martin Luther King perceived an identity between freedom from bondage in the Old Testament Exodus and in twentieth century America. This sense of a shared identity among separate events is the primary vision of myth, too, as it is with poetry and dreams.

For myth is the detector of the long, slow rhythms of human behavior that drum beneath the staccato beats of temporality. Myth sees history not as a series of isolated events, but as a continuum, a pulse that moves beneath the episodic janglings. Myth catches the constants in human actions, reflects the shared identity of a woman conceiving a child, a family planting a crop, an Aeneas founding a city, a Milton writing an epic poem, an astronaut touching down on the moon. Mythic awareness begins with believing in what James Joyce called "the grave and constant" in life.

When the grave and the constant are acceptable to a given society, then myth is accepted as a celebrant. In contemporary America, for instance, we still openly accept the grave and constant desire for revelation and deliverance from the darkness. Consequently, we go on retelling the Prometheus myth. Prometheus, we recall, defied Zeus, who did not want the human race to have the gift of fire; but Prometheus stole fire from the Olympian forge and carried it to earth. In retaliation Zeus had Prometheus chained to a mountain, with no escape from the elements or from wild animals and birds. Prometheus is hero and martyr, martyrdom being the price paid for delivering the gift. The Berrigans, the Kennedys, Malcolm X, Martin Luther King have been our Prometheus. The myth serves as a definer and a celebrator of a force in our society.

On the other hand, it is not always to the advantage of a given society to make the grave and constant a part of its structure. Myth sometimes serves not as public celebrator but as underground sybil, keeping us nervously aware of something excluded by erupting every so often and declaring itself. A short time ago a national publication described a Rolling Stones concert as a rematch between Apollo and Marsyas. In Greek legend, Marsyas was a rough satyr who dared to challenge Apollo to a musical contest. When Marsyas lost, Apollo had him flayed alive, and hung his skin on a pine tree. The reappearance of Marsyas (called now Mick Jagger) in the aggressively ordered Apollonian world of Lawrence Welk and commercial deodorants, most of whose inhabitants would gladly flay him and hang his skin out to dry again, is a reminder out of the underground that we've been ignoring one of the grave constants, in this case demonic energy that won't be compromised or co-opted.

The sense of patterns being repeated, of the recurrent identities of events, is mythic consciousness. Teilhard de Chardin's description of "super consciousness" is strikingly similar: "We are faced with a harmonised collectivity of consciousness equivalent to a sort of superconsciousness. The idea is that of the earth not only becoming covered by myriads of grains of thought, but becoming enclosed in a single thinking envelope so as to form, functionally, no more than a single vast grain of thought on the sidereal scale, the plurality of individual reflections grouping themselves together and reinforcing one another in the act of a single unanimous reflection."[6] Mythic consciousness denies separateness, apprehending instead a communalism of human affairs no matter how widely separated in time, space, or cultures. To those who can tolerate atomic existence and the self-cloistered living styles of contemporary life, "mythic conscious-ness" is a dangerous simplification, an ignoring of complexities and differences. To those who reject the partitioning and classifying that goes on in corporate society, "mythic consciousness" is a "renewal of a lost insight,"[7] a reawakened awareness of kindredship. In *Symbols of Transformation*, Carl Jung distinguished between "reality-thinking," a cause-effect, analytic thought, and "synnomic" thinking, which is non-linear, non-teleological, multi-referenced. In short, mythological thinking. When we think mythically we recreate the oldest mental behavior of our species, we make contact with our earliest and most natural thought processes.[8]

Whichever the attitude, whether we suspect or welcome it, mythic consciousness is a fact, a *datum* that cannot be ignored. But such consciousness, by itself, is not sufficient to create *myth*. Churchyards may indeed contain mute, inglorious Miltons, as Thomas Grey imagined; but without a voice, a language, poetic visions do not become poems; and mythic consciousness does not become myth without a vehicle of its own. The necessary vehicle is movement, either narrative or dramatic. Myth is a lively image, not a static one. For myth to come into being, the apprehension of identities and recurrences must be wedded to movement. A "myth" that does not move through a storyline is no myth at all. Prometheus cannot be detached from his tale of courage, gift-giving, and punishment; and Prometheus cannot be reincarnated unless his new self is enmeshed in the same table. (This is one reason bogus myths are so detectable. They have no weight of telling and retelling behind them, but are manufactured for an occasion. What venerable narrative is retold by the Victorian prude or the soybean?)

Consequently, for a myth to be it must be told; and for a myth to be understood, the symbols within the tale need to be understood. The story itself may be envisioned as moving horizontally through time. (This happened, and then this, and then this.) The constant factors, the symbolic spines that resist the temporal and the changing, stand vertically. The structure of a full myth is so:

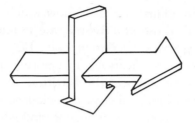

Comprehension of a myth requires both movement and penetration—movement for it to be a myth, penetration to understand the myth.[9] The details of the horizontal sequence are changeable, and reflect changes over time and of place. The details of the vertical symbolic stanchions are constant, reflecting the constant unity of human action.

This wedding of flux and constancy need not be ponderous, monumental, or calculated. Myths can be reborn even in the most casual and entertaining and frivolous of circumstances. When we think of myth, we too often think in terms of the massive, a Milton recreating Genesis for instance. But myth can be lighthearted, too. Consider an episode in the life of King Midas, the same unfortunate whose touch turned everything into gold. Midas, who was a follower of Dionysos, was one of those who attended the competition between Apollo and Marsyas. Even after Apollo had been declared the victor, Midas took exception to the judgment of the umpire, the river-god Tmolus. Tmolus retaliated by giving Midas a pair of donkey's ears. For a long while Midas was able to hide the deformity under a tall cap, but eventually the secret was discovered—by Midas' barber. The secret was too good to keep, but the barber rightly suspected that if he blabbed he'd be killed by Midas. So, to release the tension of having such a fine story to tell, the barber dug a hole in a river-bank and shouted into it, "Midas has donkey's ears!" Relieved of his secret, the barber filled in the hole and went away feeling secure. But a reed grew from the river bank, and when it rustled in the wind, the reed repeated the barber's words for all to hear. Disgraced and outraged, Midas executed the barber and then took his own life.

It's a good story, with an intriguing blend of comedy and melo-drama. It also has serious symbolic components, particularly the an-tagonism between order and disorder (Midas, a follower of mad Dionysos, judged against Apollo) and the irreversibility of divine judgment (Apollo was declared the winner by a river-god who would tolerate no nonsense from the contrary Midas).

Consider now one of Agatha Christie's fine detective stories, A Murder is Announced, featuring Miss Marple, the antiquated spinster-sleuth. Inhabitants of a small English village are puzzled by an an-nouncement in the local newspaper that a murder will take place at 6:30 that evening at the home of Laetitia Blacklock, and friends are invited. Laetitia is only recently arrived but already well-liked, a gracious lady who lives with an old friend Dora. People arrive from the village, curious to see what will happen. At precisely 6:30 the lights go out, and a masked figure appears in the doorway and shines a powerful spotlight on the roomful of surprised people. Two shots are fired. The figure in the doorway turns, there is another shot, and he falls to the floor. When candles are lighted, the visitors see Laetitia with blood flowing from her ear-lobe, two bullet holes in the wall near her head, and the gunman, a stranger, evidently a suicide with a revolver lying next to his body.

At first, it seems a simple affair to the police. The intruder tried to kill Laetitia Blacklock, then killed himself. But Laetitia insists she doesn't know the intruder and would-be murderer. Why the elaborate charade of inviting neighbors to a killing? And why is old friend Dora so upset?

As the police investigation proceeds, more complications arise. Laetitia will soon inherit a great fortune from her now-defunct em-ployer, the estate to come to Laetitia as soon as the employer's still living but mortally ill wife dies. Should Laetitia predecease the wife, the inheritance will go to the old employer's niece and nephew. Be-fore any of this can be sorted out there are two more killings: first, old friend Dora and second, a certain Miss Murgatroyd who kept dithering that she had seen someone leave the room just before the shots that killed the intruder were fired. The constabulary is stumped.

Ancient Miss Marple solves all the problems. She deduces that

Laetitia Blacklock is not herself at all, but is really Charlotte Black-lock, sister of Laetitia. Charlotte had had a goiter on her neck through most of her youth, and had shunned society, becoming almost a re-cluse. Finally, the real Laetitia had taken her sister to a hospital in Switzerland where the goiter was removed, leaving a scar. Soon after, Laetitia died suddenly of influenza, thereby losing out on the fabulous inheritance. Charlotte saw her chance and took it: she assumed her sister's identity and the fortune that was soon to go with it. All that was required was that no one who knew her as Charlotte ever see her again.

But a young orderly from the Swiss hospital turned up in the remote English village where Charlotte-Laetitia had settled. It would only be a matter of time before he told what he knew, once he noticed that the villagers referred to Miss Blacklock as *Laetitia* and not as *Charlotte*. Before it came to that, Miss Blacklock talked him into helping her play a little trick on her friends (for a fee, of course). He would come to her house, frighten them a bit, and then disappear. A nice night's prank, a way of livening up a dull evening. But in the darkness Miss Blacklock slipped behind him, fired two bullets at where she had been standing to make it seem that she had been the intended victim, and then killed the man who could betray her secret.

Next came Dora, who knew the difference between Charlotte and Laetitia and who, growing senile, kept making slips. Miss Murgatroyd had to be disposed of because she knew that Miss Blacklock had not been in the spot where, supposedly, she had been shot at. Miss Mur-gatroyd was on the verge of discovering the whole truth, so she had to be done in.

Once Miss Marple deduced all this, the police led off the murderer, whereupon the inheritance could go to the rightful heirs. The original intention of the will is satisfied.

If the Midas story is compared with A *Murder is Announced*, there are obvious differences. The time, the setting, the customs, most details have changed between the Greek tale and the English detec-tive novel. Most, but not all. They share the element of a contest (Apollo vs. Marsyas, Laetitia vs. Charlotte), a judgment is delivered in both (Apollo wins the contest, Laetitia is to have an inheritance), the loser is disfigured (Marsyas is flayed, Midas gets donkey's ears, Charlotte is scarred), the loser attempts to disguise the disfigurement (Midas' cap, Charlotte's pearl choker), but a confidant discovers the secret (the barber, Dora), surreptitiously announces it (the barber's hole in the river bank, Dora's slips of the tongue), and all the principals pay the penalty (Midas and the barber die, Charlotte is captured, and Dora dies), so that the original judgment is left intact (the river-god's decree is upheld, the inheritance reaches the proper heirs). For all the *horizontal* changes, the *vertical* values are the same: order vs. disorder, and the irreversibility of a powerful judgment. The myth still lives in spite of all the changes that have occurred between Midas and Miss Marple.

This is how myth exists, on the two planes of time and symbol, change and constancy, reminding us of "the plurality of individual reflections grouping themselves together and reinforcing one another in the act of a single unanimous reflection."[10]

# NOTES

1. Mary Barnard, *The Mythmakers* (Ohio, Ohio University Press, 1966), p. 24.

2. These definitions of myth will be found, in order, in: Mary Barnard, *The Mythmakers;* Andrew Lang, *Custom and Myth* (1885); Max Muller, *Contributions to the Science of Mythology* (1897); Bronislaw Malinowski, *Myth in Primitive Psychology* (1926); Richard Weaver, *Visions of Order* (1964); Clyde Kluckhohn, "Myths and Rituals," in *Myth and Literature,* ed. John Vickery (1966); Mircea Eliade, *Cosmos and History* (1954); Carl Jung, *Two Essays on Analytical Psychology* (1928); Joseph Campbell, *Myths to Live By* (1972). An historical survey of changing definitions of myth was undertaken by Richard Chase in *Quest For Myth* (1949), and a critical review of leading theorists of myth is G.S. Kirk's *Myth: Its Meaning and Functions in Ancient and Other Cultures* (1970).

3. On the origins of myth, the work of Gilbert Murray and Jane Ellen Harrison (e.g., *Five Stages of Greek Religion* (1926), *Prolegomena to the Study of Greek Religion* (1903), and *Themis* (1912); on the structure of myth, Claude Levi-Strauss, *Structural Anthropology* (1963), and

Northrop Frye, *Fables Of Identity* (1963); on the function of myth, Paul Ricoeur, "Symbolic Functions of Myth," *The Symbolism of Evil* (1967).

4. Daniel Hoffman's *Barbarous Knowledge* (1967) is an illuminating essay on myth in the poetry of W.B. Yeats, Robert Graves, and Edwin Muir. D. Streatfeild's *Persephone: A Study of Two Worlds* (1959) analyzes popular detective fiction as myth. Harry Slochower's *Mythopoesis: Mythic Patterns in the Literary Classics* (1970), and Walter Strauss' *Descent and Return* (1971) present a broad survey of the place of myth in serious literature. Raphael Pati's *Myth and Modern Man* (1972) relates myth to contemporary political and cultural behavior. Alan Watts' *Myth and Ritual in Christianity* (1953) is a good place to begin on an immensely complicated topic.

5. If a feminist history of myth is attempted, it will have to take into account Esther Harding's important *Woman's Mysteries*, an historical and psychoanalytic study of female myths, rituals, and dreams.

6. Teilhard de Chardin, *The Phenomenon of Man* (New York, Harper and Row, 1965), pp. 251–52.

7. Owen Barfield, *Saving the Appearances: A Study in Idolatry* (New York, Harcourt Brace, n.d), p. 184.

8. Carl Jung, *The Collected Works of C. G. Jung*, edited by G. Adler, M. Fordham, W. McGuire, and H. Read, translated by R.F.C. Hull, Bollingen Series XX (copyright (c) 1956 by Bollingen Foundation), volume 5, p. 23. Reprinted by permission of Princeton University Press.

9. The two-dimensionality of myth has been brilliantly elucidated by Claude Levi-Strauss in *Structural Anthropology*. His analysis of the legend of the House of Thebes in such horizontal-vertical terms demonstrates the thesis: Horizontally we tell the myth, vertically we understand the myth.

10. Teilhard de Chardin, *The Phenomenon of Man*, p. 252.

# 1

## The

## NARCISSUS

## Myth

It happened one day that Jove and Juno had an argument over who had the greatest pleasure in love-making, Jove insisting it was the woman, Juno saying it was the man. To settle the dispute, they decided to let Tiresias judge the question. Tiresias was an excellent choice as umpire. Once, on striking two snakes that he found coiled in intercourse, he had himself been changed into a woman. Seven years later, he found the same snakes, struck them again, and was returned to his male state. Having lived as both man and woman, he was in the best position to decide the quarrel.

Tiresias gave his judgment that the woman has the most pleasure in love. Enraged that she lost the argument, Juno struck Tiresias blind. Jove, to soften the misfortune, gave Tiresias the gift of prophecy.

One of the first to test Tiresias' new powers of foretelling the future was the water nymph Liriope, who had been assaulted by Cephisus, and had given birth to a boy-child, whom she called Narcissus. Liriope asked Tiresias how long her child would live, and the seer replied: to very old age, provided he never came to know himself. Just what the prophecy meant didn't become clear until later on.

By the time he reached young manhood, Narcissus had become incredibly beautiful, loved and sought after by everyone. One of those most deeply enamored of him was Echo, herself a victim, like Tiresias, of Juno's anger. Echo had once kept Juno involved in conversation so that she wouldn't discover Jove at one of his frequent dalliances with other women, and when Juno discovered the ruse she decreed that Echo would never again be able to speak properly. Since then, Echo could only repeat the last words of sentences spoken to her by others.

When Echo first saw Narcissus she became inflamed with love, followed him through the forest, and at last rushed upon him and threw her arms about him. But Narcissus drew back, refused to let her touch him, and declared he would rather die than be trapped by her love. Despondent, Echo withdrew into the forest. There she so mourned that she wasted away to nothing, until only her voice remained, still echoing the last words of those who call out.

As for Narcissus, he continued unapproachable, spurning everyone who offered him love. One of the rejected suitors called a curse down on Narcissus: let him love only himself, and let that love fail. The curse worked. One day, tired from hunting, Narcissus threw himself down beside a bright pool to quench his thirst. As he drank, he saw his own image—and was immediately entranced by the beauty he saw there. Again and again he tried to kiss the figure he saw in the pool, to embrace it, only to be frustrated repeatedly. Loving his own reflection, he was both lover and beloved, taunted and made despairing by his own loveliness. In his misery he wished to leave his own body and join the image in the pool. Like Echo, he began to waste away, and to strike himself, tearing his flesh. At last the end came. Echo found him dead beside the pool. As those who loved him came to arrange the funeral rites his body vanished, and in its place grew the gold and white flower named after him.

An unlikely pair of authors has contributed to Narcissus being one of the best-known of mythic figures: the Roman poet Ovid, and Sigmund Freud.

It was Ovid who, in Book III of the *Metamorphoses*, his re-telling of many of the ancient myths, so adroitly interwove the tales of Tiresias, Echo and Narcissus. English poets have responded warmly to Ovid's version of the myth ever since William Golding's sixteenth century translations: T. S. Eliot incorporated the Tiresias material into *The Wasteland*, and Horace Gregory's translation of the entire *Metamorphoses* is widely admired. Freud's contribution to our awareness of Narcissus was considerably different from Ovid's. In his essay *Beyond the Pleasure Principle* (1920), Freud suggested that Narcissus-love, a love that turns from the world and towards one's self, is an instance of psychoneurosis. This was not, however, Freud's final word on Narcissus. In *Civilization and Its Discontents* (1930), he theorized that narcissism is a primary stage of human awareness, a necessary part of psychological growth and development. Freud's earlier speculations on the symbolism of the Narcissus myth threw a baleful shadow around our understanding of the myth, while his later investigations put the symbolism in a much more positive light. It is curious and significant that most people agree with the earlier judgment: narcissistic has come to mean *selfish, neurotically introverted, unmindful of all but the self.*[1] This is an inaccurate interpretation of the myth that can be corrected by closer attention to Ovid and the later Freud.

First, there are some insistent recurrences in Ovid's telling of the myth that demand attention: specifically, acts of aggression and violence. Jove and Juno quarrel over the pleasures of love; Tiresias is blinded for deciding against Juno; Liriope is raped by Cephisus; Echo is stricken by Juno for having collaborated in Jove's sexual misadventures, and later disintegrates in the face of Narcissus' rejection of her; a disappointed suitor calls down a curse on Narcissus; Narcissus himself dies of unquenchable desire. All of these instances of violence are connected in one way or another with sexual antagonism. For Jove and Juno, the antagonism is essentially selfish, each partner regretting the other's pleasure. For Liriope, Echo and Narcissus, the antagonism is combative, a desiring subject being opposed by a desired object.

It is the aggression surrounding him that drives Narcissus to throw himself down beside the pool and yearn to enter it. We recall that his mother Liriope was a water-nymph. The pool is a symbol of Liriope herself, and Narcissus instinctively seeks a return to the mother as a sanctuary from violence.

But this is not simply an Oedipal fantasy, and to read Narcissus' story as only that is to fall several stages short of understanding. The imagery of poetry and myth is a spiral, leading down and down to the center of insight, and the commonest blunder in interpretation is to fail to follow the spiral long enough. We behave as Theseus might have if Ariadne's thread had been too short: the place of confrontation doesn't exist close to the entrance.

So there's another passageway beyond the evident one of Narcissus trying to return to the safety of the womb, more than a fable-version of flight from anxiety and danger. As the pool symbolically represents the womb, so too the womb has symbolic representation beyond itself. The spiral goes on. Narcissus is not simply infantile regressor. He is time-traveller and unity-seeker, drawn to the womb-pool not as the end of his quest but as the vehicle of his travel and his search. Narcissus moves toward a spot of quiet in his forest and reaches toward the pool not as a place to be, but as a way of getting to somewhere else.

Like other mythical figures, Narcissus keeps reappearing and rede-fining his own meaning. He appears, briefly, in one of Billy Pilgrim's episodes in Kurt Vonnegut's *Slaughterhouse Five*. At one point in the novel Billy falls into a time-wrinkle, and takes off on the same trip Narcissus makes and for the same reason.

Billy Pilgrim padded downstairs on his blue and ivory feet. He went into the kitchen, where the moonlight called his atten-tion to a half bottle of champagne on the kitchen table, all that was left from the reception in the tent. Somebody had stoppered it again. 'Drink me,' it seemed to say.

So Billy uncorked it with his thumb. It didn't make a pop. The champagne was dead. So it goes.

Billy looked at the clock on the gas stove. He had an hour to kill before the saucer came. He went into the living room, swinging the bottle like a dinner bell, turned on the television. He came slightly unstuck in time, saw the late movie backward, then forwards again. It was a movie about American bombers in the Second World War and the gallant men who flew them. Seen backwards by Billy, the story went like this:

American planes, full of holes and wounded men and corps-es, took off backwards from an airfield in England. Over France, a few German fighter planes flew at them backwards, sucked bullets and shell fragments from some of the planes and crewmen. They did the same for some wrecked American bombers on the ground, and those planes flew up backwards to join the forma-tion.

The formation flew backwards over a German city that was in flames. The bombers opened their bomb bay doors, exerted a miraculous magnetism which shrunk the fires, gathered them into cylindrical steel containers, and lifted the containers into the bellies of the planes. The containers were stored neatly in racks. The Germans below had miraculous devices of their own, which were long steel tubes. They used them to suck more frag-ments from the crewmen and planes. But there were still a few wounded Americans, though, and some of the bombers were in bad repair. Over France, though, German fighters came up again, made everything and everybody as good as new.

When the bombers got back to their base, the steel cylinders were taken from the racks and shipped back to the United States of America, where factories were operating night and day, dismantling the cylinders, separating the dangerous contents into minerals. Touchingly, it was mainly women who did this work. The minerals were then shipped to specialists in remote areas. It was their business to put them into the ground, to hide them cleverly, so they would never hurt anybody ever again.

The American fliers turned in their uniforms, became high school kids. And Hitler turned into a baby, Billy Pilgrim supposed. That wasn't in the movie. Billy was extrapolating. Everybody turned into a baby, and all humanity, without exception, conspired biologically to produce two perfect people named Adam and Eve, he supposed.[2]

The torn men and planes, the burning cities, Hitler, are the equivalents of all the enmities in Narcissus' world; and like Narcissus, Billy Pilgrim reaches back to the beginnings of things, the time before violence began. Narcissus stares into the pool, trying to see the pure beginnings there; Billy stares into a television picture tube, looking for the same thing.

It is curious and important that Narcissus and Billy Pilgrim both have gardens to go with their pools. In the myth Narcissus' pool is set in a quiet glade, away from the noise of the hunters. Billy's twenty-one inch pool brings him back to Adam and Eve, still within the gates of the garden of Eden. Garden re-enforces pool as a symbol of an undivided pristine serenity. This was the meaning so precisely intuited by Andrew Marvell. In his poem "The Garden," Marvell depicts a host of aggressions that bedevil man: the anxious quests for glory in politics, war, the arts; the jostle and noise of society; the cruelties of sexual aggression; the demands of passion. In contrast to all these is the garden:

Fair quiet, have I found thee here,
And Innocence thy Sister dear!

Withdrawal into the garden becomes a retreat back into one's self, and the negation of all sense of a threatening "other."

> Meanwhile the Mind, from pleasure less,
> Withdraws into its happiness:
> The Mind, that Ocean where each kind
> Does streight its own resemblance find;
> Yet it creates, transcending these,
> Far other Worlds, and other Seas:
> Annihilating all that's made
> To a green thought in a green Shade.

Freudian psychology could nicely gloss Marvell's juxtaposing *withdrawal, self-seeking, annihilation* and *peace.* In *Civilization and Its Discontents*, Freud speculated that the ego in its earliest stage of development does not distinguish itself from the external world, it has no sense of "other." The separation of reality into a subject-object arrangement is a later stage of consciousness development, accompanied by a loss of the sense of unity.[3] In *Beyond the Pleasure Principle*, Freud had speculated that "all instincts tend toward the restoration of an earlier state of things,"[4] that, as a matter of fact, "the aim of all life is death."[5] There is a natural, instinctual craving for total peace, total calm, total absence of conflict with "otherness."

Within this context, the garden symbolizes that pristine sense of unity (man in accord with nature) and the serenity that inheres in such oneness. If one needs more gardens than Marvell's to be convinced, then consider those of Adam and Buddha. In the Genesis story, differentiation and conflict are made inevitable when God commands Adam to subdue the earth and to exert his dominion over the fishes of the sea and the birds of the sky and all living things that move on the earth. (Genesis I:28) Disharmony follows on disharmony, and finally comes expulsion out of the eastern gate of Eden, the gate we've all been trying to reenter in every way we know ever since. The expulsion from the biblical garden propelled Judaeo-Christian society into anxiety; the vanished garden is the image of anxiety. The garden of Buddha was not forsaken, it never disappeared. When Siddhartha Gautama seated himself under the tree of enlightenment he enraged Mara, the chief demon of evil, who considered Gautama's aspiration to Buddhahood vainglorious. But not all Mara's forces could dislodge Gautama from his seat of serenity, for Buddha simply put his hand on the ground, thus signalling his communion with the earth, and the powers of the earth fortified him against Mara. For Buddha there is no exit and no anxiety.[6]

The longing to reenter the lost garden is one version of the recovery of lost innocence, of becoming childlike again, of reexperiencing unity and serenity. The deep appeal of that rearward journey is right now busily asserting itself, the myth is forcing itself on our consciousness, albeit in fragmentary and groping ways. High fashion mimics the modes of the twenties and thirties; television series try to recapture the thirties and forties; the music of the fifties is competing with the music of the seventies; our theatres happily regress to *No, No, Nanette*, or *The Great Gatsby*; old radio programs are rebroadcast; in their clothes, adornments and speech inflections young people hark back to an agrarian society. A fine Victorian novelist (who happens to be writing in the 1970s), R. F. Delderfield, receives critical praise for eschewing the modern nonsense of ambiguity and complexity. The childlike fantasies of C. S. Lewis, Antoine de Saint Exupery, and Richard Bach (*The Narnian Chronicles, The Little Prince, Jonathan Livingston Seagull*) have a devoted adult reading audience. Our Narcissus is named Nostalgia.

Two recent novels in particular have assumed cultic significance for those who want to turn off and drop out of aggressive society, and step into Narcissus' pool. One is Brian Aldiss' science-fiction work, *Cryptozoic!* and the other is Richard Brautigan's *In Watermelon Sugar*.

Aldiss' novel is set in the not-too-distant future (2090 A.D.) when science has perfected time travel. Curiously, travel into the extremely remote past is quite simply done: the mind and the astral body (the physical body remains in a time chamber as the port of reentry when the travelling is concluded) can beam far backwards into the earliest geological ages, but travel to the immediate past is impossible for all but a few. Though such time travel is incredibly expensive, the state of society is so depressing and repressive that mind travel is widely practiced.

Edward Bush, an especially adept mind-traveller, is pressed into service by the government to go back through time and locate a renegade scientist, Dr. Silverstone, who has been decreed an enemy of the state and has escaped into time. It is believed that he possesses some forbidden knowledge that, if announced, would lead to the overthrow of organized society.

When Bush locates Silverstone and his secret, he learns the startling truth: the real movement of time is not forward, but backward. Earth is evolving not towards greater and greater complexity, but towards increasing simplicity and, ultimately, to basic cellular existence and then extinction. The deepest unconscious of man (called here the "undermind") has always known the truth; but the analytic and ratiocinative intelligence (the "overmind") has increasingly distorted and concealed the real nature of time from mankind. The overmind, and all it has created—science, industry, social systems —is in control and, naturally, anxious to remain in control. Hence, the "criminality" of a man like Silverstone who speaks for the power of the undermind. His knowledge is indeed forbidden, because it shatters the very roots of organized societal behavior. "We are the Himalayan generation," he tells Bush, "the great hump over which the human race goes down to a future that we already know, the increasing simplification of human society and the human mind, until first individuality and then humanity itself is lost into the amorphous being of the early—sorry, late!—primates, tarsiers, and so on."[7]

Aldiss' novel deserves its reputation: it may very well be the first science fiction novel to be built on a thoroughly informed grasp of Jungian psychology, and Aldiss has achieved a splendid union of analytical psychology and narrative excitement. But the appeal of the book is not to be explained by its fidelity to the Jungian concepts of archetypes and the collective unconscious, but to its dramatization of the Narcissus theme: the way out is the way back, and the end of the journey is re-absorption into the All.

Richard Brautigan's gentle novel, *In Watermelon Sugar*, has the surface naivete of a fairy tale, and the wispy illogic of a dream or a drug trip. There is a minimum of transitional scenes in the narrative, the sketchiest of character development, a total absence of authorial rumination on the significance of the action, a casual disregard of most of the traditional arts of storytelling. One chapter, for example, reads in its entirety:

> Pauline and Al together cooked an early dinner that we had late in the afternoon. It was very hot outside, so they prepared something light. They made a potato salad that somehow ended up having a lot of carrots in it.[8]

Or consider Pauline:

> She told a little story about a lamb going for a walk.
> 'The lamb sat down in the flowers,' she said. 'The lamb was all right,' and that was the end of the story.[9]

The landscape of the novel is dotted with statues of potatoes, rutabagas, grass; sometimes the sun shines red, sometimes golden, sometimes gray or black or white or blue or brown, depending on the day of the week; most things from windowpanes to building planks, are made from pressed watermelon sugar; the dead are buried in crystalline tombs set in softly-lit pools of water. And yet, for all this, the people in the novel are not aware of any surrealism. They go softly and tenderly about their business of being together, sleeping, eating, making love, evidently not caring that they're living in a Daliesque world.

The trance-like setting of the novel identifies it as one of the gateways into the unconscious, an opening into the passageway trodden by dreams, myths, and other messengers from the subterranean regions of the mind. If we accept that dreams and fantasies may be annunciations, then we can estimate *In Watermelon Sugar* rightly: it is an annunciation of the Narcissus myth.

The simplicity of the tale maddeningly resists paraphrase, but briefly the narrative is as follows. A small group of people live in a place called IDEATH. Theirs is a life without servile labor, without unnecessary possessions, and without animosities. The storyteller loves Pauline, and is loved also by Margaret, who has begun to stray away from the community at IDEATH and to frequent the Place of Forgotten Works. There, she has gotten into the habit of collecting things (whose use most people have forgotten), and to associate with the decidedly ungentle INBOIL and his gang, all of whom resent the life going on at IDEATH. INBOIL and his cronies come one day to IDEATH, and in a rage cut off their own fingers, noses, ears, and bleed to death. Margaret hangs herself, she is buried in a glass tomb in the river, and musicians prepare to play at a dance: "The musicians were poised with their instruments. They were ready to go. It would only be a few seconds now, I wrote."[10] And that, as Pauline might say, is the end of the story.

While the atmosphere of the novel is gauzelike, softly imprecise, the locales and the blockings of characters and themes are arranged with geometric hardness. One lifestyle is acted out in IDEATH, the opposing lifestyle at the Place of Forgotten Works. IDEATH is I-Death, Ego-Death, the annihilation of single identity. The place itself has no fixed, definable borders. At one point, the narrator remarks, "Just before I arrived at IDEATH, it changed. IDEATH's like that: always changing." (p. 16) Space shifts and melds: "I walked across the living room toward the kitchen. There was nobody in the room, nobody sitting on the couches along the river. That's where people usually gather in the room or they stand in the trees by the big rocks, but there was nobody there either. There were many lanterns shining along the river and in the trees. It was very close to dinner." (p. 16) Images of coalescence help define the condition of IDEATH: "It was about dark when I arrived at IDEATH. The two evening stars were now shining side by side. The smaller one had moved over to the big one. They were very close now, almost touching, and then they went together and became one very large star." (p. 16) Spatial distinctions and object identities hardly exist: "I know a river that is half-an-inch wide. I know because I measured it and sat beside it for a whole day. It started raining in the middle of the afternoon. We call everything a river here. We're that kind of people." (p. 2) The watermelon sugar of the title symbolizes the collectivity of experience, it is an image of the fused, organic, all-at-one state of IDEATH:

> Some of the bridges are made of watermelon sugar. I like those bridges best. We make a great many things out of watermelon sugar here—I'll tell you about it—including this book being written near IDEATH.
> All this will be gone into, travelled in watermelon sugar.
> (p. 2)

Even as IDEATH has no insistent, single identity, neither does the narrator. In the chapter entitled "My Name," we discover that the *self* of the narrator is indistinguishable from its contexts. It does not exist singly and alone.

### My Name

> I guess you are kind of curious as to who I am, but I am one of those who do not have a regular name. My name depends on you. Just call me whatever is in your mind.
> If you are thinking about something that happened a long time ago: Somebody asked you a question and you did not know the answer.
> That is my name.
> Perhaps it was raining very hard.
> That is my name.
> Or somebody wanted you to do something. You did it. Then they told you what you did was wrong—'Sorry for the mistake,'—and you had to do something else.
> That is my name.
> Perhaps it was a game that you played when you were a child or something that came idly into your mind when you were old and sitting in a chair near the window.
> That is my name.
> Or you walked someplace. There were flowers all around.
> That is my name.

Perhaps you stared into a river. There was somebody near you who loved you. They were about to touch you. You could feel this before it happened. Then it happened.

That is my name.

Or you heard someone calling from a great distance. Their voice was almost an echo.

That is my name.

Perhaps you were lying in bed, almost ready to go to sleep and you laughed at something, a joke unto yourself, a good way to end the day.

That is my name.

Or you were eating something good and for a second forgot what you were eating, but still went on, knowing it was good.

That is my name.

Perhaps it was around midnight and the fire tolled like a bell inside the stove.

That is my name.

Or you felt bad when she said that thing to you. She could have told it to someone else: Somebody who was more familiar with her problems.

That is my name.

Perhaps the trout swam in the pool but the river was only eight inches wide and the moon shone on IDEATH and the watermelon fields glowed out of proportion, dark and the moon seemed to rise from every plant.

That is my name. (pp. 4–5)


The Forgotten Works and INBOIL, who lives there, are very different from IDEATH and the story-teller. The Forgotten Works (like Kurt Vonnegut's not-so-unreal Ilium) is harsh, metallic, devoid of any human warmth, and filled with *things* whose use has been forgotten. The Forgotten Works is, in fact, The City or, rather, that culture whose chief symbol is the City with its emphasis on production rather than people or any living thing. INBOIL, major resident of Forgotten Works, *is* his name (unlike the nameless narrator): he is inner turmoil, inner rage, inner soreness. Once a dweller at IDEATH, he has rejected that way of life, and disagrees violently with those who maintain it.

> INBOIL and that gang of his lived in a little bunch of lousy shacks with leaky roofs near the Forgotten Works. They lived there until they were dead. I think there were about twenty of them. All men, like INBOIL, that were no good.
>
> First there was just INBOIL who lived there. He got in a big fight one night with Charley and told him to go to hell and said he would sooner live by the Forgotten Works than in IDEATH.
>
> 'To hell with IDEATH,' he said, and went and built himself a lousy shack by the Forgotten Works. He spent his time digging around in there and making whiskey from things. (p. 61)

INBOIL has no patience with the communal and collective spirit of IDEATH. Instead, he opts for isolation and singularity: "He began spending a lot of time at the Forgotten Works, and Charley would ask him what he was doing and INBOIL would say, 'Oh, nothing. Just off by myself." (p. 62) If the Forgotten Works is uncomfortably like the cities in which we live, INBOIL is uncomfortably like most of the people who live there.

Caught between the two is Margaret, strongly attracted to IDEATH but waywardly drawn to the Forgotten Works, where she collects *things* and fills her room with them. She is the figure of dilemma, the representative of all who are torn between a gentle pastoralism that owns nothing and a harsh urbanism that owns a great deal. That Margaret has not been able to adapt to IDEATH is imaged in her most annoying habit: she always steps on the one squeaky board on the bridge leading to IDEATH. "I can walk across the bridge hundreds of times without stepping on that board, but Margaret always steps on it." (p. 3) Intentionally or not, she announces herself—she has not been able to silence her own loud identity.

IDEATH and INBOIL share Margaret, and they share one other thing: remembrance of the tigers. The citizens at IDEATH remember the tigers with ambivalent fondness: they had "beautiful voices" (the phrase is said of them many times), they were fond of children, they spoke and thought as children. But when they came, they destroyed the parents.

One morning the tigers came in while we were eating breakfast and before my father could grab a weapon they killed him and they killed my mother. My parents didn't even have time to say anything before they were dead. I was still holding the spoon from the mush I was eating.

'Don't be afraid,' one of the tigers said. 'We're not going to hurt you. We don't hurt children. Just sit there where you are and we'll tell you a story.'

One of the tigers started eating my mother. He bit her arm off and started chewing on it. 'What kind of story would you like to hear? I know a good story about a rabbit.'

'I don't want to hear a story,' I said.

'OK,' the tiger said, and he took a bite out of my father. I sat there for a long time with the spoon in my hand, and then I put it down.

'Those were my folks,' I said finally.

'We're sorry,' one of the tigers said. 'We really are.'

'Yeah,' the other tiger said. 'We wouldn't do this if we didn't have to, if we weren't absolutely forced to. But this is the only way we can keep alive'." (p. 33)


Since then, the tigers have gone; and although they are remembered in IDEATH without rancor, and even with pleasure ("they had beautiful voices"), it is generally agreed that it is good they are no longer among the people. When the tigers had gone, there was both relief and regret.


I was six years old when they killed the last one. I remember the hunters bringing it to IDEATH. There were hundreds of people with them. The hunters said they had killed it up in the hills that day, and it was the last tiger.

They brought the tiger to IDEATH and everybody came with them. They covered it with wood and soaked the wood down with watermelon-trout oil. Gallons and gallons of it. I remember people threw flowers on the pile and stood around crying because it was the last tiger. (p. 31)

The tigers were a force, destructive of authority and control, but in no way culpable. "We're awfully sorry we had to kill your parents and eat them. Please try to understand. We tigers are not evil. This is just a thing we have to do." (p. 35) Sated, they become harmless and finally extinct.

The tigers, in a word, are the instincts, unrepressed, passion-spent, libidinal energy transformed into the folklore of IDEATH itself.

It is not at all strange that INBOIL wishes for the tigers to return. As spokesman for the productive, acquisitive, and competitive society, INBOIL knows his Sigmund Freud well. In *Civilization and Its Discontents,* Freud demonstrated that society, protective of its own existence, demands that the instincts be sublimated, safely channeled into endeavors that mask the ferocity and voracity of their energy. Free expression of the instincts would surely gratify the individual, but only at the expense of others. For society to exist, "the members of the community [must] restrict themselves in their possibilities of satisfaction, whereas the individual [knows] no restrictions."[11] But the society-challenging instincts cannot be erased, they must be redirected, manipulated, contorted into forms that won't threaten group security. The nuclear family, by inhibiting the sexual instinct and concentrating its energies away from promiscuity and toward the small domestic unit, is an instance of redirected instinct; the business community, by narrowing and refining the hunting instinct, is a sublimation of combative energy; team sports, as they are ritualizations of aggression, are controlled manifestations of instinct-energy. Society cannot eradicate the tigers, but it must muzzle them.

It can be said that society *needs* the tigers, since so many of the operations and institutions of society are muzzled tigers. The tigers are taught to be useful, to become agents of productivity, the hunting pack converted into the corporation.

INBOIL knows all this: he knows that the tigers must come back if he and his gang and the Forgotten Works are to survive. What he does *not* know is what IDEATH means. He cannot understand *ego-death*, as the story-teller does, the absorption of the individual into a collective consciousness, the recovery of Nirvana. To INBOIL, IDEATH means surrender of identity to the corporation, to the manufacturing society.[12] He chooses to bring back the tigers by a violent mutilation of himself, a bloody summoning through an appropriate sacrifice.

> 'The tigers should never have been killed. The tigers were the true meaning of IDEATH. Without the tigers there would be no IDEATH, and you killed the tigers and so IDEATH went away, and you've lived here like a bunch of clucks ever since. I'm going to bring back IDEATH. We're all going to bring back IDEATH. My gang here and me. I've been thinking about it for years and now we're going to do it. IDEATH will be again.'
> INBOIL reached into his pocket and took out a jackknife.
> 'What are you going to do with that knife?' Charley said.
> 'I'll show you,' INBOIL said. He pulled the blade out. It looked sharp. 'This is IDEATH,' he said, and took the knife and cut off his thumb . . . INBOIL was still up and cutting fingers off his hands. 'This is IDEATH,' he said. 'Oh, boy. This is really IDEATH.' Finally he had to sit down, too, so he could bleed to death.[13] (pp. 93–95)

INBOIL's first offering is his thumb—the tool of the creating, producing man, the essential digit of the tool-maker and tool-handler. No thumbs, no Forgotten Works; no tigers, no city. Following the slaughter, the people of IDEATH burn the houses of INBOIL and his gang.

> As the flames diminished to very little, a strong wind came out of the Forgotten Works and scattered ashes rapidly through the air. After a while Fred yawned. I dreamt. (p. 102)

The good citizens of IDEATH have shared Siddhartha's experience at the river. Siddhartha's serenity had been achieved when he put behind him all selfish quests for fulfillment, and had surrendered himself to the voice of collectivity and submersion into the wholeness of experience.

Siddhartha listened. He was now listening intently, completely absorbed, taking in everything. He felt that he had now completely learned the art of listening. He had often heard all this before, all these numerous voices in the river, but today they sounded different. He could no longer distinguish the different voices—the merry voice from the weeping voice, the childish voice from the manly voice. They all belonged to each other; the lament of those who yearn, the laughter of the wise, the cry of indignation and the groan of dying. They were all interwoven and interlocked, entwined in a thousand ways. And all the vices, all the goals, all the yearnings, all the sorrows, all the pleasures, all the good and evil, all of them together was the world. All of them together was the stream of events, the music of life. When Siddhartha listened attentively to this river, to this song of a thousand voices; when he did not listen to the sorrow or laughter, when he did not bind his soul to any one particular voice and absorb it in his Self, but heard them all, the whole, the unity; then the great song of a thousand voices consisted of one word: Om—perfection.[14]

The appeal of the Narcissus-trip is undeniable, particularly so in times of personal and social stress. Our endless attempts to return to the garden testify to the strength of that drive, all our different nostalgias reaffirm its importance to us. The lure of the pool is multiform: simplicity, changelessness, freedom from anxiety and combat, unrepressed acceptance of the unconscious and the instincts, at-one-ness with all being. The dream indeed has been the motive force behind great religious aspiration,[15] and may be the hallmark of a newly liberated social system.[16] According to this view, society's neuroses, hang-ups, and anxieties stem from the repression of our instincts. Free the Instincts, free the person, free the society: it is a nervous but alluring dream, and it satisfies the dwellers at IDEATH.

But what if INBOIL was right? There are cautionary voices, reminding us of the psychic and civil dangers of IDEATH. Carl Jung, for all his reverence of the unconscious and the creative energies therein, anticipated INBOIL's sense that ego-death could mean literal destruction:

A collective attitude is always a threat to the individual, even when it is a necessity. It is dangerous because it is very apt to check and smother all personal differentiation. . . . Collective thinking and feeling and collective effort are relatively easy in comparison with individual functioning and performance; and from this may arise, all too easily, a dangerous threat to the development or personality through enfeeblement of the personal function.[17]

Jung commented on the two basic disorders that frequently result from reabsorption into the collective unconscious:

The process of assimilating the unconscious leads to some very remarkable phenomena. It produces in some patients an unmistakable and often unpleasant increase of self-confidence and conceit: they are full of themselves, they know everything, they imagine themselves to be fully informed of everything concerning their unconscious, and are persuaded that they understand perfectly everything that comes out of it. . . . Others on the contrary feel themselves more and more crushed under the contents of the unconscious, they lose their self-confidence and abandon themselves with dull resignation to all the extraordinary things that the unconscious produces.[18]

INBOIL does accuse the residents of IDEATH of Jung's first malady, their persuasion that only they understand what comes out of the unconscious; and as for the second malady, loss of productive activity, we note that the story-teller is unable to complete a piece of sculpture he's been working on—and he doesn't especially care.

'How's it coming?' [Margaret] said.
'It's finished,' I said.
'It doesn't look finished,' she said.
'It's finished,' I said. (p. 67)

In IDEATH a gentle life has become the art form and if forgotten things are not made there, neither are complete poems or complete statues. Freudian psychology proposes that art is a sublimated expression of a powerful psychic drive that has been thwarted in its urge to be freely expressed. That same psychic energy seeks release through symbolic expression: self-destructiveness may lead then not to suicide but to a poem, rage may lead then not to violence but to a sculpture, lust may lead then not to assault but to dance. Were the instincts not initially repressed, and thus forced to discover the symbolic release, there would be no art. The oyster unirritated by a grain of sand produces no pearl; a life unirritated produces no art.

Rollo May's concern is that primal innocence, the kind sought by Narcissus and lived at IDEATH, is socially suicidal. May's theme in *Power and Innocence* is that childlikeness and sincerity are not enough, that the cruel myth of the sacrifice of children to the Minotaur will be inevitably reenacted, if the retreat to innocence is encouraged—for the devourers are always with us. May's discussion of the Kent State killings, and his analysis of Herman Melville's *Billy Budd* affirm that the garden is no complete sanctuary:

> [The innocent ones] are thorns in the flesh of the world; they threaten to annihilate 'law and order,' the police, and the authority of government. The symbolic action of Allison Krause [one of the students killed at Kent State] in dropping a flower down the barrel of the guardsman's gun defies all of the accepted beliefs about the power of guns. Thus, innocence threatens to upset the world as we know it.[19]
>
> Let no one think for an instant that we, in our vaunted modern civilization, have gone 'beyond the primitive human sacrifice.' We do it as well, not only in sevens, but by the tens of thousands. And the name of the god to whom we sacrifice them is Moloch. More than fifty thousand of our youths have been sacrificed in Vietnam, and if we add the Vietnamese, as we surely must, the sacrifice goes into the millions. . . . Our modern Moloch is greedy—which means we have much inner aggression and violence to project.[20]

The place of the Forgotten Works does have the capability of send-
ing out raiding parties.

But for all the warnings, Narcissus keeps his allure, since the legend
is an invitation to myth itself, and myth we cannot do without. The
unconscious keeps to its old ways of recognizing the similes and
metaphors that inhere in all experience. The mythic way of seeing
connects and relates and assembles, in defiance of all our analytic
separations and will continue to do so no matter how refined our
systems of classification become. In myth, as in other voices of the
unconscious, lies "the hidden treasure upon which mankind ever and
anon has drawn, and from which it has raised up its gods and demons,
and all those potent and mighty thoughts without which man ceases
to be man;"[21] and it is a treasure that has been there from the beginning, the primeval form of mental operation.[22] We have had to learn
*not* to think mythically, we have had to unlearn our atavistic sense of
unity. "The development of Western philosophy during the last two
centuries has succeeded in isolating the mind in its own sphere and in
severing it from its primordial oneness with the universe."[23] The recovery of mythic thought is an immediate challenge, demanding and
dangerous (as the following chapter will try to show). Nonmythic
thought is analytic, the perception of dualities, differences, oppositions. Mythic thought is synthetic, an overcoming of any antagonism
between desire and need, man and nature, self and other, thought and
instinct: and it is evidently the elder of the two thought forms. Myth,
and especially the Narcissus myth, speaks of itself, for "the return to
the origins and to primordiality is a basic feature of every
mythology."[24] "Mythology provides a foundation insofar as the teller
of myths, by living out his story, finds his way back to primordial
times."[25] "Myth narrates a sacred history; it relates an event that took
place in primordial Time, the fabled time of the 'beginnings'."[26] The
earliest state of things that is the subject of myth is not only "historical" time, but psychological and psychogenetic time. That is, in dealing with origins, myth is telling us of our own earliest and most basic
thought forms, and of the earliest thought forms of *Homo sapiens*.
Narcissus is the symbol of the mind in search of its own roots, the
renewal of mythic thought, both personal and collective. He is there

in the portico, beckoning us back into myth and into an encounter with Dionysos, Orpheus, and Christ, each necessary images of the discovered self.

# NOTES

1. See, for instance, Grace Stuart's lively *Narcissus: A Psychological Study of Self-Love* (London, Allen and Unwin, 1956), where Narcissus is identified with self-destructiveness through withdrawal, as contrasted with healthy eroticism, in which self-fulfillment is achieved through giving.

2. Kurt Vonnegut, Jr., *Slaughterhouse Five*. Copyright © by Kurt Vonnegut, Jr. Used by permission of Delacorte Press/Seymour Lawrence.

3. Sigmund Freud, *Civilization and Its Discontents* (London, Hogarth Press, 1949), p. 13. For a brilliantly expanded treatment of this theme of unity vs. differentiation, and its relationship to the development of consciousness, see Erich Neumann, *The Origins and History of Consciousness* (Princeton, Princeton University Press, 1954).

4. *Beyond the Pleasure Principle* (London, Hogarth Press, 1955), p. 37.

5. *Ibid.*, p. 38. Note also: "[The sexual instincts] operate against the purpose of the other instincts which lead by reason of their function to death." (*Ibid.*, p. 40)

6. Cf. Padraic Colum, *Myths of the World* (New York, Grosset and Dunlap, n.d.), pp. 231–34.

7. Brian W. Aldiss, *Cryptozoic!* (New York, Doubleday and Company, 1967), p. 156.

8. Richard Brautigan, *In Watermelon Sugar*. Copyright © 1968 by Richard Brautigan. Used by permission of Delacorte Press/Seymour Lawrence.

9. *Ibid.*, p. 37.

10. *Ibid.*, p. 138.

11. Freud, *Civilization and Its Discontents*, p. 42.

12. I have seen INBOIL's puzzlement on the Boston Common, when lunch-bound executives pass by the chanting monks of Hare Krishna.

13. INBOIL's manner of dying is reminiscent of an ancient ritual death described by Sir James George Frazer in *The Golden Bough*. Frazer relates that the king of a certain Indian province had at one time a fixed twelve-year reign, at the end of which he publicly sacrificed himself before his subjects, cutting off his fingers, ears, nose and as much of himself as

possible with sharp knives, before bleeding to death. The purpose of such immolation and INBOIL's act is the same: the continuation of a kind of society by the sacrificial death of the current ruler. See *The Golden Bough* (New York, Macmillan, 1960), p. 320.

14. Herman Hesse, *Siddhartha* (New York, New Directions, 1957), pp. 110–111.

15. Cf. Norman O. Brown, *Life Against Death* (Middletown, Conn., Wesleyan University Press, 1970), p. 90.

16. Herbert Marcuse, *Eros and Civilization* (New York, Alfred A. Knopf, Inc., 1962), p. 160, pp. 210–211. Also, Brown, p. 307.

17. Carl Jung, "The Structure of the Unconscious," *Two Essays on Analytical Psychology* (copyright 1953 and © 1966 by Bollingen Foundation), p. 277. Reprinted by permission of Princeton University Press.

18. "Phenomena Resulting From the Assimilation of the Unconscious," *Two Essays on Analytical Psychology*, p. 139.

19. Rollo May, *Power and Innocence* (New York, W. W. Norton, 1972), p. 207.

20. *Ibid.*, p. 214.

21. Jung, "The Personal and the Collective Unconscious," *Two Essays on Analytical Psychology*, p. 67.

22. Jung, *Two Essays*, p. 66; and Neumann, *Origins and History of Consciousness*, p. 11.

23. Jung, "The Difference Between Eastern and Western Thinking," *Symbols of Transformation*, *Works*, V, 184.

24. C. G. Jung and C. Kerenyi, *Essays on a Science of Mythology*, trans. by R. F. C. Hull, Bollingen Series XXII (copyright 1949, © 1959 and 1963 by Bollingen Foundation), p. 7. Reprinted by permission of Princeton University Press.

25. *Ibid.*, p. 8.

26. Mircea Eliade, *Myth and Reality* (New York, Harper and Row, 1963), p. 5.

O how I long to travell back
And tread again that ancient track!
That I might once more reach that plaine,
Where first I left my glorious traine,
From whence th'Inlightened spirit sees
That shady City of Palme trees;
But (ah!) my soul with too much stay
Is drunk, and staggers in the way.
Some men a forward motion love,
But I by backward steps would move,
And when this dust falls to the urn
In that state I came return.

Henry Vaughan, *The Retreate*

# Dr. Heidegger's Experiment

*Nathaniel Hawthorne*

That very singular man, old Dr. Heidegger, once invited four venerable friends to meet him in his study. There were three white-bearded gentlemen, Mr. Medbourne, Colonel Killigrew, and Mr. Gascoigne, and a withered gentlewoman, whose name was the Widow Wycherly. They were all melancholy old creatures, who had been unfortunate in life, and whose greatest misfortune it was that they were not long ago in their graves. Mr. Medbourne, in the vigor of his age, had been a prosperous merchant, but had lost his all by a frantic speculation, and was now little better than a mendicant. Colonel Killigrew had wasted his best years, and his health and substance, in the pursuit of sinful pleasures, which had given birth to a brood of pains, such as the gout, and divers other torments of soul and body. Mr. Gascoigne was a ruined politician, a man of evil fame, or at least had been so till time had buried him from the knowledge of the present generation, and made him obscure instead of infamous. As for the Widow Wycherly, tradition tells us that she was a great beauty in her day; but, for a long while past, she had lived in deep seclusion, on account of certain scandalous stories which had prejudiced the gentry of the town against her. It is a circumstance worth mentioning that each of these three old gentlemen, Mr. Medbourne, Colonel Killigrew, and Mr. Gascoigne, were early lovers of the Widow Wycherly, and had once been on the point of cutting each other's throats for her sake. And, before proceeding further, I will merely hint that Dr. Heidegger and all his four guests were sometimes thought to be a little beside themselves, —as is not unfrequently the case with old people, when worried either by present troubles or woeful recollections.

"My dear old friends," said Dr. Heidegger, motioning them to be seated, "I am desirous of your assistance in one of those little experiments with which I amuse myself here in my study."

If all stories were true, Dr. Heidegger's study must have been a very curious place. It was a dim, old-fashioned chamber, festooned with cobwebs, and besprinkled with antique dust. Around the walls stood several oaken bookcases, the lower shelves of which were filled with rows of gigantic folios and black-letter quartos, and the upper with little parchment-covered duodecimos. Over the central bookcase was a bronze bust of Hippocrates, with which, according to some authorities, Dr. Heidegger was accustomed to hold consultations in all difficult cases of his practice. In the obscurest corner of the room stood a tall and narrow oaken closet, with its door ajar, within which doubtfully appeared a skeleton. Between two of the bookcases hung a looking-glass, presenting its high and dusty plate within a tarnished gilt frame. Among many wonderful stories related of this mirror, it was fabled that the spirits of all the doctor's deceased patients dwelt within its verge, and would stare him in the face whenever he looked thitherward. The opposite side of the chamber was ornamented with the full-length portrait of a young lady, arrayed in the faded magnificence of silk, satin, and brocade, and with a visage as faded as her dress. Above half a century ago, Dr. Heidegger had been on the point of marriage with this young lady; but, being affected with some slight disorder, she had swallowed one of her lover's prescriptions, and died on the bridal evening. The greatest curiosity of the study remains to be mentioned; it was a ponderous folio volume, bound in black leather, with massive silver clasps. There were no letters on the back, and nobody could tell the title of the book. But it was well known to be a book of magic; and once, when a chambermaid had lifted it, merely to brush away the dust, the skeleton had rattled in its closet, the picture of the young lady had stepped one foot upon the floor, and several of the ghastly faces had peeped forth from the mirror; while the brazen head of Hippocrates frowned, and said, —"Forbear!"

Such was Dr. Heidegger's study. On the summer afternoon of our tale, a small round table, as black as ebony, stood in the centre of the room, sustaining a cut-glass vase of beautiful form and elaborate workmanship. The sunshine came through the window, between the heavy festoons of two faded damask curtains, and fell directly across this vase; so that a mild splendor was reflected from it on the ashen visages of the five old people who sat around. Four champagne glasses were also on the table.

"My dear old friends," repeated Dr. Heidegger, "may I reckon on your aid in performing an exceedingly curious experiment?"

Now Dr. Heidegger was a very strange old gentleman, whose eccentricity had become the nucleus for a thousand fantastic stories. Some of these fables, to my shame be it spoken, might possibly be traced back to my own veracious self; and if any passages of the present tale should startle the reader's faith, I must be content to bear the stigma of a fiction-monger.

When the doctor's four guests heard him talk of his proposed experiment, they anticipated nothing more wonderful than the murder of a mouse in an air pump, or the examination of a cobweb by the microscope, or some similar nonsense, with which he was constantly in the habit of pestering his intimates. But without waiting for a reply, Dr. Heidegger hobbled across the chamber, and returned with the same ponderous folio, bound in black leather, which common report affirmed to be a book of magic. Undoing the silver clasps, he opened the volume, and took from among its black-letter pages a rose, or what was once a

rose, though now the green leaves and crimson petals had assumed one brownish hue, and the ancient flower seemed ready to
crumble to dust in the doctor's hands.

"This rose," said Dr. Heidegger, with a sigh, —"This same
withered and crumbling flower, blossomed five and fifty years
ago. It was given me by Sylvia Ward, whose portrait hangs yonder; and I meant to wear it in my bosom at our wedding. Five and
fifty years it has been treasured between the leaves of this old
volume. Now, would you deem it possible that this rose of half a
century could ever bloom again?"

"Nonsense!" said the Widow Wycherly, with a peevish toss
of her head. "You might as well ask whether an old woman's
wrinkled face could ever bloom again."

"See!" answered Dr. Heidegger.

He uncovered the vase, and threw the faded rose into the
water which it contained. At first, it lay lightly on the surface of
the fluid, appearing to imbibe none of its moisture. Soon, however, a singular change began to be visible. The crushed and
dried petals stirred, and assumed a deepening tinge of crimson, as
if the flower were reviving from a deathlike slumber; the slender
stalk and twigs of foliage became green; and there was the rose of
half a century, looking as fresh as when Sylvia Ward had first
given it to her lover. It was scarcely full blown; for some of its
delicate red leaves curled modestly around its moist bosom,
within which two or three dewdrops were sparkling.

"That is certainly a very pretty deception," said the
doctor's friends; carelessly, however, for they had witnessed greater miracles at a conjurer's show; "pray, how was it effected?"

"Did you never hear of the 'Fountain of Youth'?" asked Dr.
Heidegger, "which Ponce De Leon, the Spanish adventurer,
went in search of, two or three centuries ago?"

"But did Ponce De Leon ever find it?" asked the Widow
Wycherly.

"No," answered Dr. Heidegger, "for he never sought it in
the right place. The famous Fountain of Youth, if I am rightly
informed, is situated in the southern part of the Floridian penin-
sula, not far from Lake Macaco. Its source is overshadowed by
several gigantic magnolias, which, though numberless centuries
old, have been kept as fresh as violets by the virtues of this

wonderful water. An acquaintance of mine, knowing my curiosity in such matters, has sent me what you see in the vase."

"Ahem!" said Colonel Killigrew, who believed not a word of the doctor's story; "and what may be the effect of this fluid on the human frame?"

"You shall judge for yourself, my dear colonel," replied Dr. Heidegger; "and all of you, my respected friends, are welcome to so much of this admirable fluid as may restore to you the bloom of youth. For my own part, having had much trouble in growing old, I am in no hurry to grow young again. With your permission, therefore, I will merely watch the progress of the experiment."

While he spoke, Dr. Heidegger had been filling the four champagne glasses with the water of the Fountain of Youth. It was apparently impregnated with an effervescent gas, for little bubbles were continually ascending from the depths of the glasses, and bursting in silvery spray at the surface. As the liquor diffused a pleasant perfume, the old people doubted not that it possessed cordial and comfortable properties; and though utter sceptics as to its rejuvenescent power, they were inclined to swallow it at once. But Dr. Heidegger besought them to stay a moment.

"Before you drink, my respectable old friends," said he, "it would be well that, with the experience of a lifetime to direct you, you should draw up a few general rules for your guidance, in passing a second time through the perils of youth. Think what a sin and shame it would be, if, with your peculiar advantages, you should not become patterns of virtue and wisdom to all the young people of the age!"

The doctor's four venerable friends made him no answer, except by a feeble and tremulous laugh; so very ridiculous was the idea that, knowing how closely repentance treads behind the steps of error, they should ever go astray again.

"Drink, then," said the doctor, bowing: "I rejoice that I have so well selected the subjects of my experiment."

With palsied hands, they raised the glasses to their lips. The liquor, if it really possessed such virtues as Dr. Heidegger imputed to it, could not have been bestowed on four human beings who needed it more woefully. They looked as if they had never known what youth or pleasure was, but had been the offspring of Nature's dotage, and always the gray, decrepit, sapless, miserable creatures, who now sat stooping round the doctor's table, without life enough in their souls or bodies to be animated even by the prospect of growing young again. They drank off the water, and replaced their glasses on the table.

Assuredly there was an almost immediate improvement in the aspect of the party, not unlike what might have been produced by a glass of generous wine, together with a sudden glow of cheerful sunshine brightening over all their visages at once. There was a healthful suffusion on their cheeks, instead of the ashen hue that had made them look so corpse-like. They gazed at one another, and fancied that some magic power had really begun to smooth away the deep and sad inscriptions which Father Time had been so long engraving on their brows. The Widow Wycherly adjusted her cap, for she felt almost like a woman again.

"Give us more of this wondrous water!" cried they eagerly. "We are younger—but we are still too old! Quick—give us more!"

"Patience, patience!" quoth Dr. Heidegger, who sat watching the experiment with philosophic coolness. "You have been a long time growing old. Surely, you might be content to grow young in half an hour! But the water is at your service."

Again he filled their glasses with the liquor of youth, enough of which still remained in the vase to turn half the old people in the city to the age of their own grandchildren. While the bubbles were yet sparkling on the brim, the doctor's four guests snatched their glasses from the table, and swallowed the contents at a single gulp. Was it delusion? even while the draught was passing down their throats, it seemed to have wrought a change on their whole systems. Their eyes grew clear and bright; a dark shade deepened among their silvery locks; they sat around the table, three gentlemen of middle age, and a woman hardly beyond her buxom prime.

"My dear widow, you are charming!" cried Colonel Killigrew, whose eyes had been fixed upon her face, while the shadows of age were flitting from it like darkness from the crimson daybreak.

The fair widow knew, of old, that Colonel Killigrew's compliments were not always measured by sober truth; so she started up and ran to the mirror, still dreading that the ugly visage of an old woman would meet her gaze. Meanwhile, the three gentlemen behaved in such a manner as proved that the water of the Fountain of Youth possessed some intoxicating qualities; unless, indeed, their exhilaration of spirits were merely a lightsome dizziness caused by the sudden removal of the weight of years. Mr. Gascoigne's mind seemed to run on political topics, but whether relating to the past, present, or future, could not easily be determined, since the same ideas and phrases have been in vogue these fifty years. Now he rattled forth full-throated sentences about patriotism, national glory, and the people's rights; now he muttered some perilous stuff or other, in a sly and doubtful whisper, so cautiously that even his own conscience could scarcely catch the secret; and now, again, he spoke in measured accents, and a deeply deferential tone, as if a royal ear were listening to his well-turned periods. Colonel Killigrew all this time had been trolling forth a jolly bottle-song, and ringing his glass in symphony with the chorus, while his eyes wandered toward the buxom figure of the Widow Wycherly. On the other side of the table, Mr. Medbourne was involved in a calculation of dollars and cents, with which was strangely intermingled a project for supplying the East Indies with ice, by harnessing a team of whales to the polar icebergs.

As for the Widow Wycherly, she stood before the mirror curtsying and simpering to her own image, and greeting it as the friend whom she loved better than all the world beside. She thrust her face close to the glass, to see whether some long-remembered wrinkle or crow's foot had indeed vanished. She examined whether the snow had so entirely melted from her hair that the venerable cap could be safely thrown aside. At last, turning briskly away, she came with a sort of dancing step to the table.

"My dear old doctor," cried she, "pray favor me with another glass!"

"Certainly, my dear madam, certainly!" replied the complaisant doctor; "see! I have already filled the glasses."

There, in fact, stood the four glasses, brimful of this wonderful water, the delicate spray of which, as it effervesced from the surface, resembled the tremulous glitter of diamonds. It was now so nearly sunset that the chamber had grown duskier than ever; but a mild and moonlike splendor gleamed from within the vase, and rested alike on the four guests and on the doctor's venerable figure. He sat in a highbacked, elaborately carved, oaken armchair, with a gray dignity of aspect that might have well befitted that very Father Time, whose power had never been disputed, save by this fortunate company. Even while quaffing the third draught of the Fountain of Youth, they were almost awed by the expression of his mysterious visage.

But, the next moment, the exhilarating gush of young life shot through their veins. They were now in the happy prime of youth. Age, with its miserable train of cares and sorrows and diseases, was remembered only as the trouble of a dream, from which they had joyously awoke. The fresh gloss of the soul, so early lost, and without which the world's successive scenes had been but a gallery of faded pictures, again threw its enchantment over all their prospects. They felt like new-created beings in a new-created universe.

"We are young! We are young!" they cried exultingly.

Youth, like the extremity of age, had effaced the strongly marked characteristics of middle life, and mutually assimilated them all. They were a group of merry youngsters, almost maddened with the exuberant frolicsomeness of their years. The most singular effect of their gayety was an impulse to mock the infirmity and decrepitude of which they had so lately been the victims. They laughed loudly at their old-fashioned attire, the wide-skirted coats and flapped waistcoats of the young men, and the ancient cap and gown of the blooming girl. One limped across the floor like a gouty grandfather; one set a pair of spectacles astride of his nose, and pretended to pore over the black-letter pages of the book of magic; a third seated himself in an armchair, and strove to imitate the venerable dignity of Dr. Heidegger. Then all shouted mirthfully, and leaped about the room. The Widow Wycherly—if so fresh a damsel could be called a widow—tripped up to the doctor's chair, with a mischievous merriment in her rosy face.

"Doctor, you dear old soul," cried she, "get up and dance with me!" And then the four young people laughed louder than ever, to think what a queer figure the poor old doctor would cut.

"Pray excuse me," answered the doctor quietly. "I am old and rheumatic, and my dancing days were over long ago. But either of these gay young gentlemen will be glad of so pretty a partner."

"Dance with me, Clara!" cried Colonel Killigrew.

"No, no, I will be her partner!" shouted Mr. Gascoigne.

"She promised me her hand, fifty years ago!" exclaimed Mr. Medbourne.

They all gathered round her. One caught both her hands in his passionate grasp—another threw his arm about her waist—the third buried his hand among the glossy curls that clustered beneath the widow's cap. Blushing, panting, struggling, chiding, laughing, her warm breath fanning each of their faces by turns, she strove to disengage herself, yet still remained in their triple embrace. Never was there a livelier picture of youthful rivalship, with bewitching beauty for the prize. Yet, by a strange deception, owing to the duskiness of the chamber and the antique dresses which they still wore, the tall mirror is said to have reflected the figures of the three old, gray, withered grandsires, ridiculously contending for the skinny ugliness of a shrivelled grandam.

But they were young: their burning passions proved them so. Inflamed to madness by the coquetry of the girl-widow, who neither granted nor quite withheld her favors, the three rivals began to interchange threatening glances. Still keeping hold of the fair prize, they grappled fiercely at one another's throats. As they struggled to and fro, the table was overturned, and the vase dashed into a thousand fragments. The precious Water of Youth flowed in a bright stream across the floor, moistening the wings of a butterfly, which, grown old in the decline of summer, had alighted there to die. The insect fluttered lightly through the chamber, and settled on the snowy head of Dr. Heidegger.

"Come, come, gentlemen!—come, Madam Wycherly," exclaimed the doctor, "I must protest against this riot."

They stood still and shivered; for it seemed as if gray Time were calling them back from their sunny youth, far down into the chill and darksome vale of years. They looked at old Dr. Heidegger, who sat in his carved armchair, holding the rose of half a century, which he had rescued from among the fragments of the shattered vase. At the motion of his hand, the four rioters resumed their seats; the more readily, because their violent exertions had wearied them, youthful though they were.

"My poor Sylvia's rose!" ejaculated Dr. Heidegger, holding it in the light of the sunset clouds; "it appears to be fading again."

And so it was. Even while the party were looking at it, the flower continued to shrivel up, till it became as dry and fragile as when the doctor had first thrown it into the vase. He shook off the few drops of moisture which clung to its petals.

"I love it as well thus as in its dewy freshness," observed he, pressing the withered rose to his withered lips. While he spoke, the butterfly fluttered down from the doctor's snowy head, and fell upon the floor.

His guests shivered again. A strange chillness, whether of the body or spirit they could not tell, was creeping gradually over them all. They gazed at one another, and fancied that each fleeting moment snatched away a charm, and left a deepening furrow where none had been before. Was it an illusion? Had the changes of a lifetime been crowded into so brief a space, and were they now four aged people, sitting with their old friend, Dr. Heidegger?

"Are we grown old again, so soon?" cried they dolefully.

In truth they had. The Water of Youth possessed merely a virtue more transient than that of wine. The delirium which it created had effervesced away. Yes! they were old again. With a shuddering impulse, that showed her a woman still, the widow clasped her skinny hands before her face, and wished that the coffin lid were over it, since it could be no longer beautiful.

"Yes, friends, ye are old again," said Dr. Heidegger, "and lo! the Water of Youth is all lavished on the ground. Well—I bemoan it not; for if the fountain gushed at my very doorstep, I would not stoop to bathe my lips in it—no, though its delirium were for years instead of moments. Such is the lesson ye have taught me!"

But the doctor's four friends had taught no such lesson to themselves. They resolved forthwith to make a pilgrimage to Florida, and quaff at morning, noon, and night, from the Fountain of Youth.

Note. —In an English review, not long since, I have been accused of plagiarizing the idea of this story from a chapter in one of the novels of Alexandre Dumas. There has undoubtedly been a plagiarism on one side or the other; but as my story was written a good deal more than twenty years ago, and as the novel is of considerably more recent date, I take pleasure in thinking that M. Dumas has done me the honor to appropriate one of the fanciful conceptions of my earlier days. He is heartily welcome to it; nor is it the only instance, by many, in which the great French romancer has exercised the privilege of commanding genius by confiscating the intellectual property of less famous people to his own use and behoof.

*September,* 1860.

2

The

DIONYSOS

Myth

There is some dispute about the ancestry of Dionysos. Some say his mother was Demeter, the earth-goddess; others, that she was Persephone, the death-goddess; or Lethe, the goddess of forgetfulness. The most widely accepted version is that his mother was Semele, a mortal woman and daughter of Cadmus, King of Thebes. Zeus came to Semele disguised as a mortal, and Semele conceived a child by him. When Hera heard of the affair she was enraged, and prepared a plan to destroy her rival. Adopting a disguise herself, as an old woman, she coaxed Semele into believing that her lover was not an ordinary man, and that she should have no further relations with him until he revealed himself to her as he really was. When Semele told this to Zeus he did manifest himself—in a great blast of lightning, which destroyed Semele.

But the unborn child in her womb was not destroyed. Hermes took the foetus and sewed it inside Zeus' thigh, and in due time, the child was delivered. His name means "twice-born."

Hera's jealousy was not appeased, and she ordered the Titans to destroy the infant Dionysos, which they did by tearing him to pieces. But he was reassembled by Zeus and given for safe-keeping to Persephone, who in turn gave him to King Athamas and his wife Ino. To hide Dionysos' identity, this royal couple disguised the child as a girl and reared him in the women's part of the palace. But Hera was not deceived, and in revenge drove Athamas and Ino mad. In his madness Athamas killed his own son, mistaking him for a stag.

Zeus then instructed Hermes to once again save Dionysos from Hera. Hermes did this by transforming the child into a ram and carrying him to Mount Nysa, where he resumed his former shape and was attended by nymphs. It was during this sojourn that Dionysos invented wine.

When Dionysos reached manhood he was recognized by Hera and, as she had done to King Athamas, she drove him mad. He wandered all over the world, accompanied by wild satyrs and maenads, alternatively delighting people of other countries by introducing wine, or terrifying them with his armed and frightening entourage. During his travels through Egypt he was finally revenged on the Titans who had once tried to destroy him: he led an army of Amazons against the Titans, and defeated them.

Turning toward India, Dionysos and his followers were opposed by the King of Damascus, who did not want such an unaccountable visitor in his kingdom. Dionysos had him flayed alive, and then proceeded through the whole country, teaching the art of winemaking, building great cities, and establishing temples devoted to himself.

When he returned to Egypt he was attacked by his one-time allies, the Amazons, and in the ensuing battle, Dionysos and his troops destroyed most of their antagonists. He then made his way to Europe where once again he was opposed. This time Dionysos was soundly beaten, by King Lycurgus of Thrace, who captured Dionysos' whole army. Dionysos himself escaped by plunging into the sea, where he took refuge with Thetis, a water-goddess. But Lycurgus' triumph was short-lived. He went mad, and in his madness he cut down his own son with an ax, believing him to be a vine. As if in answer to this horror, all of Thrace grew barren. Dionysos, returned from the sea, predicted that the curse would stay on the land until Lycurgus was killed, so his subjects had him pulled apart by wild horses.

Leaving Thrace and entering Thebes, Dionysos invited the Theban women to join him in his revels. King Pentheus, attempting to restore order, attacked and tried to imprison Dionysos and all his maenads. But Pentheus too went mad. He captured a bull, believing it was Dionysos, and so let slip any chance he had of warring against his real adversary; then the maenads turned on him and tore him apart. Pentheus' own mother took part in the general frenzy, and tore off his head.

There were three women, though, who had refused to join in the mad revelries. They were the daughters of Minyas, and Dionysos came to them personally (disguised as a girl) to persuade them to answer his summons. When they still refused, he changed into a series of frightening apparitions—a lion, a bull, a panther—and drove them mad. The three women chose one of their own children as a sacrifice, tore him to pieces, devoured him, and then raced across the mountains in a wild rapture until Dionysos turned them into bats.

By now all lands recognized Dionysos' power, but there were still episodes of violence in his career. Once a band of pirates, not recognizing Dionysos, tried to kidnap him. Dionysos transformed their ship into a great vine, their oars into snakes, and himself into a lion.

Crazed, the pirates leapt into the sea and became dolphins. Another time, the heroic Perseus made the mistake of opposing Dionysos. In retaliation, the women of his kingdom were driven mad, and devoured their children. Perseus dropped his opposition at once, and appeased Dionysos by building a temple in his honor.

At last Dionysos ascended Olympus, to become one of the twelve great gods. In a final victory he arranged that his mother, Semele, be brought from the place of the dead and installed in Olympus, for final vengeance against Hera.

Dionysos is one of the most puzzling and disturbing of all mythic figures. There is an element of mystery and elusiveness in all myth, an edge of shadow that frustrates single definition. But in the case of Dionysos, the absence of hard-edged, single meaning is striking. He is a terrible and destructive force, but on occasion he is effeminate; he brings the blessings of horticulture, and he founds cities, but he also destroys kingdoms; he demands total allegiance, but he demolishes all other forms of rule and order. This paradox, this ambiguity is central to his nature, "the variety and contradictions inherent in the worship of Dionysos" are at the heart of his meaning:

> [Dionysos] presents us with the spectacle of annual festivals in the towns or fields in spring—and with biennial festivals on the bare mountain-tops in winter; with daylight celebrations and torchlit midnight rovings; it has its joyous and bountiful side and its grim and gruesome side, for the same god is hailed as the giver of all good gifts and feared as the eater of raw flesh and the man-tearer; he has animal incarnations, aniconic forms closely connected with tree-worship, a definite connection with ships and the sea; he offers ecstasy and spiritual union and wild intoxication in which he himself is the leader, so that he can be called mad, the raving god; at the same time what disconcerts his adversaries and singles him out from them is an uncanny stillness and calm, and stillness and calm too are among the gifts he bestows

on his infatuated worshippers; sexual license as a feature of his *orgia* is now admitted, now denied; his frenzied women votaries, in the passionate abandonment of his service, take young beasts in their arms and with maternal tenderness give them breast—the same women who with scarcely conceivable savagery tear the limbs from the young creatures and fasten their teeth on them.[1]

Dionysos is "the enigmatic god, the spirit of a dual nature and of paradox."[2] This strong aura of paradox, the final mysteriousness of Dionysos does not, of course, mean that he cannot be partially understood. We can begin by analyzing the recurrent motifs of the myth.[3] He comes abruptly, and is opposed by the guardians of order (by Hera, patroness of the family, by the King of Damascus, by Lycurgus, Pentheus, and Perseus). He is frequently disguised so that he cannot be prepared for, his disguises varying from the terrible (panther, tiger, bull) to the seductive (he appeared at first to the daughters of Minyas as a young girl). Pandemonium, frequently music, trances and loss of self-identity characterize his revelries. He is associated with intoxication (the invention of wine) and with the underground (some legends emphasize this in naming Demeter or Persephone his mother, both of them subterranean dwellers; he is also allied to vegetation and the seasonal rhythm of the earth). There is an insistent connection with water (to escape Lycurgus he flees to the protection of the sea-goddess, and the sea becomes his ally in the episode with the pirates), and with women (he is tutored by nymphs, frequently disguised as a woman, and the maenads, crazed women, are his most frequent companions). Most important, and binding all the episodes, is the theme of madness: he is the crazed god, his followers are frenzied, he destroys his enemies with madness. An envelope of fury surrounds his story.

But this brief analysis does not satisfy our need to know who or what Dionysos is. To move to the matter directly: he is the unconscious itself. Narcissus is *myth*, the inviter to the unconscious; and Dionysos is what we meet if we accept Narcissus' beckoning.

Carl Jung distinguished

> three psychic levels: (1) consciousness, (2) the personal un-
> conscious, and (3) the collective unconscious. The personal un-
> conscious consists firstly of all those contents that became uncon-
> scious either because they lost their intensity and were forgotten
> or because consciousness was withdrawn from them (repression),
> and secondly of contents, some of them sense-impressions, which
> never had sufficient intensity to reach consciousness but have
> somehow entered the psyche. The collective unconscious, how-
> ever, as the ancestral heritage of possibilities of representation, is
> not individual but common to all men, and perhaps even to all
> animals, and is the true basis of the individual psyche.[4]

The language of the collective unconscious, when it crosses the
threshold that divides it from the conscious state, is primarily myth; it
is in the symbols of myth (and dreams) that the vast array of hidden
psychic energy reveals itself. All the desires, needs, demands, appe-
tites that are and always have been part of the human condition
manifest themselves symbolically; and the symbols themselves point
back and down to this transpersonal, universally-shared unconscious.
"The collective unconscious . . . appears to consist of mythological
motifs or primordial images, for which reason the myths of all nations
are its real exponents. In fact, the whole of mythology could be taken
as a sort of projection of the collective unconscious."[5] The unconscious "is the deposit of all human experience right back to its re-
motest beginnings;"[6] "the collective unconscious contains the whole
spiritual heritage of mankind's evolution, born anew in the brain
structure of every individual."[7]

What is there in the collective unconscious that provokes identification with Dionysos? To the rational and conscious mind the collective unconscious is incredible, frightening;[8] it is radical, capable of
altering the more staid world of consciousness,[9] so much so that "consciousness struggles in a regular panic against being swallowed up in
the primitivity and unconsciousness of sheer instinctuality."[10] While
it is destructive of serenity and order, it is also creative, indeed the
source of the creative impulse;[11] it is identical with instinctual
energy,[12] it denies individuation and lures us to a nonpersonalized

state of being.[13] The collective unconscious is an extension of man beyond himself, a death of personal being and a rebirth in a new dimension.[14] If inhibited or denied, the instinctual energy of the unconscious will yet break forth, violently if too strongly repressed.[15] Its most common symbols are water,[16] and Woman (the *Anima*)[17]: it is through these images especially that the unconscious reveals itself.

Dionysos is associated with the deepest psychic levels (Demeter, Persephone[18]), with the nonpersonalized state (Lethe), opposed by established systems of governance (Lycurgus, Pentheus), particularly violent when unheeded (daughters of Minyas), disruptive of serenity and yet creative (unwelcome in Damascus and yet the gift-bearer and builder), always accompanied by the emblems of the unconscious (the maenads) and symbolizing radically altered consciousness (he is the twice-born).

We can speculate almost endlessly on *what* is Dionysos. But *why* is Dionysos? For what purpose does he come to Damascus, to Thrace, to Thebes?

The psyche is a complex, self-regulating organism, striving continually for a realization of its whole self. Thinking, feeling, sensing, intuiting; instinct and intellect; consciousness and unconsciousness—they are all integral parts of the entire personality. Should any part be excluded, denied, ignored, then the primal drive to wholeness will assert itself. Should the conscious mind, for its own interests, attempt to relegate the instinctual forces to the dark chambers of forgetfulness, those instinctual forces will assert themselves, to redress the upset balance. "Whenever life proceeds one-sidedly in any given direction, the self-regulation of the organism produces in the unconscious an accumulation of all those factors which play too small a part in the individual's conscious existence;[19] "the further we remove ourselves from [the unconscious] with our enlightenment and our rational superiority, the more it fades into the distance, but is made all the more potent by everything that falls into it, thrust out by our one-sided rationalism. This lost bit of nature seeks revenge."[20] As the unconscious has the function of providing that which has been lost, so consciousness has the obligation to accept the offer: "it is the function of consciousness not only to recognize and assimilate the external world through the gateway of the senses, but to translate into visible reality the world within us."[21]

This is the significance of Dionysos' confrontations. Lycurgus and Pentheus denied him, and so were destroyed; Perseus built him a temple, translated him into visible reality, and so escaped his fury. He comes from great psychic depths, his motive to transform the ordered, placid world. The established order fears him, since his transformative energy might easily be destructive, not creative. Ironically, the more he is feared and repressed, the greater the likelihood he will manifest himself as destruction.

We might say that as of this moment we are the daughters of Minyas. We sit in the safe circle of our civilized world, content to maintain the ordered regularity of our lives. All the while, Dionysos keeps appearing to us in different shapes, telling us to leave our sanctuary of orderliness and join his revels. The question is: will we, Minyas' daughters, listen?

There is certainly no lack of voices asserting Dionysos' claim. What Albert LaValley called "The New Consciousness"[22] is a many-voiced expression of the Dionysiac transformation: the renewed interest in Zen and yoga, the invitations extended by Ken Kesey and Timothy Leary to alter consciousness through LSD, Oscar Ichazo's Arica Institute with its emphasis on ego-destruction and communal consciousness, Norman O. Brown's philosophy of radical ego-change ("The human ego must face the Dionysian reality, and therefore a great work of self-transformation lies ahead of it"):[23] these are all urgings to admit extrarational awareness into our lives and thus to alter our lives. And still the voices of Dionysos go on. Pop music, most particularly of the Mick Jagger or Alice Cooper variety, extols Dionysian abandonment and even violence. The whole "back-to-the-earth" movement, with its panoply of rural communalism, organic food craze, even the earth colors of casual dress[24] are whisperings of a return to our affiliations with Dionysos, the god of vegetation. We are becoming more and more intrigued by the condition of trance, by a wisdom achieved outside the perimeters of traditional rationality: witness the amazing popularity of Carlos Castaneda's books, *The Teachings of Don Juan*, *A Separate Reality*, and *Journey to Ixtlan*, or the Sioux

shaman's visions in John Neihardt's *Black Elk Speaks*. Or consider the
new apostolate of "madness" (or rather, what the established order
defines as madness), a psychiatry that does not attempt to mollify,
bridle or "explain" psychic disturbance, but instead describes the re-
creative and transfigurative powers of the dark and hidden places.
Joseph Campbell has commented on the mythic dimensions of the
new psychiatry, as he described the work of John Weir Perry, M.D.:

> Now it was Dr. Perry's thesis . . . that in certain cases the
> best thing is to let the schizophrenic process run its course, not to
> abort the psychosis by administering shock treatments and the
> like, but, on the contrary, to help the process of disintegration
> and reintegration along. However, if a doctor is to be helpful in
> this way, he has to understand the image language of mythology.
> He has himself to understand what the fragmentary signs and
> signals signify that his patient, totally out of touch with rationally
> ordered manners of thought and communication, is trying to
> bring forth in order to establish some kind of contact. Interpreted
> from this point of view, a schizophrenic breakdown is an inward
> and backward journey to recover something missed or lost, and to
> restore, thereby, a vital balance. So let the voyager go. He has
> tipped over and is sinking, perhaps drowning; yet, as in the old
> legend of Gilgamesh and his long, deep dive to the bottom of the
> cosmic sea to pluck the watercress of immortality, there is the one
> green value of his life down there. Don't cut him off from it: help
> him through.[25]

R. D. Laing is surely the most important spokesman for what can
fairly be called the meeting with Dionysos, the acceptance of the
potential transfigurer. "We are a generation of men," he sardonically
notes in *The Politics of Experience*, "so estranged from the inner world
that many are arguing that it does not exist; and that even if it does
exist, it does not matter. Even if it has some significance, it is not the
hard stuff of science, and if it is not, then let's make it hard. Let it be
measured and counted. Quantify the heart's agony and ecstasy in a
world in which, when the inner world is first discovered, we are liable

to find ourselves bereft and derelict. For without the inner the outer loses its meaning, and without the outer the inner loses its substance."[26] Laing so well understands the fearful inertia of an established order, Lycurgus' reluctance to let Dionysos cross his borders: "in our present world, which is both so terrified and so unconscious of the other world, it is not surprising that when 'reality,' the fabric of this world bursts, and a person enters the other world, he is completely lost and terrified."[27] But we ought not to deny that god entrance: "Madness need not be all breakdown. It may also be breakthrough. It is potentially liberation and renewal as well as enslavement and existential death,"[28] always the paradoxical god.

It is possible to imagine that the politics of liberation owe much of their strength to the fact that they touch a mythic nerve. The images of dreams speak to the individual psyche, the images of liberation movements speak to the communal psyche. The world of "common sense," of course, rejects dreams; a society enslaved by its own choice in its own establishments rejects freedom; a narrow rationalism rejects the para-rational; and every such denial is ultimately a denial of something of our own.[29]

Just as we are the inheritors of a species-history, so too are we the inheritors of instinctual behavior that is older and deeper than literacy, civilization and technology. Cerebral and cultural behavior is a late-comer to humankind, a patina overlaying the Dionysiac depths, "the most recent construction on a very old site."[30] The partitions between *here* and *there, now* and *then*, civilized man and Dionysiac man, consciousness and unconsciousness are indeed, as John Dryden said, thin, and easily crossed.

Joseph Conrad's *Heart of Darkness* is about such a crossing. To be more precise, Conrad's novel is about two journeys into the hidden self. One of the journeys is horrifying, ending in personality destruction and death; the other journey is restorative, wisdom-producing, a gateway to wholeness. Conrad has seized on the paradoxical quality of the descent into the unconscious, revealing, in the characters of Kurtz and Marlow, the two faces of Dionysos: "liberation and renewal as well as enslavement and existential death."[31]

Conrad's Kurtz is a monumental version of Western man: a

rationalist, a technocrat, of boundless ego-sense, activated by his conscious will, a colonizer not only of African soil but of the African soul.
"He is a prodigy," says one of his colleagues in The Company, a
European establishment devoted to the exploitation and "civilizing"
of the African interior. "He is an emissary of pity and science and
progress, and devil knows what else."[32] Kurtz has been allowed by
The Company (increasingly clearly a symbol of that myopic empire-
building fixation that Kipling so adored and that we are so slow to
abandon) to establish a series of outposts in the interior, to serve not
only as trading centers but also as instruction areas for the natives.
"Each station should be like a beacon on the road towards better
things, a centre for trade of course, but also for humanizing, improv-
ing, instructing." (p. 54) "All Europe contributed to the making of
Kurtz; and by and by I learned that, most appropriately, The Interna-
tional Society for the Suppression of Savage Customs had intrusted
him with the making of a report, for its future guidance." (p. 83) It
was in that report that Kurtz' real attitude toward Africa, the heart of
darkness, his own, Everyman's, genetic and psychic home, was revealed. Commenting on the report, Marlow recounted that "it was
very simple, and at the end of that moving appeal to every altruistic
sentiment it blazed at you, luminous and terrifying, like a flash of
lightning in a serene sky: 'Exterminate all the brutes!'" (p. 84) What
Kurtz truly hopes to exterminate, deny, repress is a part of himself—it
is Lycurgus' and Pentheus' course of action.

For it, he suffers the same consequence as his mythic brothers.
Pushing deeper and deeper into the jungle, Kurtz lapses into madness
and murder. Having first denied and then confronted his own darkness, "his soul was mad. Being alone in the wilderness, it had looked
within itself, and, by heavens! I tell you, it had gone mad." (p. 113)
Kurtz' last words, "The horror! The horror!", (p. 118) sum up the
Jungian insight that "from the same root that produces wild, untamed,
blind instinct there grow up the natural laws and cultural forms that
tame and break its pristine power. But when the animal in us is split
off from consciousness by being repressed, it may easily burst out in full
force, quite unregulated and uncontrolled. An outburst of this sort
always ends in catastrophe—the animal destroys itself."[33]

Marlow—who tells Kurtz' story—follows Kurtz into the jungle, with the purpose of locating him for The Company. The stages of his journey, the long penetration of the dark self, are the same as Kurtz'; but because Marlow accepts and participates in the Dionysiac journey, he is not destroyed: instead he achieves enlightenment, a fuller realization of himself. As Kurtz is the reembodiment of Lycurgus and Pentheus, Marlow reincarnates Perseus, the accepter. The story he tells us is, in a sense, the equivalent of the temple Perseus dedicated to the power of Dionysos.

Even before he began his search for Kurtz, before he took employment with The Company, Marlow had been fascinated by the prospect of exploring the jungle. On the map, he had seen the waterway into the jungle as a great snake: archetypally, as the inhabitant and messenger of the underground regions, the unconscious itself:[34]

> It had become a place of darkness. But there was in it one river especially, a mighty big river, that you could see on the map, resembling an immense snake uncoiled, with its head in the sea, its body at rest curving afar over a vast country, and its tail lost in the depths of the land . . . The snake had charmed me. (p. 11)

Seeing the jungle interior as a snake, as symbolically the unconscious, it was appropriate that Marlow should have begun on his journey with the help of women, Woman, the Anima, the greatest symbol of the unconscious.[35] When he applied for employment with The Company to skipper a boat into those dark places, Marlow was rebuffed until he had help from the women:

> The man said 'My dear fellow,' and did nothing. Then—would you believe it?—I tried the women. I, Charlie Marlow, set the women to work—to get a job. Heavens! Well, you see, the notion drove me. I had an aunt, a dear enthusiastic soul. She wrote: 'It will be delightful. I am ready to do anything, anything for you. It is a glorious idea. I know the wife of a very high personage in the Administration'. . . I got the appointment—of course. (p. 12)

At The Company's first outpost, perched on the edge between "civilization" and "jungle," the spectacle of brutalizing and exploiting the African people appears, The Company's version of Kurtz' dictate "Exterminate the brutes!" Marlow describes the station:

> Black shapes crouched, lay, sat between the trees leaning against the trunks, clinging to the earth, half coming out, half effaced within the dim light, in all the attitudes of pain, abandonment, and despair. [A] mine on the cliff went off, followed by a slight shudder of the soil under my feet. The work was going on. The work! And this was the place where some of the helpers had withdrawn to die.
>
> They were dying slowly—it was very clear. They were not enemies, they were not criminals, they were nothing earthly now—nothing but black shadows of disease and starvation, lying confusedly in the greenish gloom. Brought from all the recesses of the coast in all the legality of time contracts, lost in uncongenial surroundings, fed on unfamiliar food, they sickened, became inefficient, and were then allowed to crawl away and rest. (p. 26)

This fratricide, this white erasure of the older black brothers, is overseen by an absolute walking vision of system, efficiency, "civilization": "near the buildings I met a white man, in such an unexpected elegance of getup that in the first moment I took him for a sort of vision. I saw a high starched collar, white cuffs, a light alpaca jacket, snowy trousers, a clean necktie, and varnished boots. No hat. Hair parted, brushed, oiled, under a green-lined parasol held in a big white hand. He was amazing, and had a penholder behind his ear." (p. 28)

When Marlow, after delays, begins his journey into the interior, he senses that he moves not only in space but in time ("Going up that river was like travelling back to the earliest beginnings of the world." (p. 55) Quite true, of course. The white-cuffed, penholder-behind-the-ear apparition stood at the nearer end of time, while behind him stretched aeons; and those aeons began with the black man. Marlow's journey is thus spatial (into the African interior), temporal (back to the origins of man), and psychic (to the roots of his own unconscious). In that many-meaninged interior, the equations of power are quite different from what they are outside. Outside the interior, civilization and efficiency, the infants of history, dominate, and the man in the light alpaca jacket watches black men die. Within the interior, the products of modernity and technology are ludicrous compared to the power of the dark continent. Marlow recalls an episode:

> Once, I remember, we came upon a man-of-war anchored off the coast. There wasn't even a shed there, and she was shelling the bush. It appears the French had one of their wars going on thereabouts. Her ensign drooped like a rag; the muzzles of the long six-inch guns stuck out all over the low hull; the greasy, slimy swell swung her up lazily and let her down, swaying her thin masts. In the empty immensity of earth, sky, and water, there she was, incomprehensible, firing into a continent. Pop, would go one of the six-inch guns; a small flame would disappear, a tiny projectile would give a feeble screech—and nothing happened. Nothing could happen. (p. 21)

It is an ironic prediction of Kurtz himself, firing his puny weaponry of culture, colonialism and civilized intelligence into the darkness of himself. "There was a touch of insanity in the proceeding," Marlow remarks of the French man-of-war (but the remark is equally applicable to Kurtz' behavior), "a sense of lugubrious drollery in the sight; and it was not dissipated by somebody on board assuring me earnestly there was a camp of natives—he called them enemies!—hidden out of sight somewhere." (p. 21)

As he moves nearer and nearer to Kurtz, Marlow sees three apparitions. The first is of the station-master, symbolic of the veneer of civilization. The second is of a harlequin figure, a companion of Kurtz who had been left behind part way through Kurtz' passage inward and who becomes Marlow's guide on the last stage of the trek inland. It is he who waves Marlow ashore and leads him to Kurtz. His appearance is striking:

> His aspect reminded me of something I had seen—something funny I had seen somewhere. As I maneuvered to get alongside, I was asking myself, 'What does this fellow look like?' Suddenly, I got it. He looked like a harlequin. His clothes had been made of some stuff that was brown holland probably, but it was covered with patches all over, with bright patches, blue, red, and yellow—patches on the back, patches on the front, patches on elbows, knees; colored binding around his jacket, scarlet edging at the bottom of his trousers; and the sunshine made him look extremely gay and wonderfully neat withal, because you could see how beautifully all this patching had been done. (pp. 88–9)

The station-master had been all of a piece; this figure is patchwork. The station-master had been at the outer edge, beyond the darkness; the harlequin is part way into the darkness, a bridge between the two worlds of conscious and unconscious. As harlequin, he is cousin-germane to other figures of fun, such as the jester, the court fool, the madcap Robins in the history of foolery,[36] and ultimately to the trickster figure, the hobgoblin of legend and fairy tale. Jung has written of the symbolism of such a figure, pointing out that he is "the reflection of an earlier, rudimentary stage of consciousness.[37] He is a metaphor for the mind's ineradicable link with its own history and at the same time of the mind's reluctance to accept that link. "Outwardly people are more or less civilized, but inwardly they are still primitives. Something in man is profoundly disinclined to give up all his beginnings, and something else believes it has long since got beyond all that."[38] Conrad's harlequin represents this ambivalence.

The third apparition coincides with the end of Marlow's quest for Kurtz and for himself. It is a superb, blazing apparition of Woman, the grand archetype of the unconscious, consort of the mad Kurtz, and the goal of Marlow's inner search. Beginning his quest with the aid of women, Marlow completes his exploration by seeing Her, the Unconscious. As he finally comes upon Kurtz,

> Dark human shapes could be made out in the distance, flitting indistinctly against the gloomy border of the forest, and near the river two bronze figures, leaning on tall spears, stood in the

sunlight under fantastic head-dresses of spotted skins, warlike and still in statuesque repose. And from right to left along the lighted shore moved a wild and gorgeous apparition of a woman.

She walked with measured steps, draped in striped and fringed clothes, treading the earth proudly, with a slight jingle and flash of barbarous ornaments. She carried her head high; her hair was done in the shape of a helmet; she had brass leggings to the knees, brass wire gauntlets to the elbow, a crimson spot on her tawny cheek, innumerable necklaces of glass beads on her neck; bizarre things, charms, gifts of witch-men, that hung about her, glittered and trembled at every step. She must have had the value of several elephant tusks upon her. She was savage and superb, wild-eyed and magnificent; there was something ominous and stately in her deliberate progress. And in the hush that had fallen suddenly upon the whole sorrowful land, the immense wilderness, the colossal body of the fecund and mysterious life seemed to look at her, pensive, as though it had been looking at the image of its own tenebrous and passionate soul. (pp. 102–3)

The image of the dark and passionate soul, the image of the jungle and of the unconscious itself; and she is the last such image that Marlow sees as he moves out of the jungle, back to civilization with the dying Kurtz—she stands at the end and "stretched tragically her bare arms after us over the sombre and glittering river." (p. 115)

(That same image returns to Marlow later on. Having promised himself to report Kurtz' death to his betrothed, he goes to the woman's house. When she speaks to Marlow, she stretches out her arms, and the image of the dark woman superimposes itself over that gesture. [p. 130] But Marlow finds that he cannot tell this white woman the truth of Kurtz' madness and death—she is the antithesis of that smouldering and passionate woman in the heart of darkness. This woman has been labelled by Kurtz My intended, she is will and consciousness; she is surrounded, encased, protected by the trappings of civilization and culture,[39] she is cerebration and the mind,[40] unable to apprehend the mystery of the other woman or of Kurtz' dark journey. So Marlow leaves her with a lie and her own manageable version of his death.)

Drawn deeper and deeper into the interior, into his racial past, into himself, Marlow accepts his enmeshment: "It was written I should be loyal to the nightmare of my choice," he said when his journey was over; "I was anxious to deal with this shadow by myself alone." (p. 109) Indeed, he even regretted that he had not gone as deep as Kurtz, into the final stage of madness and confrontation with the ultimate deep:

> [Kurtz] had made that last stride, he had stepped over the edge, while I had been permitted to draw back my hesitating foot. And perhaps in this is the whole difference; perhaps all the wisdom, and all truth, and all sincerity, are just compressed into that inappreciable moment of time in which we step over the threshold of the invisible. Perhaps! I like to think my summing-up would not have been a word of careless contempt. Better his cry—much better. It was an affirmation, a moral victory paid for by innumerable defeats, by abominable terror, by abominable satisfactions. But it was a victory! (p. 120)

By receiving the darkness, Marlow attains enlightenment. Three times Conrad describes him as Buddha-like, symbol of wisdom.[41]

In his student days, Carl Jung had a dream which, as he recalled in his memoirs, both frightened and encouraged him:

> It was night in some unknown place, and I was making slow and painful headway against a mighty wind. Dense fog was flying along everywhere. I had my hands cupped around a tiny light which threatened to go out at any moment. Everything depended on my keeping this little light alive. Suddenly I had the feeling that something was coming up behind me. I looked back, and saw a gigantic black figure following me. But at the same moment I was conscious, in spite of my terror, that I must keep my little light going through night and wind, regardless of all dangers. When I awoke I realized at once that the figure was . . . my own shadow on the swirling mists, brought into being by the

little light I was carrying. I knew, too, that this little light was my consciousness, the only light I have. My own understanding is the sole treasure I possess, and the greatest. Though infinitely small and fragile in comparison with the powers of darkness, it is still a light, my only light.[42]

Jung's awareness that the darkness is a part of himself, that to deny the darkness would be a self-mutilation,[43] and that awareness is not erased but is heightened by a recognition of that dark self: this is Marlow's discovery. In *Heart of Darkness*, Joseph Conrad has superbly dramatized "the enigmatic god, the spirit of a dual nature and of paradox,"[44] Dionysos, both the destructive and the creative force within.

# NOTES

1. W. K. C. Guthrie, *The Greeks and Their Gods* (Boston, Houghton Mifflin, 1971), pp. 145–6.
2. Walter F. Otto, *Dionysus: Myth and Cult.* Tr. Robert D. Palmer (Bloomington, Indiana University, 1965), p. 73.
3. The following tabulation is greatly indebted to W. F. Otto's enthusiastic, sympathetic, and polemical study first published in Germany in 1933.
4. Carl Jung, *The Structure and Dynamics of the Psyche* (copyright 1953 and © 1960 by Bollingen Foundation and © 1969 by Princeton University Press), pp. 151–152. Reprinted by permission of Princeton University Press.
5. *Ibid.*, 152.
6. *Ibid.*, 157.
7. *Ibid.*, 158.
8. *Ibid.* Also, "The Role of the Unconscious" in *Civilization in Transition* (© 1964 by Bollingen Foundation), pp. 11–12.
9. *Ibid.*, 178.
10. *Ibid.*, 212.
11. *Ibid.*, 157.

12. Jung, *Two Essays on Analytical Psychology, Works*, VII, 116.
13. Jung, "Psychological Types," in *Civilization in Transition*, p. 10. Reprinted by permission of Princeton University Press.
14. Jung, *The Role of the Unconscious, Works*, X, 10.
15. *Ibid.*, 21, 26–7.
16. Jung, *The Archetypes and the Collective Unconscious* ( © 1959 and 1969 by Bollingen Foundation), p. 18. Reprinted by permission of Princeton University Press.
17. Jung, *Aion: Researches into the Phenomenology of the Self* (Copyright © 1959 and 1968 by Bollingen Foundation), p. 13; and *Two Essays on Analytical Psychology, Works*, XII, 195.
18. Semele herself is perhaps a goddess of the underground rather than a mortal woman. She may be derived from *Zemelo*, one of the earth goddesses of ancient Asia Minor. Cf. Erich Neumann, *Art and the Creative Unconscious* (Princeton, Princeton University Press, 1971), p. 70.
19. Jung, *The Role of the Unconscious*, p. 15.
20. *Ibid.*, pp. 26–7. See also *Structure and Dynamics of the Psyche*, pp. 216–23.
21. Jung, *The Structure and Dynamics of the Psyche*, p. 158. See also *Two Essays on Analytical Psychology*, p. 54.
22. Albert J. LaValley, *The New Consciousness* (Cambridge, Mass., Winthrop, 1972).
23. Norman O. Brown, *Life Against Death*, p. 175.
24. The image value of current dress fads was remarked on by Charles Reich in *The Greening of America*.
25. Joseph Campbell, *Myths to Live By* (New York, Viking Press, 1972), p. 203. The technique described here by Campbell has been used in actual situations. A number of terminally ill patients at the Maryland Psychiatric Research Center in Catonsville, Maryland, have, through counselling and the use of LSD, been initiated into this inner journey. The experience is very often terrifying; but the patient is encouraged to go through the agony rather than around it. The hoped for and usually achieved result is a strong sense of unity with all of creation and a diminishment of individual pain and suffering. The entire procedure is described by Jerry Avorn in "Beyond Dying," *Harper's*, March 1973, pp. 56–64. Avorn's account tends to corroborate Dr. Perry's thesis. Norman O. Brown's is probably the most eloquent voice raised on behalf of Dionysos: "The mad truth: the boundary between sanity and insanity is a false one. The proper outcome of psychoanalysis is the abolition of the boundary, the healing of the split, the integration of the human race . . . Dionysus, the mad god, breaks down the boundaries; releases the prisoners; abolishes repression; and abolishes the *principium individuationis*, substituting for it the unity of man and the unity of man with nature." (*Love's Body*, Toronto, Random House, 1966, pp. 160–1)
26. R. D. Laing, *The Politics of Experience* (New York, Ballantine Books, Inc., 1967), pp. 54–5.
27. *Ibid.*, p. 125.
28. *Ibid.*, p. 133.
29. Philip Slater's thoughtful study, *The Pursuit of Loneliness* (Boston, Beacon Press, 1971), analyzed the so-called "generation gap" of the sixties from this point of view of the deniers being the self-destructors. The elders of society, Slater argued, secretly envy the freedom of the young, and their attempts to repress youthful lifestyles stem not from righteousness but regret. "If we can't have it, neither can they."
30. Robert Ardrey, *African Genesis* (New York, Atheneum, 1965), p. 315.
31. Laing, *The Politics of Experience*, p. 133.
32. Joseph Conrad, *Heart of Darkness* (New York, 1961), p. 41.

33. Jung, *The Role of the Unconscious*, p. 21.
34. The snake is traditionally recognized as a symbol of the underground. See Neumann, *Origins and History of Consciousness*, pp. 49, 276–7.
35. Jung, *The Development of Personality, Works*, XVII, 198.
36. Cf. Enid Welsford, *The Fool: His Social and Literary History* (London, Faber and Faber, 1935).
37. Jung, "On the Psychology of the Trickster Figure," *Works*, IX, part 1, 261.
38. *Ibid.*, pp. 268–9.
39. "I had to wait [to see her] in a lofty drawingroom with three long windows from floor to ceiling that were like three luminous and bedraped columns. The bent gilt legs and backs of the furniture shone in indistinct curves. The tall marble fireplace had a cold and monumental whiteness. A grand piano stood massively in a corner; with dark gleams on the flat surfaces like a sombre and polished sarcophagus." (pp. 125–6)
40. "'You knew him best,' I repeated. And perhaps she did. But with every word spoken the room was growing darker, and only her forehead, smooth and white, remained illumined by the unextinguishable light of belief and love." (p. 127)
41. "[Marlow] had sunken cheeks, a yellow complexion, a straight back, an ascetic aspect, and, with his arms dropped, the palms of his hands outwards, resembled an idol." (p. 4)
    ". . . he had the pose of a Buddha preaching in European clothes and without a lotus-flower." (p. 9)
    "Marlow ceased, and sat apart, indistinct and silent, in the pose of a meditating Buddha." (p. 131)
42. C. G. Jung, *Memories, Dreams, Reflections*. Recorded and edited by Amelia Jaffe, translated by Richard and Clara Winston (New York, Vintage Books, 1965), pp. 87–8.
43. *Ibid.*, p. 89.
44. Otto, *Dionysus*, p. 73.

# SECOND INTERLUDE:
# THE TERRIBLE TREASURE

As I was walking among the fires of Hell,
delighted with the enjoyments of Genius,
which to Angels look like torment
and insanity, I collected some of their
Proverbs . . . *The tigers of wrath are wiser
than the horses of instruction.*

William Blake, *The Marriage of Heaven and Hell*

# The Woman Who Rode Away

*D. H. Lawrence*

She had thought that this marriage, of all marriages, would
be an adventure. Not that the man himself was exactly magical to
her. A little, wiry, twisted fellow, twenty years older than herself,
with brown eyes and greying hair, who had come to America a
scrap of a wastrel, from Holland, years ago, as a tiny boy, and
from the gold-mines of the west had been kicked south into
Mexico, and now was more or less rich, owning silver-mines in
the wilds of the Sierra Madre: it was obvious that the adventure
lay in his circumstances, rather than his person. But he was still a
little dynamo of energy, in spite of accidents survived, and what
he had accomplished he had accomplished alone. One of those
human oddments there is no accounting for.

When she actually *saw* what he had accomplished, her
heart quailed. Great green-covered, unbroken mountain-hills,
and in the midst of the lifeless isolation, the sharp pinkish
mounds of the dried mud from the silver-works. Under the
nakedness of the works, the walled-in, one-storey adobe house,
with its garden inside, and its deep inner veranda with tropical
climbers on the sides. And when you looked up from this shut-in

flowered patio, you saw the huge pink cone of the silver-mud refuse, and the machinery of the extracting plant against heaven above. No more.

To be sure, the great wooden doors were often open. And then she could stand outside, in the vast open world. And see great, void, tree-clad hills piling behind one another, from nowhere into nowhere. They were green in autumn-time. For the rest, pinkish, stark dry and abstract.

And in his battered Ford car her husband would take her into the dead, thrice-dead little Spanish town forgotten among the mountains. The great, sun-dried dead church, the dead portales, the hopeless covered market-place, where the first time she went, she saw a dead dog lying between the meat-stalls and the vegetable array, stretched out as if for ever, nobody troubling to throw it away. Deadness within deadness.

Everybody feebly talking silver, and showing bits of ore. But silver was at a standstill. The great war came and went. Silver was a dead market. Her husband's mines were closed down. But she and he lived on in the adobe house under the works, among the flowers that were never very flowery to her.

She had two children, a boy and a girl. And her eldest, the boy, was nearly ten years old before she aroused from her stupor of subjected amazement. She was now thirty-three, a large, blue-eyed, dazed woman, beginning to grow stout. Her little, wiry, tough, twisted, brown-eyed husband was fifty-three, a man as tough as wire, tenacious as wire, still full of energy, but dimmed by the lapse of silver from the market, and by some curious inaccessibility on his wife's part.

He was a man of principles, and a good husband. In a way, he doted on her. He never quite got over his dazzled admiration of her. But essentially, he was still a bachelor. He had been thrown out on the world, a little bachelor, at the age of ten. When he married he was over forty, and had enough money to marry on. But his capital was all a bachelor's. He was boss of his own works, and marriage was the last and most intimate bit of his own works.

He admired his wife to extinction, he admired her body, all her points. And she was to him always the rather dazzling Californian girl from Berkeley, whom he had first known. Like any sheikh, he kept her guarded among those mountains of Chihuahua. He was jealous of her as he was of his silver-mine: and that is saying a lot.

At thirty-three she really was still the girl from Berkeley, in all but physique. Her conscious development had stopped mysteriously with her marriage, completely arrested. Her husband had never become real to her, neither mentally nor physically. In spite of his late sort of passion for her, he never meant anything to her, physically. Only morally he swayed her, downed her, kept her in an invincible slavery.

So the years went by, in the adobe house strung round the sunny patio, with the silver-works overhead. Her husband was never still. When the silver went dead, he ran a ranch lower down, some twenty miles away, and raised pure-bred hogs, splendid creatures. At the same time, he hated pigs. He was a squeamish waif of an idealist, and really hated the physical side of life. He loved work, work, work, and making things. His marriage, his children, were something he was making, part of his business, but with a sentimental income this time.

Gradually her nerves began to go wrong: she must get out. She must get out. So he took her to El Paso for three months. And at least it was the United States.

But he kept his spell over her. The three months ended: back she was, just the same, in her adobe house among those eternal green or pinky-brown hills, void as only the undiscovered is void. She taught her children, she supervised the Mexican boys who were her servants. And sometimes her husband brought visitors, Spaniards or Mexicans or occasionally white men.

He really loved to have white men staying on the place. Yet he had not a moment's peace when they were there. It was as if his wife were some peculiar secret vein of ore in his mines, which no one must be aware of except himself. And she was fascinated by the young gentlemen, mining engineers, who were his guests at times. He, too, was fascinated by a real gentleman. But he was an old-timer miner with a wife, and if a gentleman looked at his wife, he felt as if his mine were being looted, the secrets of it pried out.

It was one of these young gentlemen who put the idea into her mind. They were all standing outside the great wooden doors of the patio, looking at the outer world. The eternal, motionless hills were all green, it was September, after the rains. There was no sign of anything, save the deserted mine, the deserted works, and a bunch of half-deserted miners' dwellings.

"I wonder," said the young man, "what there is behind those great blank hills."

"More hills," said Lederman. "If you go that way, Sonora and the coast. This way is the desert—you came from there —and the other way, hills and mountains."

"Yes, but what *lives* in the hills and the mountains? *Surely* there is something wonderful? It looks *so* like nowhere on earth: like being on the moon."

"There's plenty of game, if you want to shoot. And Indians, if you call *them* wonderful."

"Wild ones?"

"Wild enough."

"But friendly?"

"It depends. Some of them are quite wild, and they don't let anybody near. They kill a missionary at sight. And where a missionary can't get, nobody can."

"But what does the government say?"

"They're so far from everywhere, the government leaves 'em alone. And they're wily; if they think there'll be trouble, they send a delegation to Chihuahua and make a formal submission. The government is glad to leave it at that."

"And do they live quite wild, with their own savage customs and religion?"

"Oh yes. They use nothing but bows and arrows. I've seen them in town, in the Plaza, with funny sort of hats with flowers round them, and a bow in one hand, quite naked except for a sort of shirt, even in cold weather—striding round with their savage's bare legs."

"But don't you suppose it's wonderful, up there in their secret villages?"

"No. What would there be wonderful about it? Savages are savages, and all savages behave more or less alike: rather low-down and dirty, unsanitary, with a few cunning tricks, and struggling to get enough to eat."

"But surely they have old, old religions and mysteries—it *must* be wonderful, surely it must."

"I don't know about mysteries—howling and heathen practices, more or less indecent. No, I see nothing wonderful in that kind of stuff. And I wonder that you should, when you have lived in London or Paris or New York—"

"Ah, *everybody* lives in London or Paris or New York" —said the young man, as if this were an argument.

And this particular vague enthusiasm for unknown Indians found a full echo in the woman's heart. She was overcome by a foolish romanticism more unreal than a girl's. She felt it was her destiny to wander into the secret haunts of these timeless, mysterious, marvellous Indians of the mountains.

She kept her secret. The young man was departing, her husband was going with him down to Torreon, on business: would be away for some days. But before the departure, she made her husband talk about the Indians: about the wandering tribes, resembling the Navajo, who were still wandering free; and the Yaquis of Sonora: and the different groups in the different valleys of Chihuahua State.

There was supposed to be one tribe, the Chilchuis, living in a high valley to the south, who were the sacred tribe of all the Indians. The descendants of Montezuma and the old Aztec or Totonac kings still lived among them, and the old priests still kept up the ancient religion, and offered human sacrifices—so it was said. Some scientists had been to the Chilchui country, and had come back gaunt and exhausted with hunger and bitter privation, bringing various curious, barbaric objects of worship, but having seen nothing extraordinary in the hungry, stark village of savages.

Though Lederman talked in this off-hand way, it was obvious he felt some of the vulgar excitement at the idea of ancient and mysterious savages.

"How far away are they?" she asked.

"Oh—three days on horseback—past Cuchitee and a little lake there is up there."

Her husband and the young man departed. The woman made her crazy plans. Of late, to break the monotony of her life, she had harassed her husband into letting her go riding with him, occasionally, on horseback. She was never allowed to go out alone. The country truly was not safe, lawless and crude.

But she had her own horse, and she dreamed of being free as she had been as a girl among the hills of California.

Her daughter, nine years old, was now in a tiny convent in the little half-deserted Spanish mining-town five miles away.

"Manuel," said the woman to her house-servant, "I'm going to ride to the convent to see Margarita, and take her a few things. Perhaps I shall stay the night in the convent. You look after Freddy and see everything is all right till I come back."

"Shall I ride with you on the master's horse, or shall Juan?" asked the servant.

"Neither of you. I shall go alone."

The young man looked her in the eyes, in protest. Absolutely impossible that the woman should ride alone!

"I shall go alone," repeated the large, placid-seeming, fair-complexioned woman, with peculiar overbearing emphasis. And the man silently, unhappily yielded.

"Why are you going alone, mother?" asked her son, as she made up parcels of food.

"Am I *never* to be let alone? Not one moment of my life?" she cried, with sudden explosion of energy. And the child, like the servant, shrank into silence.

She set off without a qualm, riding astride on her strong roan horse, and wearing a riding-suit of coarse linen, a riding-skirt over her linen breeches, a scarlet neck-tie over her white blouse, and a black felt hat on her head. She had food in her saddle-bags, an army canteen with water, and a large, native blanket tied on behind the saddle. Peering into the distance, she set off from her home. Manuel and the little boy stood in the gateway to watch her go. She did not even turn to wave them farewell.

But when she had ridden about a mile, she left the wild road and took a small trail to the right, that led into another valley, over steep places and past great trees, and through another deserted mining settlement. It was September, the water was running freely in the little stream that had fed the now-abandoned mine. She got down to drink, and let the horse drink too.

She saw natives coming through the trees, away up the slope. They had seen her, and were watching her closely. She watched in turn. The three people, two women and a youth, were making a wide detour, so as not to come too close to her. She did not care. Mounting, she trotted ahead up the silent valley, beyond the silver-works, beyond any trace of mining. There was still a rough trail that led over rocks and loose stones into the valley beyond. This trail she had already ridden, with her husband. Beyond that she knew she must go south.

Curiously she was not afraid, although it was a frightening country, the silent, fatal-seeming mountain slopes, the occasional distant, suspicious, elusive natives among the trees, the great carrion birds occasionally hovering, like great flies, in the distance, over some carrion or some ranch-house or some group of huts.

As she climbed, the trees shrank and the trail ran through a thorny scrub, that was trailed over with blue convolvulus and an occasional pink creeper. Then these flowers lapsed. She was nearing the pine trees.

She was over the crest, and before her another silent, void, green-clad valley. It was past midday. Her horse turned to a little runlet of water, so she got down to eat her midday meal. She sat in silence looking at the motionless unliving valley, and at the sharp-peaked hills, rising higher to rock and pine trees, southwards. She rested two hours in the heat of the day, while the horse cropped around her.

Curious that she was neither afraid nor lonely. Indeed, the loneliness was like a drink of cold water to one who is very thirsty. And a strange elation sustained her from within.

She travelled on, and camped at night in a valley beside a stream, deep among the bushes. She had seen cattle and had crossed several trails. There must be a ranch not far off. She heard the strange wailing shriek of a mountain-lion, and the answer of dogs. But she sat by her small camp-fire in a secret hollow place and was not really afraid. She was buoyed up always by the curious, bubbling elation within her.

It was very cold before dawn. She lay wrapped in her blanket looking at the stars, listening to her horse shivering, and feeling like a woman who has died and passed beyond. She was not sure that she had not heard, during the night, a great crash at the centre of herself, which was the crash of her own death. Or else it was a crash at the centre of the earth, and meant something big and mysterious.

With the first peep of light she got up, numb with cold, and made a fire. She ate hastily, gave her horse some pieces of oil-seed cake, and set off again. She avoided any meeting—and since she met nobody, it was evident that she in turn was avoided. She came at last in sight of the village of Cuchitee, with its black houses with their reddish roofs, a sombre, dreary little cluster below another silent, long-abandoned mine. And beyond, a long, great mountain-side, rising up green and light to the darker, shaggier green of pine trees. And beyond the pine trees stretches of naked rock against the sky, rock slashed already and brindled with white stripes of snow. High up, the new snow had already begun to fall.

And now, as she neared, more or less, her destination, she began to go vague and disheartened. She had passed the little lake among yellowing aspen trees whose white trunks were round and suave like the white round arms of some woman. What a lovely place! In California she would have raved about it. But here she looked and saw that it was lovely, but she didn't care. She was weary and spent with her two nights in the open, afraid of the coming night. She didn't know where she was going, or what she was going for. Her horse plodded dejectedly on, towards that immense and forbidding mountain-slope, following a stony little trail. And if she had had any will of her own left, she would have turned back, to the village, to be protected and sent home to her husband.

But she had no will of her own. Her horse splashed through a brook, and turned up a valley, under immense yellowing cottonwood trees. She must have been near nine thousand feet above sea-level, and her head was light with the altitude and with weariness. Beyond the cottonwood trees she could see, on each side the steep sides of mountain-slopes hemming her in, sharp-plumaged with overlapping aspen, and, higher up, with sprouting, pointed spruce and pine tree. Her horse went on automatically. In this tight valley, on this slight trail, there was nowhere to go but ahead, climbing.

Suddenly her horse jumped, and three men in dark blankets were on the trail before her.

"Adios!" came the greeting, in the full, restrained Indian voice.

"Adios!" she replied in her assured, American woman's voice.

"Where are you going?" came the quiet question, in Spanish.

The men in the dark sarapes had come closer, and were looking up at her.

"On ahead," she replied coolly, in her hard, Saxon Spanish.

These were just natives to her: dark-faced, strongly-built men in dark sarapes and straw hats. They would have been the same as the men who worked for her husband, except, strangely, for the long black hair that fell over their shoulders. She noted this long black hair with a certain distaste. These must be the wild Indians she had come to see.

"Where do you come from?" the same man asked. It was always the one man who spoke. He was young, with quick, large, bright black eyes that glanced sideways at her. He had a soft black moustache on his dark face, and a sparse tuft of beard, loose hairs on his chin. His long black hair, full of life, hung unrestrained on his shoulders. Dark as he was, he did not look as if he had washed lately.

His two companions were the same, but older men, powerful and silent. One had a thin black line of moustache, but was beardless. The other had the smooth cheeks and the sparse dark hairs marking the lines of his chin with the beard characteristic of the Indians.

"I come from far away," she replied, with half-jocular evasion.

This was received in silence.

"But where do you live?" asked the young man, with that same quiet insistence.

"In the north," she replied airily.

Again there was a moment's silence. The young man conversed quietly, in Indian, with his two companions.

"Where do you want to go, up this way?" he asked suddenly, with challenge and authority, pointing briefly up the trail.

"To the Chilchui Indians," answered the woman laconically.

The young man looked at her. His eyes were quick and black, and inhuman. He saw, in the full evening light, the faint sub-smile of assurance on her rather large, calm, fresh-complexioned face; the weary, bluish lines under her large blue eyes; and in her eyes, as she looked down at him, a half-childish, half-arrogant confidence in her own female power. But in her eyes also, a curious look of trance.

"*Usted es Sēnora?* You are a lady?" the Indian asked her.

"Yes, I am a lady," she replied complacently.

"With a family?"

"With a husband and two children, boy and girl," she said.

The Indian turned to his companion and translated, in the low, gurgling speech, like hidden water running. They were evidently at a loss.

"Where is your husband?" asked the young man.

"Who knows?" she replied airily. "He has gone away on business for a week."

The black eyes watched her shrewdly. She, for all her weariness, smiled faintly in the pride of her own adventure and the assurance of her own womanhood, and the spell of the madness that was on her.

"And what do *you* want to do?" the Indian asked her.

"I want to visit the Chilchui Indians—to see their houses and to know their gods," she replied.

The young man turned and translated quickly, and there was a silence almost of consternation. The grave elder men were glancing at her sideways, with strange looks, from under their decorated hats. And they said something to the young man, in deep chest voices.

The latter still hesitated. Then he turned to the woman.

"Good!" he said. "Let us go. But we cannot arrive until to-morrow. We shall have to make a camp to-night."

"Good!" she said. "I can make a camp."

Without more ado, they set off at a good speed up the stony trail. The young Indian ran alongside her horse's head, the other two ran behind. One of them had taken a thick stick, and occasionally he struck her horse a resounding blow on the haunches to urge him forward. This made the horse jump, and threw her back in the saddle, which, tired as she was, made her angry.

"Don't do that!" she cried, looking round angrily at the fellow. She met his black, large, bright eyes, and for the first time her spirit really quailed. The man's eyes were not human to her, and they did not see her as a beautiful white woman. He looked at her with a black, bright inhuman look, and saw no woman in her at all. As if she were some strange, unaccountable *thing*, incomprehensible to him, but inimical. She sat in her saddle in wonder, feeling once more as if she had died. And again he struck her horse, and jerked her badly in the saddle.

All the passionate anger of the spoilt white woman rose in her. She pulled her horse to a standstill, and turned with blazing eyes to the man at her bridle.

"Tell that fellow not to touch my horse again," she cried.

She met the eyes of the young man, and in their bright black inscrutability she saw a fine spark, as in a snake's eye, of derision. He spoke to his companion in the rear, in the low tones of the Indian. The man with the stick listened without looking. Then, giving a strange low cry to the horse, he struck it again on the rear, so that it leaped forward spasmodically up the stony trail, scattering the stones, pitching the weary woman in her seat.

The anger flew like a madness into her eyes, she went white at the gills. Fiercely she reined in her horse. But before she could turn, the young Indian had caught the reins under the horse's throat, jerked them forward, and was trotting ahead rapidly, leading the horse.

The woman was powerless. And along with her supreme anger there came a slight thrill of exultation. She knew she was dead.

The sun was setting, a great yellow light flooded the last of the aspens, flared on the trunks of the pine trees, the pine needles bristled and stood out with dark lustre, the rocks glowed with unearthly glamour. And through the effulgence the Indian at her horse's head trotted unweariedly on, his dark blanket swinging, his bare legs glowing with a strange transfigured ruddiness in the powerful light, and his straw hat with its half-absurd decorations of flowers and feathers shining showily above his river of long black hair. At times he would utter a low call to the horse, and then the other Indian, behind, would fetch the beast a whack with the stick.

The wonder-light faded off the mountains, the world began to grow dark, a cold air breathed down. In the sky, half a moon was struggling against the glow in the west. Huge shadows came down from steep rocky slopes. Water was rushing. The woman was conscious only of her fatigue, her unspeakable fatigue, and the cold wind from the heights. She was not aware how moonlight replaced daylight. It happened while she travelled unconscious with weariness.

For some hours they travelled by moonlight. Then suddenly they came to a standstill. The men conversed in low tones for a moment.

"We camp here," said the young man.

She waited for him to help her down. He merely stood holding the horse's bridle. She almost fell from the saddle, so fatigued.

They had chosen a place at the foot of rocks that still gave off a little warmth of the sun. One man cut pine boughs, another erected little screens of pine boughs against the rock for shelter, and put boughs of balsam pine for beds. The third made a small fire, to heat tortillas. They worked in silence.

The woman drank water. She did not want to eat—only to lie down.

"Where do I sleep?" she asked.

The young man pointed to one of the shelters. She crept in and lay inert. She did not care what happened to her, she was so weary, and so beyond everything. Through the twigs of spruce she could see the three men squatting round the fire on their hams, chewing the tortillas they picked from the ashes with their dark fingers, and drinking water from a gourd. They talked in low muttering tones, with long intervals of silence. Her saddle and saddle-bags lay not far from the fire, unopened, untouched. The men were not interested in her nor her belongings. There they squatted with their hats on their heads, eating, eating mechanically, like animals, the dark sarape with its fringe falling to the ground before and behind, the powerful dark legs naked and squatting like an animal's showing the dirty white shirt and the sort of loin-cloth which was the only other garment, underneath. And they showed no more sign of interest in her than if she had been a piece of venison they were bringing home from the hunt, and had hung inside a shelter.

After a while they carefully extinguished the fire, and went inside their own shelter. Watching through the screen of boughs, she had a moment's thrill of fear and anxiety, seeing the dark forms cross and pass silently in the moonlight. Would they attack her now?

But no! They were as if oblivious to her. Her horse was hobbled; she could hear it hopping wearily. All was silent, mountain-silent, cold, deathly. She slept and woke and slept in a semiconscious numbness of cold and fatigue. A long, long night, icy and eternal, and she aware that she had died.

## II

Yet when there was a stirring, and a clink of flint and steel, and the form of a man crouching like a dog over a bone, at a red splutter of fire, and she knew it was morning coming, it seemed to her the night had passed too soon.

When the fire was going, she came out of her shelter with one real desire left: for coffee. The men were warming more tortillas.

"Can we make coffee?" she asked.

The young man looked at her, and she imagined the same faint spark of derision in his eyes. He shook his head.

"We don't take it," he said. "There is no time."

And the elder men, squatting on their haunches, look up at her in the terrible paling dawn, and there was not even derision in their eyes. Only that intense, yet remote, inhuman glitter which was terrible to her. They were inaccessible. They could not see her as a woman at all. As if she *were* not a woman. As if, perhaps, her whiteness took away all her womanhood, and left her as some giant, female white ant. That was all they could see in her.

Before the sun was up, she was in the saddle again, and they were climbing steeply, in the icy air. The sun came, and soon she was very hot, exposed to the glare in the bare places. It seemed to her they were climbing to the roof of the world. Beyond against heaven were slashes of snow.

During the course of the morning, they came to a place where the horse could not go farther. They rested for a time with a great slant of living rock in front of them, like the glossy breast of some earth-beast. Across this rock, along a wavering crack, they had to go. It seemed to her that for hours she went in torment, on her hands and knees, from crack to crevice, along the slanting face of this pure rock-mountain. An Indian in front and an Indian behind walked slowly erect, shod with sandals of braided leather. But she in her riding-boots dared not stand erect.

Yet what she wondered, all the time, was why she persisted in clinging and crawling along these mile-long sheets of rock. Why she did not hurl herself down, and have done! The world was below her.

When they emerged at last on a stony slope, she looked back, and saw the third Indian coming carrying her saddle and saddle-bags on his back, the whole hung from a band across his forehead. And he had his hat in his hand, as he stepped slowly, with the slow, soft, heavy tread of the Indian, unwavering in the chinks of rock, as if along a scratch in the mountain's iron shield.

The stony slope led downwards. The Indians seemed to grow excited. One ran ahead at a slow trot, disappearing round the curve of stones. And the track curved round and down, till at last in the full blaze of the mid-morning sun, they could see a valley below them, between walls of rock, as in a great wide chasm let in the mountains. A green valley, with a river, and trees, and clusters of low flat sparkling houses. It was all tiny and perfect, three thousand feet below. Even the flat bridge over the stream, and the square with the houses around it, the bigger buildings piled up at opposite ends of the square, the tall cotton-wood trees, the pastures and stretches of yellow-sere maize, the patches of brown sheep or goats in the distance, on the slopes, the railed enclosures by the stream-side. There it was, all small and perfect, looking magical, as any place will look magical, seen from the mountains above. The unusual thing was that the low houses glittered white, white-washed, looking like crystals of salt, or silver. This frightened her.

They began the long, winding descent at the head of the barranca, following the stream that rushed and fell. At first it was all rocks; then the pine trees began, and soon, the silver-limbed aspens. The flowers of autumn, big daisy-like flowers, and white ones, and many yellow flowers, were in profusion. But she had to sit down and rest, she was so weary. And she saw the bright flowers shadowily, as pale shadows hovering, as one who is dead must see them.

At length came grass and pasture-slopes between mingled aspen and pine trees. A shepherd, naked in the sun save for his hat and his cotton loin-cloth, was driving his brown sheep away. In a grove of trees they sat and waited, she and the young Indian. The one with the saddle had also gone forward.

They heard a sound of someone coming. It was three men, in fine sarapes of red and orange and yellow and black, and with brilliant feather head-dresses. The oldest had his grey hair braided with fur, and his red and orange-yellow sarape was covered with curious black markings, like a leopard-skin. The other two were not grey-haired, but they were elders too. Their blankets were in stripes, and their head-dresses not so elaborate.

The young Indian addressed the elders in a few quiet words. They listened without answering or looking at him or at the woman, keeping their faces averted and their eyes turned to the ground, only listening. And at length they turned and looked at the woman.

The old chief, or medicine-man, whatever he was, had a deeply wrinkled and lined face of dark bronze, with a few sparse grey hairs round the mouth. Two long braids of grey hair, braided with fur and coloured feather, hung on his shoulders. And yet, it was only his eyes that mattered. They were black and of extraordinary piercing strength, without a qualm of misgiving in their demonish, dauntless power. He looked into the eyes of the white woman with a long piercing look, seeking she knew not what. She summoned all her strength to meet his eyes and keep up her guard. But it was no good. He was not looking at her as one human being looks at another. He never even perceived her resistance or her challenge, but looked past them both, into she knew not what.

She could see it was hopeless to expect an human communication with this old being.

He turned and said a few words to the young Indian.

"He asks what do you seek here?" said the young man in Spanish.

"I? Nothing! I only came to see what it was like."

This was again translated, and the old man turned his eyes on her once more. Then he spoke again, in his low muttering tone, to the young Indian.

"He says, why does she leave her house with the white men? Does she want to bring the white man's God to the Chilchui?"

"No," she replied, foolhardy. "I came away from the white man's God myself. I came to look for the God of the Chilchui."

Profound silence followed, when this was translated. Then the old man spoke again, in a small voice almost of weariness.

"Does the white woman seek the gods of the Chilchui because she is weary of her own God?" came the question.

"Yes, she does. She is tired of the white man's God," she replied, thinking that was what they wanted her to say. She would like to serve the gods of the Chilchui.

She was aware of an extraordinary thrill of triumph and exultance passing through the Indians, in the tense silence that followed when this was translated. Then they all looked at her with piercing black eyes, in which a steely covetous intent glittered incomprehensible. She was the more puzzled, as there was nothing sensual or sexual in the look. It had a terrible glittering purity that was beyond her. She was afraid, she would have been paralysed with fear, had not something died within her, leaving her with a cold, watchful wonder only.

The elders talked a little while, then the two went away, leaving her with the young man and the oldest chief. The old man now looked at her with a certain solicitude.

"He says are you tired?" asked the young man.

"Very tired," she said.

"The men will bring you a carriage," said the young Indian.

The carriage, when it came, proved to be a litter consisting of a sort of hammock of dark woollen frieze, slung on to a pole which was borne on the shoulders of two long-haired Indians. The woollen hammock was spread on the ground, she sat down on it, and the two men raised the pole to their shoulders. Swinging rather as if she were in a sack, she was carried out of the grove of trees, following the old chief, whose leopard-spotted blanket moved curiously in the sun-light.

They had emerged in the valley-head. Just in front were the maize-fields, with ripe ears of maize. The corn was not very tall, in this high altitude. The well-worn path went between it, and all she could see was the erect form of the old chief, in the flame and black sarape, stepping soft and heavy and swift, his head forward, looking neither to right nor left. Her bearers followed, stepping rhythmically, the long blue-black hair glistening like a river down the naked shoulders of the man in front.

They passed the maize, and came to a big wall or earthwork made of earth and adobe bricks. The wooden doors were open. Passing on, they were in a network of small gardens, full of flowers and herbs and fruit trees, each garden watered by a tiny ditch of running water. Among each cluster of trees and flowers was a small, glittering white house, windowless, and with closed door. The place was a network of little paths, small streams, and little bridges among square, flowering gardens.

Following the broadest path—a soft narrow track between leaves and grass, a path worn smooth by centuries of human feet, no hoof of horse nor any wheel to disfigure it—they came to the little river of swift bright water, and crossed on a log bridge. Everything was silent—there was not a human being anywhere. The road went on under magnificent cottonwood trees. It emerged suddenly outside the central plaza or square of the village.

This was a long oblong of low white houses with flat roofs, and two bigger buildings, having as it were little square huts piled on top of bigger long huts, stood at either end of the oblong, facing each other rather askew. Every little house was a dazzling white, save for the great round beam-ends which projected under the flat eaves, and for the flat roofs. Round each of the bigger buildings, on the outside of the square, was a stockyard fence, inside which was garden with trees and flowers, and various small houses.

Not a soul was in sight. They passed silently between the houses into the central square. This was quite bare and arid, the earth trodden smooth by endless generations of passing feet, passing across from door to door. All the doors of the windowless houses gave on to this blank square, but all doors were closed. The firewood lay near the threshold, a clay oven was still smoking, but there was no sign of moving life.

The old man walked straight across the square to the big house at the end, where the two upper storeys, as in a house of toy bricks, stood each one smaller than the lower one. A stone staircase, outside, led up to the roof of the first storey.

At the foot of this staircase the litter-bearers stood still, and lowered the woman to the ground.

"You will come up," said the young Indian who spoke Spanish.

She mounted the stone stairs to the earthen roof of the first house, which formed a platform round the wall of the second storey. She followed around this platform to the back of the big house. There they descended again, into the garden at the rear.

So far they had seen no one. But now two men appeared, bare-headed, with long braided hair, and wearing a sort of white shirt gathered into a loin-cloth. These went along with the three newcomers, across the garden where red flowers and yellow flowers were blooming, to a long, low white house. There they entered without knocking.

It was dark inside. There was a low murmur of men's voices. Several men were present, their white shirts showing in the gloom, their dark faces invisible. They were sitting on a great log of smooth old wood, that lay along the far wall. And save for this log, the room seemed empty. But no, in the dark at one end was a couch, a sort of bed, and someone lying there, covered with furs.

The old Indian in the spotted sarape, who had accompanied the women, now took off his hat and his blanket and his sandals. Laying them aside, he approached the couch, and spoke in a low voice. For some moments there was no answer. Then an old man with the snow-white hair hanging round his darkly-visible face, roused himself like a vision, and leaned on one elbow, looking vaguely at the company, in tense silence.

The grey-haired Indian spoke again, and then the young Indian, taking the woman's hand, led her forward. In her linen riding-habit, and black boots and hat, and her pathetic bit of a red tie, she stood there beside the fur-covered bed of the old, old man, who sat reared up, leaning on one elbow, remote as a ghost, his white hair streaming in disorder, his face almost black, yet with a far-off intentness, not of this world, leaning forward to look at her.

His face was so old, it was like dark glass, and the few curling hairs that sprang white from his lips and chin were quite incredible. The long white locks fell unbraided and disorderly on either side of the glassy dark face. And under a faint powder of white eyebrows, the black eyes of the old chief looked at her as if from the far, far dead, seeing something that was never to be seen.

At last he spoke a few deep, hollow words, as if to the dark air.

"He says, do you bring your heart to the god of the Chilchui?" translated the young Indian.

"Tell him yes," she said, automatically.

There was a pause. The old Indian spoke again, as if to the air. One of the men present went out. There was a silence as if of eternity in the dim room that was lighted only through the open door.

The woman looked round. Four old men with grey hair sat on the log by the wall facing the door. Two other men, powerful and impassive, stood near the door. They all had long hair, and wore white shirts gathered into a loin-cloth. Their powerful legs were naked and dark. There was a silence like eternity.

At length the man returned, with white and dark clothing on his arm. The young Indian took them, and holding them in front of the woman, said:

"You must take off your clothes, and put these on."

"If all you men will go out," she said.

"No one will hurt you," he said quietly.

"Not while you men are here," she said.

He looked at the two men by the door. They came quickly forward, and suddenly gripped her arms as she stood, without hurting her, but with great power. Then two of the old men came, and with curious skill slit her boots down with keen knives, and drew them off, and slit her clothing so that it came away from her. In a few moments she stood there white and uncovered. The old man on the bed spoke, and turned her round for him to see. He spoke again, and the young Indian deftly took the pins and comb from her fair hair, so that it fell over her shoulders in a bunchy tangle.

Then the old man spoke again. The Indian led her to the bedside. The white-haired, glassy-dark old man moistened his finger-tips at his mouth, and most delicately touched her on the breasts and on the body, then on the back. And she winced strangely each time, as the finger-tips drew along her skin, as if Death itself were touching her.

And she wondered, almost sadly, why she did not feel shamed in her nakedness. She only felt sad and lost. Because nobody felt ashamed. The elder men were all dark and tense with some other deep, gloomy, incomprehensible emotion, which suspended all her agitation, while the young Indian had a strange look of ecstasy on his face. And she, she was only utterly strange and beyond herself, as if her body were not her own.

They gave her the new clothing: a long white cotton shift, that came to her knees: then a tunic of thick blue woollen stuff, embroidered with scarlet and green flowers. It was fastened over one shoulder only, and belted with a braid sash of scarlet and black wool.

When she was thus dressed, they took her away, barefoot, to a little house in the stockaded garden. The young Indian told her she might have what she wanted. She asked for water to wash herself. He brought it in a jar, together with a long wooden bowl. Then he fastened the gate-door of her house, and left her a prisoner. She could see through the bars of the gate-door of her house, the red flowers of the garden, and a humming-bird. Then from the roof of the big house she heard the long, heavy sound of a drum, unearthly to her in its summons, and an uplifted voice calling from the house-top in a strange language, with a far-away emotionless intonation, delivering some speech or message. And she listened as if from the dead.

But she was very tired. She lay down on a couch of skins, pulling over her the blanket of dark wool, and she slept, giving up everything.

When she woke it was late afternoon, and the young Indian was entering with a basket-tray containing food, tortillas,
and corn-mush with bits of meat, probably mutton, and a drink
made of honey, and some fresh plums. He brought her also a long
garland of red and yellow flowers with knots of blue buds at the
end. He sprinkled the garland with water from a jar, then offered
it to her, with a smile. He seemed very gentle and thoughtful,
and on his face and in his dark eyes was a curious look of triumph
and ecstasy, that frightened her a little. The glitter had gone from
the black eyes, with their curving dark lashes, and he would look
at her with this strange soft glow of ecstasy that was not quite
human, and terribly impersonal, and which made her uneasy.

"Is there anything you want?" he said, in his low, slow,
melodious voice, that always seemed withheld, as if he were
speaking aside to somebody else, or as if he did not want to let the
sound come out to her.

"Am I going to be kept a prisoner here?" she asked.

"No, you can walk in the garden to-morrow," he said
softly. Always this curious solicitude.

"Do you like that drink?" he said, offering her a little
earthenware cup. "It is very refreshing."

She sipped the liquor curiously. It was made with herbs and
sweetened with honey, and had a strange, lingering flavour. The
young man watched her with gratification.

"It has a peculiar taste," she said.

"It is very refreshing," he replied, his black eyes resting on
her always with that look of gratified ecstasy. Then he went
away. And presently she began to be sick, and to vomit violently,
as if she had no control over herself.

Afterwards she felt a great soothing languor steal over her,
her limbs felt strong and loose and full of languor, and she lay on
her couch listening to the sounds of the village, watching the
yellowing sky, smelling the scent of burning cedar wood, or pine
wood. So distinctly she heard the yapping of tiny dogs, the shuffle
of far-off feet, the murmur of voices, so keenly she detected the
smell of smoke, and flowers, and evening falling, so vividly she
saw the one bright star infinitely remote, stirring above the sunset, that she felt as if all her senses were diffused on the air, that
she could distinguish the sound of evening flowers unfolding, and

the actual crystal sound of the heavens, as the vast belts of the world-atmosphere slid past one another, and as if the moisture ascending and the moisture descending in the air resounded like some harp in the cosmos.

She was a prisoner in her house, and in the stockaded garden, but she scarcely minded. And it was days before she realised that she never saw another woman. Only the men, the elderly men of the big house, that she imagined must be some sort of temple, and the men priests of some sort. For they always had the same colours, red, orange, yellow, and black, and the same grave, abstracted demeanour.

Sometimes an old man would come and sit in her room with her, in absolute silence. None spoke any language but Indian, save the one younger man. The older men would smile at her, and sit with her for an hour at a time, sometimes smiling at her when she spoke in Spanish, but never answering save with this slow, benevolent-seeming smile. And they gave off a feeling of almost fatherly solicitude. Yet their dark eyes, brooding over her, had something away in their depths that was awesomely ferocious and relentless. They would cover it with a smile, at once, if they felt her looking. But she had seen it.

Always they treated her with this curious impersonal solicitude, this utterly impersonal gentleness, as an old man treats a child. But underneath it she felt there was something else, something terrible. When her old visitor had gone away, in his silent, insidious, fatherly fashion, a shock of fear would come over her; though of what she knew not.

The young Indian would sit and talk with her freely, as if with great candour. But with him, too, she felt that everything real was unsaid. Perhaps it was unspeakable. His big dark eyes would rest on her almost cherishingly, touched with ecstasy, and his beautiful, slow, langourous voice would trail out its simple, ungrammatical Spanish. He told her he was the grandson of the old, old man, son of the man in the spotted sarape: and they were caciques, kings from the old, old days, before even the Spaniards came. But he himself had been in Mexico City, and also in the United States. He had worked as a labourer, building the roads in Los Angeles. He had travelled as far as Chicago.

"Don't you speak English, then?" she asked.

His eyes rested on her with a curious look of duplicity and conflict, and he mutely shook his head.

"What did you do with your long hair, when you were in the United States?" she asked. "Did you cut it off?"

Again, with the look of torment in his eyes, he shook his head.

"No," he said, in a low, subdued voice, "I wore a hat, and a handkerchief tied round my head."

And he relapsed into silence, as if of tormented memories.

"Are you the only man of your people who has been to the United States?" she asked him.

"Yes. I am the only one who has been away from here for a long time. The others come back soon, in one week. They don't stay away. The old men don't let them."

"And why did you go?"

"The old men want me to go—because I shall be the cacique—"

He talked always with the same naïveté, and almost childish candour. But she felt that this was perhaps just the effect of his Spanish. Or perhaps speech altogether was unreal to him. Anyhow, she felt that all the real things were kept back.

He came and sat with her a good deal—sometimes more than she wished—as if he wanted to be near her. She asked him if he was married. He said he was—with two children.

"I should like to see your children," she said.

But he answered only with that smile, a sweet, almost ecstatic smile, above which the dark eyes hardly change from their enigmatic abstraction.

It was curious, he would sit with her by the hour, without ever making her self-conscious, or sex-conscious. He seemed to have no sex, as he sat there so still and gentle and apparently submissive with his head bent a little forward, and the river of glistening black hair streaming maidenly over his shoulders.

Yet when she looked again, she saw his shoulders broad and powerful, his eyebrows black and level, the short, curved, obstinate black lashes over his lowered eyes, the small, fur-like line of moustache above his blackish, heavy lips, and the strong chin, and she knew that in some other mysterious way he was darkly and powerfully male. And he, feeling her watching him, would glance up at her swiftly with a dark lurking look in his eyes, which he veiled with that half-sad smile.

The days and the weeks went by, in a vague kind of contentment. She was uneasy sometimes, feeling she had lost the power over herself. She was not in her own power, she was under the spell of some other control. And at times she had moments of terror and horror. But then these Indians would come and sit with her, casting their insidious spell over her by their very silent presence, their silent, sexless, powerful physical presence. As they sat they seemed to take her will away, and leaving her will-less and victim to her own indifference. And the young man would bring her sweetened drink, often the same emetic drink, but sometimes other kinds. And after drinking, the languor filled her heavy limbs, her senses seemed to float in the air, listening, hearing. They had brought her a little female dog, which she called Flora. And once, in the trance of her senses, she felt she *heard* the little dog conceive, in her tiny womb, and begin to be complex, with young. And another day she could hear the vast sound of the earth going round, like some immense arrow-string booming.

But as the days grew shorter and colder, when she was cold, she would get a sudden revival of her will, and a desire to go out, to go away. And she insisted to the young man, she wanted to go out.

So one day, they let her climb to the topmost roof of the big house where she was, and look down the square. It was the day of the big dance, but not everybody was dancing. Women with babies in their arms stood in their doorways, watching. Opposite, at the other end of the square, there was a throng before the other big house, and a small, brilliant group on the terrace roof of the first storey, in front of wide open doors of the upper storey. Through these wide open doors she could see fire glinting in darkness and priests in head-dresses of black and yellow and scarlet feathers, wearing robe-like blankets of black and red and yellow, with long green fringes, were moving about. A big drum was beating slowly and regularly, in the dense, Indian silence. The crowd below waited.

Then a drum started on a high beat, and there came the deep, powerful burst of men singing a heavy, savage music, like a wind roaring in some timeless forest, many mature men singing in one breath, like the wind; and long lines of dancers walked out from under the big house. Men with naked, golden-bronze bodies and streaming black hair, tufts of red and yellow feathers on their arms, and kilts of white frieze with a bar of heavy red and black and green embroidery round their waists, bending slightly forward and stamping the earth in their absorbed, monotonous stamp of the dance, a fox-fur, hung by the nose from their belt behind, swaying with the sumptuous swaying of a beautiful fox-fur, the tip of the tail writhing above the dancer's heels. And after each man, a woman with a strange elaborate head-dress of feathers and sea-shells, and wearing a short black tunic, moving erect, holding up tufts of feathers in each hand, swaying her wrists rhythmically and subtly beating the earth with her bare feet.

So, the long line of the dance unfurling from the big house opposite. And from the big house beneath her, strange scent of incense, strange tense silence, then the answering burst of in-human male singing, and the long line of the dance unfurling.

It went on all day, the insistence of the drum, the cavern-ous, roaring, storm-like sound of male singing, the incessant swinging of the fox-skins behind the powerful, gold-bronze, stamp-ing legs of the men, the autumn sun from a perfect blue heaven pouring on the rivers of black hair, men's and women's, the valley all still, the walls of rock beyond, the awful huge bulking of the mountain against the pure sky, its snow seething with sheer whiteness.

For hours and hours she watched, spellbound, and as if drugged. And in all the terrible persistence of the drumming and the primeval, rushing deep singing, and the endless stamping of the dance of fox-tailed men, the tread of heavy, bird-erect women in their black tunics, she seemed at last to feel her own death; her own obliteration. As if she were to be obliterated from the field of life again. In the strange towering symbols on the heads of the changeless, absorbed women she seemed to read once more the *Mene Mene Tekel Upharsin*. Her kind of woman-hood, intensely personal and individual, was to be obliterated again, and the great primeval symbols were to tower once more over the fallen individual independence of woman. The sharp-ness and the quivering nervous consciousness of the highly-bred white woman was to be destroyed again, womanhood was to be cast once more into the great stream of impersonal sex and impersonal passion. Strangely, as if clairvoyant, she saw the immense sacrifice prepared. And she went back to her little house in a trance of agony.

After this, there was always a certain agony when she heard the drums at evening, and the strange uplifted savage sound of men singing round the drum, like wild creatures howling to the invisible gods of the moon and the vanished sun. Something of the chuckling, sobbing cry of the coyote, something of the exultant bark of the fox, the far-off wild melancholy exultance of the howling wolf, the torment of the puma's scream, and the insistence of the ancient fierce human male, with his lapses of tenderness and his abiding ferocity.

Sometimes she would climb the high roof after nightfall, and listen to the dim cluster of young men round the drum on the bridge just beyond the square, singing by the hour. Sometimes there would be a fire, and in the fire-glow, men in their white shirts or naked save for a loin-cloth, would be dancing and stamping like spectres, hour after hour in the dark cold air, within the fire-glow, forever dancing and stamping like turkeys, or dropping squatting by the fire to rest, throwing their blankets round them.

"Why do you all have the same colours?" she asked the young Indian. "Why do you all have red and yellow and black, over your white shirts? And the women have black tunics?"

He looked into her eyes, curiously, and the faint, evasive smile came on to his face. Behind the smile lay a soft, strange malignancy.

"Because our men are the fire and the day-time, and our women are the spaces between the stars at night," he said.

"Aren't the women even stars?" she said.

"No. We say they are the spaces between the stars, that keep the stars apart."

He looked at her oddly, and again the touch of derision came into his eyes.

"White people," he said, "they know nothing. They are like children, always with toys. We know the sun, and we know the moon. And we say, when a white woman sacrifice herself to our gods, then our gods will begin to make the world again, and the white man's gods will fall to pieces."

"How sacrifice herself?" she asked quickly.

And he, as quickly covered, covered himself with a subtle smile.

"She sacrifice her own gods and come to our gods, I mean that," he said soothingly.

But she was not reassured. An icy pang of fear and certainty was at her heart.

"The sun he is alive at one end of the sky," he continued, "and the moon lives at the other end. And the man all the time have to keep the sun happy in his side of the sky, and the woman have to keep the moon quiet at her side of the sky. All the time she have to work at this. And the sun can't ever go into the house of the moon, and the moon can't ever go into the house of the sun, in the sky. So the woman, she asks the moon to come into her cave, inside her. And the man, he draws the sun down till he has the power of the sun. All the time he do this. Then when the man gets a woman, the sun goes into the cave of the moon, and that is how everything in the world starts."

She listened, watching him closely, as one enemy watches another who is speaking with double meaning.

"Then," she said, "why aren't you Indians masters of the white men?"

"Because," he said, "the Indian got weak, and lost his power with the sun, so the white men stole the sun. But they can't keep him—they don't know how. They got him, but they don't know what to do with him, like a boy who catch a big grizzly bear, and can't kill him, and can't run away from him. The grizzly bear eats the boy that catch him, when he want to run away from him. White men don't know what they are doing with the sun, and white women don't know what they do with the moon. The moon she got angry with white women, like a puma when someone kills her little ones. The moon, she bites white women—here inside," and he pressed his side. "The moon, she is angry in a white woman's cave. The Indian can see it. And soon," he added, "the Indian women get the moon back and keep her quiet in their house. And the Indian men get the sun, and the power over all the world. White men don't know what the sun is. They never know."

He subsided into a curious exultant silence.

"But," she faltered, "why do you hate us so? Why do you hate me?"

He looked up suddenly with a light on his face, and a startling flame of a smile.

"No, we don't hate," he said softly, looking with a curious glitter into her face.

"You do," she said, forlorn and hopeless.

And after a moment's silence, he rose and went away.

## III

Winter had now come, in the high valley, with snow that melted in the day's sun, and nights that were bitter cold. She lived on, in a kind of daze, feeling her power ebbing more and more away from her, as if her will were leaving her. She felt always in the same relaxed, confused, victimised state, unless the sweetened herb drink would numb her mind altogether, and release her senses into a sort of heightened, mystic acuteness and a feeling as if she were diffusing out deliciously into the harmony of things. This at length became the only state of consciousness she really recognised: this exquisite sense of bleeding out into the higher beauty and harmony of things. Then she could actually hear the great stars in heaven, which she saw through her door, speaking from their motion and brightness, saying things perfectly to the cosmos, as they trod in perfect ripples, like bells on the floor of heaven, passing one another and grouping in the timeless dance, with the spaces of dark between. And she could hear the snow on a cold, cloudy day twittering and faintly whistling in the sky, like birds that flock and fly away in autumn, suddenly calling farewell to the invisible moon, and slipping out of the plains of the air, releasing peaceful warmth. She herself would call to the arrested snow to fall from the upper air. She would call to the unseen moon to cease to be angry, to make peace again with the unseen sun like a woman who ceases to be angry in her house. And she would smell the sweetness of the moon relaxing to the sun in the wintry heaven, when the snow fell in a faint, cold-perfumed relaxation, as the peace of the sun mingled again in a sort of unison with the peace of the moon.

She was aware too of the sort of shadow that was on the Indians of the valley, a deep stoical disconsolation, almost religious in its depth.

"We have lost our power over the sun, and we are trying to get him back. But he is wild with us, and shy like a horse that has got away. We have to go through a lot." So the young Indian said to her, looking into her eyes with a strained meaning. And she, as if bewitched, replied:

"I hope you will get him back."

The smile of triumph flew over his face.

"Do you hope it?" he said.

"I do," she answered fatally.

"Then all right," he said. "We shall get him."

And he went away in exultance.

She felt she was drifting on some consummation, which she had no will to avoid, yet which seemed heavy and finally terrible to her.

It must have been almost December, for the days were short, when she was taken again before the aged man, and stripped of her clothing, and touched with the old finger-tips.

The aged cacique looked her in the eyes, with his eyes of lonely, far-off, black intentness, and murmured something to her.

"He wants you to make the sign of peace," the young man translated, showing her the gesture. "Peace and farewell to him."

She was fascinated by the black, glass-like, intent eyes of the old cacique, that watched her without blinking, like a basilisk's, overpowering her. In their depths also she saw a certain fatherly compassion, and pleading. She put her hand before her face, in the required manner, making the sign of peace and farewell. He made the sign of peace back again to her, then sank among his furs. She thought he was going to die, and that he knew it.

There followed a day of ceremonial, when she was brought out before all the people, in a blue blanket with white fringe, and holding blue feathers in her hands. Before an altar of one house she was perfumed with incense and sprinkled with ash. Before the altar of the opposite house she was fumigated again with incense by the gorgeous, terrifying priests in yellow and scarlet and black, their faces painted with scarlet paint. And then they threw water on her. Meanwhile she was faintly aware of the fire on the altar, the heavy, heavy sound of a drum, the heavy sound of men beginning powerfully, deeply, savagely to sing, the swaying of the crowd of faces in the plaza below, and the formation for a sacred dance.

But at this time her commonplace consciousness was numb, she was aware of her immediate surroundings as shadows, almost immaterial. With refined and heightened senses she could hear the sound of the earth winging on its journey, like a shot arrow, the ripple-rustling of the air, and the boom of the great arrow-string. And it seemed to her there were two great influences in the upper air, one golden towards the sun, the one invisible silver; the first travelling like rain ascending to the gold presence sunwards, the second like rain silverily descending the ladders of space towards the hovering, lurking clouds over the snowy mountain-top. Then between them, another presence, waiting to shake himself free of moisture, of heavy white snow that had mysteriously collected about him. And in summer, like a scorched eagle, he would wait to shake himself clear of the weight of heavy sunbeams. And he was coloured like fire. And he was always shaking himself clear, of snow or of heavy heat, like an eagle rustling.

Then there was a still stranger presence standing watching from the blue distance, always watching. Sometimes running in upon the wind, or shimmering in the heat-waves. The blue wind itself, rushing, as it were, out of the holes into the sky, rushing out of the sky down upon the earth. The blue wind, the go-between, the invisible ghost that belonged to two worlds, that played upon the ascending and the descending chords of the rains.

More and more her ordinary personal consciousness had left her, she had gone into that other state of passional cosmic consciousness, like one who is drugged. The Indians, with their heavily religious natures, had made her succumb to their vision.

Only one personal question she asked the young Indian:

"Why am I the only one that wears blue?"

"It is the colour of the wind. It is the colour of what goes away and is never coming back, but which is always here, waiting like death among us. It is the colour of the dead. And it is the colour that stands away off, looking at us from the distance, that cannot come near to us. When we go near, it goes farther. It can't be near. We are all brown and yellow and black hair, and white teeth and red blood. We are the ones that are here. You with blue eyes, you are the messengers from the far-away, you cannot stay, and now it is time for you to go back."

"Where to?" she asked.

"To the way-off things like the sun and the blue mother of rain, and tell them that we are the people on the world again, and we can bring the sun to the moon again, like a red horse to a blue mare; we are the people. The white women have driven back the moon in the sky, won't let her come to the sun. So the sun is angry. And the Indian must give the moon to the sun."

"How?" she said.

"The white woman got to die and go like a wind to the sun, tell him the Indians will open the gate to him. And the Indian women will open the gate to the moon. The white women don't let the moon come down out of the blue coral. The moon used to come down among the Indian women, like a white goat among the flowers. And the sun want to come down to the Indian men, like an eagle to the pine trees. The sun, he is shut out behind the white man, and the moon she is shut out behind the white woman, and they can't get away. They are angry, everything in the world gets angrier. The Indian says he will give the white woman to the sun, so the sun will leap over the white man and come to the Indian again. And the moon will be surprised, she will see the gate open, and she not know which way to go. But the Indian woman will call to the moon: *Come! Come! Come back into my grasslands. The wicked white woman can't harm you any more.* Then the sun will look over the heads of the white men, and see the moon in the pastures of our women, with the Red Men standing around like pine trees. Then he will leap over the heads of the white men, and come running past to the Indians through the spruce trees. And we, who are red and black and yellow, we who stay, we shall have the sun on our right hand and the moon on our left. So we can bring the rain down out of

the blue meadows, and up out of the black; and we can call the
wind that tells the corn to grow, when we ask him, and we shall
make the clouds to break, and the sheep to have twin lambs. And
we shall be full of power, like a spring day. But the white people
will be a hard winter, without snow—"

"But," said the white woman, "I don't shut out the
moon—how can I?"

"Yes," he said, "you shut the gate, and then laugh, think
you have it all your own way."

She could never quite understand the way he looked at her.
He was always so curiously gentle, and his smile was so soft. Yet
there was such a glitter in his eyes, and an unrelenting sort of hate
came out of his words, a strange, profound, impersonal hate.
Personally he liked her, she was sure. He was gentle with her,
attracted by her in some strange, soft, passionless way. But imper-
sonally he hated her with a mystic hatred. He would smile at her,
winningly. Yet if, the next moment, she glanced round at him
unawares, she would catch that gleam of pure after-hate in his
eyes.

"Have I got to die and be given to the sun?" she asked.

"Some time," he said, laughing evasively. "Some time we
all die."

They were gentle with her, and very considerate with her.
Strange men, the old priests and the young cacique alike, they
watched over her and cared for her like women. In their soft,
insidious understanding, there was something womanly. Yet their
eyes, with that strange glitter, and their dark, shut mouths that
would open to the broad jaw, the small, strong, white teeth, had
something very primitively male and cruel.

One wintry day, when snow was falling, they took her to a
great dark chamber in the big house. The fire was burning in a
corner on a high raised dais under a sort of hood or canopy of
adobe-work. She saw in the fire-glow the glowing bodies of the
almost naked priests, and strange symbols on the roof and walls of
the chamber. There was no door or window in the chamber, they
had descended by a ladder, from the roof. And the fire of
pinewood danced continually, showing walls painted with
strange devices, which she could not understand, and a ceiling of
poles making a curious pattern of black and red and yellow, and

alcoves or niches in which were curious objects she could not discern.

The older priests were going through some ceremony near the fire, in silence, intense Indian silence. She was seated on a low projection of the wall, opposite the fire, two men seated beside her. Presently they gave her a drink from a cup, which she took gladly, because of the semi-trance it would induce.

In the darkness and in the silence she was accurately aware of everything that happened to her: how they took off her clothes, and, standing her before a great, weird device on the wall, coloured blue and white and black, washed her all over with water and the amole infusion; washed even her hair, softly, carefully, and dried it on white cloths, till it was soft and glistening. Then they laid her on a couch under another great indecipherable image of red and black and yellow, and now rubbed all her body with sweet-scented oil, and massaged all her limbs, and her back, and her sides, with a long, strange, hypnotic massage. Their dark hands were incredibly powerful, yet soft with a watery softness she could not understand. And the dark faces, leaning near her white body, she saw were darkened with red pigment, with lines of yellow round the cheeks. And the dark eyes glittered absorbed, as the hands worked upon the soft white body of the woman.

They were so impersonal, absorbed in something that was beyond her. They never saw her as a personal woman: she could tell that. She was some mystic object to them, some vehicle of passions too remote for her to grasp. Herself in a state of trance, she watched their faces bending over her, dark, strangely glistening with the transparent red paint, and lined with bars of yellow. And in this weird, luminous-dark mask of living face, the eyes were fixed with an unchanging steadfast gleam, and the purplish-pigmented lips were closed in a full, sinister, sad grimness. The immense fundamental sadness, the grimness of ultimate decision, the fixity of revenge, and the nascent exultance of those that are going to triumph—these things she could read in their faces, as she lay and was rubbed into a misty glow by their uncanny dark hands. Her limbs, her flesh, her very bones at last seemed to be diffusing into a roseate sort of mist, in which her consciousness hovered like some sun-gleam in a flushed cloud.

She knew the gleam would fade, the cloud would go grey. But at present she did not believe it. She knew she was a victim; that all this elaborate work upon her was the work of victimising her. But she did not mind. She wanted it.

Later, they put a short blue tunic on her and took her to the upper terrace, and presented her to the people. She saw the plaza below her full of dark faces and of glittering eyes. There was no pity: only the curious hard exultance. The people gave a subdued cry when they saw her, and she shuddered. But she hardly cared.

Next day was the last. She slept in a chamber of the big house. At dawn they put on her a big blue blanket with a fringe, and led her out into the plaza, among the throng of silent, dark-blanketed people. There was pure white snow on the ground, and the dark people in their dark-brown blankets looked like inhabitants of another world.

A large drum was slowly pounding, and an old priest was declaiming from a house-top. But it was not till noon that a litter came forth, and the people gave that low, animal cry which was so moving. In the sack-like litter sat the old, old cacique, his white hair braided with black braid and large turquoise stones. His face was like a piece of obsidian. He lifted his hand in token, and the litter stopped in front of her. Fixing her with his old eyes, he spoke to her for a few moments, in his hollow. voice. No one translated.

Another litter came, and she was placed in it. Four priests moved ahead, in their scarlet and yellow and black, with plumed head-dresses. Then came the litter of the old cacique. Then the light drums began, and two groups of singers burst simultaneously into song, male and wild. And the golden-red, almost naked men, adorned with ceremonial feathers and kilts, the rivers of black hair down their backs, formed into two files and began to tread the dance. So they threaded out of the snowy plaza, in two long, sumptuous lines of dark red-gold and black and fur, swaying with a faint tinkle of bits of shell and flint, winding over the snow between the two bee-clusters of men who sang around the drums.

Slowly they moved out, and her litter, with its attendance of feathered, lurid dancing priests, moved after. Everybody danced the tread of the dance-step, even, subtly, the litter-bearers. And out of the plaza they went, past smoking ovens, on the trail to the great cottonwood trees, that stood like grey-silver lace against the blue sky, bare and exquisite above the snow. The river, diminished, rushed among fangs of ice. The chequer-squares of gardens within fences were all snowy, and the white houses now looked yellowish.

The whole valley glittered intolerably with pure snow, away to the walls of the standing rock. And across the flat cradle of snow-bed wound the long thread of the dance, shaking slowly and sumptuously in its orange and black motion. The high drums thudded quickly, and on the crystalline frozen air the swell and roar of the chant of savages was like an obsession.

She sat looking out of her litter with big, transfixed blue eyes, under which were the wan markings of her drugged weari-ness. She knew she was going to die, among the glisten of this snow, at the hands of this savage, sumptuous people. And as she stared at the blaze of the blue sky above the slashed and ponder-ous mountain, she thought: "I am dead already. What difference does it make, the transition from the dead I am to the dead I shall be, very soon!" Yet her soul sickened and felt wan.

The strange procession trailed on, in perpetual dance, slowly across the plain of snow, and then entered the slopes between the pine trees. She saw the copper-dark men dancing the dance-tread, onwards, between the copper-pale tree trunks. And at last, she, too, in her swaying litter, entered the pine trees.

They were travelling on and on, upwards, across the snow under the trees, past superb shafts of pale, flaked copper, the rustle and shake and tread of the threading dance, penetrating into the forest, into the mountain. They were following a stream-bed: but the stream was dry, like summer, dried up by the frozenness of the head-waters. There were dark, red-bronze wil-low bushes with wattles like wild hair, and pallid aspen trees looking cold flesh again the snow. Then jutting dark rocks.

At last she could tell that the dancers were moving forward no more. Nearer and nearer she came upon the drums as to a lair of mysterious animals. Then through the bushes she emerged into a strange amphitheatre. Facing was a great wall of hollow rock, down the front of which hung a great, dripping, fang-like spoke of ice. The ice came pouring over the rock from the precipice above, and then stood arrested, dripping out of high heaven, almost down to the hollow stones where the stream-pool should be below. But the pool was dry.

On either side of the dry pool the lines of dancers had formed, and the dance was continuing without intermission, against a background of bushes.

But what she felt was that fanged inverted pinnacle of ice, hanging from the lip of the dark precipice above. And behind the great rope of ice she saw the leopard-like figures of priests climbing the hollow cliff face, to the cave that like a dark socket bored a cavity, an orifice, half-way up the crag.

Before she could realise, her litter-bearers were staggering in the footholds, climbing the rock. She, too, was behind the ice. There it hung, like a curtain that is not spread, but hangs like a great fang. And near above her was the orifice of the cave sinking dark into the rock. She watched it as she swayed upwards.

On the platform of the cave stood the priests, waiting in all their gorgeousness of feathers and fringed robes, watching her ascent. Two of them stooped to help her litter-bearer. And at length she was on the platform of the cave, far in behind the shaft of ice, above the hollow amphitheatre among the bushes below, where men were dancing, and the whole populace of the village was clustered in silence.

The sun was sloping down the afternoon sky, on the left. She knew that this was the shortest day of the year, and the last day of her life. They stood her facing the iridescent column of ice, which fell down marvellously arrested, away in front of her.

Some signal was given, and the dance below stopped. There was now absolute silence. She was given a little to drink, then two priests took off her mantle and her tunic, and in her strange pallor she stood there, between the lurid robes of the priests, beyond the pillar of ice, beyond and above the dark-faced people. The throng below gave the low, wild cry. Then the priest turned her round, so she stood with her back to the open world, her long blonde hair to the people below. And they cried again.

She was facing the cave, inwards. A fire was burning and flickering in the depths. Four priests had taken off their robes, and were almost as naked as she was. They were powerful men in the prime of life, and they kept their dark, painted faces lowered.

From the fire came the old, old priest, with an incense-pan. He was naked and in a state of barbaric ecstasy. He fumigated his victim, reciting at the same time in a hollow voice. Behind him came another robeless priest, with two flint knives.

When she was fumigated, they laid her on a large flat stone, the four powerful men holding her by the outstretched arms and legs. Behind stood the aged man, like a skeleton covered with dark glass, holding a knife and transfixedly watching the sun; and behind him again was another naked priest, with a knife.

She felt little sensation, though she knew all that was happening. Turning to the sky, she looked at the yellow sun. It was sinking. The shaft of ice was like a shadow between her and it. And she realised that the yellow rays were filling half the cave, thought they had not reached the altar where the fire was, at the far end of the funnel-shaped cavity.

Yes, the rays were creeping round slowly. As they grew ruddier, they penetrated farther. When the red sun was about to sink, he would shine full through the shaft of ice deep into the hollow of the cave, to the innermost.

She understood now that this was what the men were waiting for. Even those that held her down were bent and twisted round, their black eyes watching the sun with a glittering eagerness, and awe, and craving. The black eyes of the aged cacique were fixed like black mirrors on the sun, as if sightless, yet containing some terrible answer to the reddening winter planet. And all the eyes of the priests were fixed and glittering on the sinking orb, in the reddening, icy silence of the winter afternoon.

They were anxious, terribly anxious, and fierce. Their ferocity wanted something, and they were waiting the moment. And their ferocity was ready to leap out into a mystic exultance, of triumph. But they were anxious.

Only the eyes of the oldest man were not anxious. Black, and fixed, and as if sightless, they watched the sun, seeing beyond the sun. And in their black, empty concentration there was power, power intensely abstract and remote, but deep, deep to the heart of the earth, and the heart of the sun. In absolute motionlessness he watched till the red sun should send his ray through the column of ice. Then the old man would strike, and strike home, accomplish the sacrifice and achieve the power.

The mastery that man must hold, and that passes from race to race.

# 3

## The

## ORPHEUS

## Myth

Orpheus was the son of Oagrus, King of Thrace, and the Muse Calliope. While still an infant he was given a lyre by Apollo, and taught its harmonies by the other Muses. He learned so well that he became the most famous of all musicians, able even to charm wild beasts with his melodies.

In his young manhood, he married Eurydice; and when she died (some say from the bite of a serpent) he boldly followed her to the underworld, hoping to win her back with the power of his music. He won his way past Charon, the ferryman of the dead, past Cerberus, the hell-hound who guards the gates of Hades, past the three terrible judges of the dead; and brought comfort to the tortured damned spirits. Hades, god of the underworld, seeing all this, granted him permission to take Eurydice back to the land of the living, but with one condition: Orpheus might not look back until both he and his beloved stood in the light of day. Together, the two made their dangerous way back to the upper world. Stepping finally into the light, Orpheus turned to see if Eurydice was safe; but she was still in the shadows, and Hades' condition had been violated. She was thus lost to Orpheus forever, returned to the underworld.

When Dionysos came to Thrace to extend his cult, Orpheus refused to honor him. Instead, he preached a new worship, one without Dionysiac frenzy and centering on devotion to Apollo. Dionysos' revenge was characteristic: his maenads broke into the temple of Apollo where Orpheus was worshipping, and tore him apart. They threw his head into a river; still singing, the head floated out to sea, and was finally recovered, as was his lyre. The head was placed in a grotto sacred to Dionysos, the lyre in a temple of Apollo. Orpheus' still-singing head was silenced finally by a command from Apollo, while the lyre was taken up by the Muses and transformed into a heavenly constellation.

An intriguing *doubling* process goes on throughout this legend of Orpheus. There are two clearly defined sections: the Eurydice material, and the cultic material. Within each segment there are binary oppositions: in the first "act," Orpheus moves between the upper and lower worlds, he wins and loses Eurydice. In the second, Orpheus is destroyed by Dionysos, but destroyed just as the god himself was once destroyed; Apollo protects Orpheus, but Orpheus' severed head is put to rest in one of Dionysos' sacred places.

There is neither contrariness nor contradictoriness here, but support and reenforcement. Underlying all the disparate elements of the myth is a single theme: the equipoise between the conscious and the unconscious, the integrity and complementarity of, on the one hand, the rationality, lucidity, self-awareness of the symbolic Apollo; and on the other hand, the pararationality, ambiguity and self-immolation of the symbolic Dionysos. Orpheus himself is the testing ground of the rival modalities, the demonstrated "proof" that both modalities do indeed exist and coexist in the living personality. Orpheus could well be taken as one of our oldest representations of what Carl Jung called "the whole individual":

> Conscious and unconscious do not make a whole when one of them is suppressed and injured by the other. If they must contend, let it at least be a fair fight with equal rights on both sides. Consciousness should defend its reason and protect itself, and the chaotic life of the unconscious should be given the chance of having its way too—as much of it as we can stand. This means open conflict and open collaboration at once. That, evidently, is the way human life should be. It is the old game of hammer and anvil: between them the patient iron is forged into an indestructible whole, an 'individual.'[1]

"The transcendent function," Jung called it,[2] this ability to make the transition between the conscious and the unconscious (to descend to Hades and yet return to the upper world) and yet never annihilate the conscious (though Eurydice be lost, yet she was brought to the verge of light). Orpheus is that transcendent function. He embodies the central elements of what Joseph Campbell has defined as the monomyth,[3] the theme of the quest and the symbolic meaning of that quest—the daring to confront *all* of the psyche and not be over-whelmed by the daring.[4] Neither Conrad's Kurtz nor his Marlow became Orpheus, Kurtz because he was overwhelmed by his journey back and down, Marlow because he drew back from completing the journey.[5]

In psychological terms, this is the meaning and significance of heroism: the unblinking meeting of one's whole self and the capacity to be aware of, expressive of, transformed by, that meeting.

> It is precisely the strongest and best among men, the heroes, who give way to their regressive longings and purposely expose themselves to the danger of being devoured by the monster of the maternal abyss. But if a man is a hero, he is a hero because, in the final reckoning, he did not let the monster devour him, but subdued it, not once but many times. Victory over the collective psyche alone yields the true value—the capture of the hoard, the invincible weapon, the magic talisman, or whatever it be that the myth deems most desirable. Anyone who identifies with the collective psyche—or, in mythological terms, lets himself be devoured by the monster—and vanishes in it, attains the treasure that the dragon guards, but he does so in spite of himself and to his own greatest harm.[6]

Orpheus as singer is the same as Orpheus the deep seeker. He has been recognized as the emblem of the creative artist, and the artist is the interiorized hero. In ultimate terms, *hero* and *artist* are the same, just as the two offices are combined in the one Orpheus. The historical hero dares to walk on the literal landscape or moonscape and then return, having liberated something from the prison of the unknown. The artist trods an inner geography—as uncharted and more vast than the physical spaces outside—and brings back images of what he has found there. As Orpheus did, the artist-hero may not bring back the whole Eurydice, but perhaps only a phantom, a memory, of that deep experience. The corporeal Eurydice vanishes at the shadowline, but this does not mean that Orpheus fails. The artist does not simply retail his experience, he cannot bring back the whole Eurydice: but he does bring back an image, a metaphor, an icon, a color, a note, a texture, a symbol; and the symbol incarnates the quest, the discovery, and the return.[7]

The importance of *symbol* to Orphism, heroic artistry, is vital. It is through Orpheus that the dark must speak to the light, the instinctual to the rational, the Dionysiac to the Apollonian. Orpheus thus needs a means of communication that is true to the whole richness of his experience—the separation, the descent, the discovery, the return—omitting nothing, sacrificing none of the strangeness, making no compromises with the elemental difference of the quest. At the same time, he needs to hold up to intelligence's gaze something formed, edged, comprehensible, so that intelligence standing on its own ground can understand.

For it is not enough simply to descend, not in mythic or psychological or aesthetic terms. Odysseus needs to come home. The mind that never returns from the depths of the unconscious is mad.[8] The powerful experience that is never imaged or given symbolic form will never be art: there can be no such thing as a mute Milton, a handless Rodin, an eyeless Renoir.[9]

The symbol, as the causeway between limited consciousness and oceanic unconsciousness, therefore, must be both illumined and obscure, direct and cryptic, focused and amorphous, to be true to its middle condition. In literary art, the symbolic statement will inhere in words—Logos, the instrument of intelligence and rationality—and in structure also, for structure is wholeness, assemblage, the re-fusion of what had stood apart. Structure itself is the image of the Orphic fusion of the two domains.

When an author deep-mines himself and then verbally and structurally symbolizes that adventure, he reenacts the Orpheus myth whether he wants to or not. Subject matter has nothing to do with it—a spelunking expedition, a space probe, a subway ride, are all potential gateways into the Orphic experience. It is depth and discovery and rescue that are important, not the path itself. And every act of participatory reading, every audience involvement, is a surrogate Orphism. In reading, we penetrate the surface of the words, seek out the treasure horde of meaning, return with it to our bounded precognitive world and find the boundaries no longer the same. We, too, become Orpheus.

"The artist is Orpheus whether he wants to be or not" does not mean, however, that he has no control. Even while the deep structure of the myth, unbidden, seizes on the author by the very act of penetration and symbolization, still there are choices. It is a commonplace that the artist and the psychotic share the dangerous underworld of the unconscious,[10] that "Great wits are sure to madness near allied,/ And thin partitions do their bounds divide." But the essential difference is that the psychotic lacks alternatives while the artist possesses them in abundance. The choice of *which* symbol, *which* structure will best express the basic myth, belongs to the artist. By his choosing, the artist attains that freedom represented by Orpheus. Orpheus tamed the darkness and the wildness, the artist gives shape and substance to his own dark journey, and that is a bond between them.

A splendid recent example of the continuing validity of the Orpheus myth, and the shaping power of the author in verbally and structurally symbolizing that myth, is James Dickey's *Deliverance*. It is one of the finest instances I know in contemporary fiction of the prevailing immediacy of myth.[11]

At the head of the novel stand two epigraphs. The first is from Georges Bataille, *Il existe à la base de la vie humaine un principe d'insuffisance*, "there is an element of incompleteness at the base of human life." The second is from the Old Testament, Obadiah, verse 3:

> The pride of thine heart hath deceited thee,
>     thou that dwellest in the clefts of the rock,
>  whose habitation is high; that saith in his heart,
>     Who shall bring me down to the ground?

The two motifs of incompleteness and being brought to the ground become entwined through the course of the novel. Obadiah becomes the response to Bataille.

Four men are seated in a tavern, planning a canoe trip down a river that will soon no longer exist—a dam is to be built and soon the river valley will be flooded to make a new lake "with its choice lots, its marinas and beer cans."[12]   Three of the men—Ed, Bobby, and Drew—are novices, comfortable in their tidy suburban lives, unfamiliar with any of the dangers of whitewater canoing. The fourth man, Lewis, will serve as their initiator and guide (but in a misguided and eventually destructive way). Very much the embodiment of the Western male *machismo* ethic, Lewis sees life as a contest, man throwing himself against the world: he "gave himself solemnly to the business of survival" (p. 42), he is contemptuous "of the sleep of mild people." (p. 36)

The narrative voice of the novel is Ed's, and it is Ed whose *deliverance* is achieved. Even in the planning session in the tavern, he feels a strange force coming at him from the prospect of a journey. The very map he pores over exudes a life, an animalism: "It unrolled slowly, forced to show its colors, curling and snapping back whenever one of us turned loose." (p. 3) The course of the river, he notices, is northeast to southwest—the same direction, it might be noted, of the river John Donne described in what was probably his last poem: "this is my South-west discoverie/ *Per fretum febris,* by these streights [I] die" (*Hymne to God my God, in my sickness*). For Donne, southwest had the meaning of descent and death (south=downward; west=occident=*occidere,* to kill); and in metaphorical terms the river of *Deliverance* will come to have the same meaning.

Plans for the journey agreed on, the four men separate, and Ed begins to walk back to his photography studio, his place of business. Without his showing any awareness of it, he crosses a symbolic landscape, a quiet message to him that the time for his special journey is now upon him, now or never, or the time will be lost to him. "The day sparkled painfully, seeming to shake on some kind of axis, and through this a leaf fell, touched with unusual color at the edges. It was the first time I had realized that autumn was close. I began to climb the last hill." (p. 15) Unaware, Ed is at a boundary situation, a possibly transformative moment. Once on the river, Lewis will say to him, "You know . . . we don't have too many more years for this kind of thing" (p. 85), and he is right: Ed is at his last hill, his autumn, the desperate instant of waning strength that Shakespeare described in his seventy-third sonnet:

> That time of year thou mayest in me behold
> When yellow leaves, or none, or few, do hang
> Upon those boughs which shake against the cold,
> Bare ruin'd choirs where late the sweet birds sang.
> In me thou see'st the twilight of such day
> As after sunset fadeth in the west,
> Which by and by black night doth take away,
> Death's second self, that seals up all in rest.

As if there were a destiny controlling him, Ed is surrounded by women—as Marlow did in *Heart of Darkness,* he sees living witnesses of the unconscious, the archetypal *anima.* "I noticed how many women there were around me. Since I had passed the Gulf station on the corner, I hadn't seen another man anywhere. I began to look for one in the cars going by, but for the few more minutes it took me to get to the building, I didn't see a one." (p. 15) This claim of the women, and what it mythically represents, pursues him into his office.

Just before a more emphatic vision of the Eternal Woman, the intuitive and the unconscious, hits him, Ed is washed over by a sense of emptiness. "The feeling of the inconsequence of whatever I would do, of anything I would pick up or think about or turn to see was at the moment being set in the very bone marrow. How does one get through this? I asked myself." (p. 18) This feeling of *l'insuffisance* is what Ed is to be delivered from, and the deliverance goes onward with his next action.

The day's work is to photograph a young woman as part of an ad campaign. As Ed watches the model, he notices:

> She was somebody I didn't mind looking in the eyes. And straight into them, too, so that if she'd permit it, the look would go deep. I did this, because on the spur of the moment I wanted to. There

was a peculiar spot, a kind of tan slice, in her left eye, and it hit
me with, I knew right away, strong powers; it was not only
recallable, but would come back of itself. (p. 21)

She turned and looked into my face at close range, and the
gold-glowing mote fastened on me; it was more gold than any real
gold could possibly be; it was alive, and it saw me. (p. 22)

In this brief encounter, Ed (still not recognizing what is happening to
him) is barraged with images of the unconscious, all latent compensa-
tions for his narrowly defined and unsatisfying life. The theme of *going
deeper* will be major: here, it is the girl's eyes; shortly it will be the river
and ultimately Ed's own self. The theme of direct gaze, of confrontation, will surface periodically through Ed's narrative. What happens
when he looks at the girl is, so to speak, a generalized prophecy of
what Ed's real adventure will be, a descent toward fuller vision.
Within this generalized framework is a specific symbol of a new kind of
life, a *deliverance*.

That symbol is the peculiarity of the girl's left eye, the slice of gold
that "was alive, and it saw me." Both factors, the crescent (or
"moon-slice" [p. 49] that Ed sees) and the gold, have specific archetypal meaning. The crescent is the moon, "the feminine principle
[which] is ruler of the night, of the unconscious . . . controller of
those mysterious forces beyond understanding."[13]  In classical
Chinese philosophy, it is *yin* (as contrasted to the rational *yang*), the
image of "everything dark, shady, cool, feminine, and this power
commences its power in the autumn."[14] Ed feels that power in this
September of his journey, even while not understanding it. The morning of September 14, just before he sets out, he makes love to his
wife—a practical kind of lovemaking, done almost routinely and
without face-to-face contact; and during that love, he sees again the
golden eye and feels its life: "in the center of Martha's heaving and
expertly working back, the gold eye shone, not with the practicality of
sex, so necessary to its survival, but the promise of it that promised
other things, another life, deliverance." (p. 28)

The common meaning of *gold* simply fortifies the moon-feminine-unconscious symbol. It represents value, that which is lacking in Ed's sense of his life. Possibly, it is even more specific: what Ed is being drawn to is a transformation, a metamorphosis of an incomplete self into a fuller self. Jung has pointed out that in the ancient science of the transformative process, alchemy, *gold* was often taken as a symbol for the *lapis philosophorum,* the philosopher's stone, the agent of transformation, and that it was frequently associated with the moon.[15] If this more occult symbolism of gold is indeed operative in the novel, then we have a great simultaneity of communications: gold–moon–*anima*–unconscious–transformation–deliverance. Fast and full as these announcements are coming, Ed is still not aware of them. He records them in his narrative with no sign that he has understood them. All the sounds of the inner world have not yet impinged on his rational consciousness.

The river expedition begins on September 14, and will end September 16, a three day ritual. When the story of Orpheus' search in the underground for Eurydice was absorbed into Christian legend, that episode became the Harrowing of Hell, Christ's three day sojourn in the internal regions between Good Friday and Easter Sunday. At the beginning of his three days, Ed reveals that part of his mind has been preparing him for this journey for quite some time.

> There was something about me that usually kept me from dreaming, or maybe kept me from remembering what I had dreamed; I was either awake or dead, and I always came back slowly. I had the feeling that if it were perfectly quiet, if I could hear nothing, I would never wake up. Something in the world had to pull me back, for every night I went down deep, and if I had any sensation during a sleep, it was of going deeper and deeper, trying to reach a point, a line or border. (p. 25)

Earlier, Ed had remarked on his feeling that his day seemed to be on some kind of axis, some turning point; now we discover that this quest for a passing-over has been championed by his own subconscious not once but many times. We've seen how the unconscious attempts to compensate for the one-sidedness of the psyche. Ed is insufficient, he lives too narrowly within the borders of routine, of harmony, of balance and order ("I liked harmoniousness and a situation where the elements didn't fight with each other or overwhelm each other." (p. 19) In dreams, one of the languages of the unconscious, he hears repeated what the girl's eyes told him—go deeper, go deeper. As he rides with Lewis on their way to the river, Ed describes his lifestyle as "sliding." "Sliding is living antifriction. Or, no, sliding is living by antifriction. It is finding a modest thing you can do, and then greasing that thing. On both sides. It is grooving with comfort." (p. 41) Lewis responds to this manifesto, just as Ed's dreams responded, with a reminder that there is more to wholeness than placidity: "You don't believe in madness, eh?" is what Lewis asks him. (p. 41) And when the four men get to the river, the river itself will become the agency prepared for by the girl's eyes, his own dreams, and Lewis's question. As he steps into the river for the first time, Ed feels himself caught by the life-power of the river (as he had when he studied the map in the tavern), and finds the river drawing him exactly as his dreams had drawn him.

> 'It's got me,' I said.
> 'What's got you?'
> 'It . . .'
> A slow force took hold of us; the bank began to go backward. I felt the complicated urgency of the current, like a thing made of many threads being pulled, and with this came the feeling I always had at the moment of losing consciousness at night, going toward something unknown that I could not avoid, but from which I would return. I dipped the paddle in. (pp. 72–3)

Before putting into the river, however, there were preparations to be made: cars to be driven to embarkation and then transported to Aintry where the journey will end. When Ed, Lewis, Bobby and Drew are taking care of these details, enlisting the services of some of the

mountain people, they are joined by a boy, a strange, uncommunica-
tive, retarded boy who "don't know nothin' but banjo-pickin'." (p.
59) This boy, Lonnie, and Drew, who had insisted on bringing his
guitar along on the trip, together and without plan create a music that
Ed describes as sheer joy, something rare and unrepeatable. Brief as
the scene is, it is crucial to the novel and requires commentary.

It is a curious fact that when the matter of mythology is recreated in
legend and fairy tale, the symbols of the nether world are strangely wizened and reduced. The great and terrible figures of Hades
and Pluto are shrunk into gnomes or dwarfs or elves. The gods of the
dark places become the tiny bearded wizard who appears to the fairy
tale hero and tells him where to dig to find the goose with the golden
feathers, or the malicious dwarf-miser who protects his horde from
Snow White and Rose Red, or the shadowy crone who imprisons
Rapunzel in the tower. But shrunken though they may be (shrunken
because we fail to really believe in what they represent?), they still
represent that other world of the dangerous but potentially redemptive
unconscious, the dark cavern where the treasure is hidden.

This is what the demented boy signifies. He is Lonnie, lunatic,
luna, the moon-force, another embodiment of the moon-slice in the
girl's left eye, offering to be Ed's initiator into the domain he has
neglected and is now being drawn into. Through his music-making
with Drew, Lonnie demonstrates communion and unification—the
music "was a lovely unimpeded flowing that seemed endless," and
"the demented country kid and the big-faced decent city man" became fused in the music. (p. 60) Dickey reasserts the motif of vision:
Lonnie's vision is double, outward but also downward; he had "pink
eyes like a white rabbit's; one of them stared off at a furious and
complicated angle. That was the eye he looked at us with, with his
face set in another direction. The sane, rational eye was fixed on
something that wasn't there, somewhere in the dust of the road." (pp.
58–9) Characteristically, Ed simply records this fact, deducing
nothing from it. Until he survives his *agon*, until he finds and crosses
over his "point, line or border" he will not transcend his trapped,
limited and unaware point of view.

Ironically, one of the deterrents to Ed's understanding the meaning of what is happening to him is Lewis, the self-appointed and unanimously accepted guide: he recognizes the thinness and incompleteness of a surface life, he has made a dark journey of his own, he speaks of the value of the irrational. And yet, he subverts the quest. The proper end of the Orphic journey is assimilation, communion, the recovery of a lost oneness. Lewis, though, sees the journey as combat and conquest, as oppositions and victories and defeats. He is *conquistador*, the man of weapons and domination, to whom even a road to the river is an enemy that must be fought and overcome. He preaches to Ed the gospel of quintessential *maleness*, *macho*, master. It is understandable that Lewis should interpret journey and quest in terms of maleness: it is an attitude endemic in the Western imagination. The Orphic rhythm of penetration and return has a natural metaphor in human sexuality, our myths are conditioned by biology. The male enters the female; in myth the hero is a man, the cavern and the treasure is the woman. In Lewis's behavior there is always the taint of genital aggression: he is man, the world is woman, he must enter and subdue.

But this is not the message coming from Lonnie or the girl's moonspecked left eye. Their gospel is the gospel of immersion, unity, reassemblage, transcendence. Lewis, offered and accepted as guide, threatens to corrupt Ed's journey to which the unconscious summons him.

Dickey's introduction of this conflict between goal and guide is wonderfully perceptive and psychologically accurate. In the figure of Lewis, the author gives us a living and credible example of what Jung referred to as "running contrariwise," *enantiodromia.* [16]

To explain: we have seen that the unconscious speaks in images, in dreams, in myths, poetry. When those images are generated not simply by the personal unconscious but by the collective unconscious, then they reveal an archetype. For example, the universal wish for completeness, wholeness, total at-one-ness may be expressed in the archetypal symbol of a garden; the universal questing for wisdom may appear archetypally as the figure of a wise old man, a guide, a *guru;* the unconscious itself will be archetypally manifest in the figure of a woman, Sophia, Mother, Goddess. It is through such metaphors that the unconscious declares itself; and, once again as we have seen, such declarations are compensatory, the entire psychic system adjusting its own balance, the neglected being attended to, one-sidedness being overcome.

However, when the elements of the unconscious are denied or repressed, these same images "run contrariwise." It is as if the unconscious, thwarted in its attempt to make contact with consciousness, becomes vengeful, and develops a malevolent negativity. Repression begets a sinister twinship, and the images that arise are dark and destructive.[17] In such circumstances the garden becomes a desert; the wise old man becomes Mephistopheles or an infantile unadept;[18] the woman becomes a witch, a devouring and terrible goddess.[19]

Ed, of course, has repressed and been unmindful of the unconscious calling on him to correct his psychic balance. He fails to understand the girl, his dreams, Lonnie; and he falls victim to "the grim law of enantiodromia,"[20] and allows himself to be led by Lewis, the flawed guide, into a flawed journey. Ed's quest is not simple: he must not only undertake the Orphic experience, he must also learn to dissociate himself from the false guide and learn for himself the true path to his goal. After getting underway (Ed experiencing "the feeling I always had at the moment of losing consciousness at night" as soon as he enters the river), there are two brief episodes that clarify the true and the false path, the Orphic way and Lewis's bent way. A prediction of one kind of journey in which dissolution ends in communion is made in a random conversation between Drew and Ed as they paddle their way through some debris.

> On the right bank some tin sheds backed down to the water; the mud was covered with rusted pieces of metal, engine parts and blue and green blinks of broken bottles. But there was something worse than any of this; some of the color was not only color; it was bright, unchangeable. Drew had been hit the same way, for another reason. 'Plastic,' he said. 'Doesn't decompose.'
> 'Does that mean you can't get rid of it,' I said, 'at all?'
> 'Doesn't go back to its elements,' he said, as though that were all right. (p. 76)

Neither Drew nor Ed notice the parable value here, the analogy between men and materials, some going back to the elements, back to the earth—and some not. By the novel's end, Drew will have gone cruelly back to the elements, his body left to decompose in the river. Ed will have achieved a different kind of elemental return. This chatter of theirs about river rubbish is prophetic of their fates, and also of Ed's real quest.

That night Ed has a nightmare in which the girl in his photography studio reappears. He dreams of her being clawed by a cat, "clawing and spitting in the middle of the air, raking the girl's buttocks and her leg-backs." (p. 87) Still not fully awake, thinking it part of the dream, Ed realizes something has hit the top of his tent. It is an owl, a predatory owl; and Ed reaches up and touches the talons that have ripped through the canvas. "All night the owl kept coming back to hunt from the top of the tent. I not only saw his feet when he came to us; I imagined what he was doing while he was gone, floating through the trees, seeing everything. I hunted with him as well as I could, there in my weightlessness. The woods burned in my head. Toward morning I could reach up and touch the claw without turning on the light." (p. 89) In the morning, before the others are awake, Ed arms himself with bow and arrow and goes out to become a hunter, to stalk and kill a deer. He feels that it is expected of him, something that "would satisfy honor." (p. 95) He fails to kill his prey, his arm wavers at the crucial moment of releasing the bowstring. Crestfallen, he admits his failure to Lewis, telling him, "What I was really thinking about up there was you." (p. 98)

The three occurrences—nightmare, owl, and deerhunt—belong together; and they all bear the stamp of the false guide, Lewis. The painful sexuality of Ed's nightmare, the contact between Ed and the hunting owl, the admission that "what I was really thinking about up there was you" drum away at Lewis's creed of male attack, domination, control. Jung speaks of the benign archetype of the wise old man being replaced by the "infantile shadow." Lewis, with his canoe, his bows and arrows, his promises of high adventure charged with opportunities for proving manhood, offers Ed an adolescent dream, a veritable Tom Sawyer paradise. As a representative of the world that Ed must come to know, Lewis functions well as an initiator: it is he who brings Ed to the river. But as guide, Lewis is Mephistophelean, promising power and thus corrupting the real object of Ed's search. Ed must learn to differentiate himself from Lewis and what Lewis represents before he can achieve any sense of his own self: "The only person who escapes the grim law of enantiodromia is the man who knows how to separate himself from the unconscious, not by repressing it—for then it simply attacks him from the rear—but by putting it clearly before him as *that which he is not.*"[21]

The terror of *Deliverance* begins that same day, September 15. Ed and Bobby set out in the lead canoe, with Lewis and Drew following. The two groups become separated from one another; to wait for them, Ed brings his canoe onto the left bank and he and Bobby disembark. They are no sooner on shore than they are confronted by two men, armed, who have come out of the woods. The quiet threat these two men carry with them explodes into violence: while Ed is tied up, Bobby is raped by one of the men, and left whimpering on the forest floor. The second of the two men begins to force Ed into an act of sodomy.

At that point Lewis, who had seen Ed's canoe, had beached his own and come stealthily on foot, uses his weapon, the hunting bow he had brought with him. Ed sees the man who had assaulted Bobby with "a foot and a half of bright red arrow . . . shoved forward from the middle of his chest." (p. 116)

Ed's tormenter breaks for the forest and escapes, leaving his dead companion and the four living men with the problem: what to do with the body. Drew speaks for order and legality—the body must be brought into the nearest town, and the whole social procedure of inquest and investigation and trial be undergone. Lewis argues that no, there would be no fair investigation, that the mountain people would protect their own, and that they, the four strangers, would be charged with murder. So all traces of the body and the incident have to be destroyed. Ed stands with Lewis, and so it is decided: the body will be carried further inland and then buried in the deep loam. Since the whole valley will shortly be flooded, discovery will be impossible.

The grisly entourage gets underway, with men who had been insulated from such macabre affairs dragging a body through the woods, their lives broken into in a way they could never have anticipated or prepared for. To Ed, the dragging of the body upstream in the canoe seems an almost inhuman activity. It is, as a matter of fact, a replica of a mythic night-journey, the terrible descent into dread, death, the *rite de passage* of myth, religion and literature, the recurrent theme of death and, perhaps, rebirth. It is a version of Orpheus descending in search of his treasure; and here it is Lewis who seems to be bearing the treasure.

> Lewis led, drawing the canoe by the bow painter, plodding bent-over upstream with the veins popping, the rope over his shoulder like a bag of gold. The trees, mostly mountain laurel and rhododendron,[22] made an arch over the creek, so that at times we had to get down on one knee or both knees and grope through leaves and branches, going right into the most direct push of water against our chests as it came through the foliage. At some places it was like a tunnel where nothing human had ever been expected to come, and at others it was like a long green hall where the water changed tones and temperatures and was much quieter than it would have been in the open. (p. 132)

As if to reinforce the echoes here of other mythic tunnel journeys, such as Theseus' probe for the Minotaur, Aladdin's journey to his lamp, Dante in the Dark Wood, Lewis does a strange thing when once they leave the river and carry the body deeper into the forest. He carefully, with full draw and classic form, shoots the death-arrow into the soft ground, and Ed imagines that "[it] could have been traveling down through muck to the soft center of the earth." (p. 135) Obviously Lewis is disposing of the murder weapon. But there is more to the act than that. He dispatches the arrow into the earth exactly as he had sent it into the body of the man. In that gesture he asserts his domination, his mastery, of the earth itself. He acts out his code, his strong self-system, as Ed calls it. (p. 139)

With the dead man buried, the four companions begin the last leg of their journey. But the terror has not ended, nor has Ed achieved his own deliverance. He is still under the tutelage of Lewis, still concentrating on survival and Lewis's strength. As the canoes shoot through a dangerous whitewater stretch of river, Drew is killed, evidently shot by the other attacker, now armed with a rifle. Both canoes capsize, and Ed, Lewis, and Bobby are hurled into the avalanche of water and bruising, smashing rocks. Before they are let loose by the river, Lewis's leg is broken. Ed catalogs their situation, all the while knowing that it is going to be he alone who can get them out alive.

> We've got a hurt man. We've got a water-logged canoe with the bottom stove in. We've got two guys who don't even know where in hell they are. He's got a rifle, and he's up above us. He knows where we are and can't help being, and we don't have the slightest notion of where he is, or even who he is. We haven't got a goddamned chance, if you and Lewis are right. If he's up there and wants to kill us, he can kill us. (p. 154)

All that Lewis can do is advise, and he does so in a way that is no surprise, it's the code again.

> 'Kill him,' Lewis said with the river.
> 'I'll kill him if I can find him,' I said.
> 'Well,' he said, lying back, 'here we are, at the heart of the Lewis Medlock country.'
> 'Pure survival,' I said.
> 'This is what it comes to,' he said. 'I told you.'
> 'Yes, you told me.' (p. 160)

But now Ed will be alone, and he knows it. "I was standing in the most entire aloneness that I had ever been given." (p. 161) As he begins the adventure that will test him as he's never been tested, he is accoutered both with Lewis's tokens and the tokens of the girl and his dream, with arrows and with the moon, with assault weapons and with that force of the unconscious whose power is most manifest in the autumn. Ed has finally come to that axis, that point or line or border that he's been fatefully drawn to; the point where he will or will not be delivered, will or will not assume the definition of *hero*, "the one who, while still alive, knows and represents the claims of the super-consciousness which throughout creation is more or less unconscious. The adventure of the hero represents the moment in his life when he achieved illumination—the nuclear moment when, while still alive, he found and opened the road to the light beyond the dark walls of our living death."[23]

To get into position to ambush the killer stalking them, Ed must scale a cliff that leaps up from the river's edge. The moon begins to rise as he starts his climb, and he experiences joy, nakedness, helplessness and intimacy, all at once. The ascent is made in two stages, and they might justifiably be called the Lewis stage and the *anima* stage, attack and union.

In the beginning, Ed assaults the cliff face. He kicks at it (p. 161), he plants his foot on it (p. 162), he labors backbreakingly against it (p. 162), he feels that he possesses the wall of rock (p. 163), he gets angry at the cliff, he fights with the wall for anything it can give him (p. 165). Strangely, in the midst of this combat, there is a contrary feeling: "With each shift to a newer and higher position I felt more and more tenderness toward the wall." (p. 163) Just as he reaches the point of panic and exhaustion, it occurs to him "not to double up my fists but to keep my hands open." (p. 165) At that instant, when he accepts the rock rather than smashing at it, the cliff seems to open to him, "strength from the stone flowed into me" (p. 165), and he finds a crevice large enough to crawl into. For most of the night he lies there, curled up in the cliff, embraced by it and drawing strength from it. With that strength he begins the second stage of his climb, and this time there is no assault. Ed thinks of this stage as an erotic exchange between the cliff and himself, a lovemaking with the earth rather than a conquest of it; and as he does so he remembers the moon-slice in the girl's eye, that early intimation that he would confront a promise, a new life, deliverance.

> Time after time I lay there sweating, having no handhold or foothold, the rubber of my toes bending back against the soft rock, my hands open. Then I would begin to try to inch upward again, moving with the most intimate motions of my body, motions I had never dared use with Martha, or with any other human woman. Fear and a kind of enormous moon-blazing sexuality lifted me, millimeter by millimeter. And yet I held madly to the human. I looked for a slice of gold like the model's in the river; some kind of freckle, something lovable in the huge serpent-shape of light. (p. 176)

This war-turning-into-Eros relationship with the cliff is a rehearsal for Ed's meeting with his enemy. He knows he must kill or be killed, and he carefully plans where to wait and how to attack his adversary. As he considers what he must do, he realizes that he is not that man's opponent, but that he has become that man; not that he, Ed, has become evil, but that his and the "enemy's" identities have become fused, merged.

> I had thought so long and hard about him that to this day I still believe I felt, in the moonlight, our minds fuse. It was not that I felt myself turning evil, but that an enormous physical indifference, as vast as the whole abyss of light at my feet, came to me: an indifference not only to the other man's body scrambling and kicking on the ground with an arrow through it, but also to mine. If Lewis had not shot his companion, he and I would have made a kind of love, painful and terrifying to me, in some dreadful way pleasurable to him, but we would have been together in the flesh, there on the floor of the woods, and it was strange to think of it. (p. 180)

Ed does kill the man, skewering him with an arrow; and almost simultaneously falls on his own second arrow and is himself skewered. Minds *and* bodies lock, Ed and his victim gored together. And then, "His brain and mine unlocked and fell apart, and in a way I was sorry to see it go." (p. 199) Briefly but horribly Ed reverts to savagery, he is caught up in blood-lust, and stands over his man like an ancient barbaric warrior chanting a death-song.

> I took the knife in my fist. What? Anything. This, also, is not going to be seen. It is not ever going to be known; you can do what you want to; nothing is too terrible. I can cut off the genitals he was going to use on me. Or I can cut off his head, looking straight into his open eyes. Or I can eat him. I can do anything I have a wish to do, and I waited carefully for some wish to come; I would do what it said.
>
> It did not come, but the ultimate horror circled me and played over the knife. I began to sing. It was a current popular favorite, a folk-rock tune. I finished and I was withdrawn from. (p. 200)

To understand the enormity of this moment, we must refer to Carl Jung's concept of *individuation,* to Narcissus, and to Dionysos.

In Jung's view, the ego is only a thin band of the entire human personality. It comprises only those phenomena that lie within the range of conscious awareness. It is hedged around by the unknown. This narrow ego-band rests on a great abyss of the unconscious, both the personal unconscious (those memories of personal experiences either forgotten or repressed) and the collective unconscious (racial or genetic memories shared by the entire race). The personality is the combination of *both* consciousness and the unconscious, ego and non-ego. Consequently, for the full personality to be realized, then narrow consciousness, *ego,* must surrender its vaunted primacy and admit that it can be subsumed by the more gigantic unknown, by non-ego and the unconscious. This is the meaning and significance of the Narcissus myth.

But to enter the domain of the unconscious is to surrender rational awareness, to experience existential death. Caught up in the collective unconscious, the conscious ego is paradoxically redeemed by making contact with its own foundations, and shattered by its companionship with the elemental and nonrational. Hence, the paradoxicality of creation and destruction, energy and terror, of the Dionysos myth.

Only when the limited ego accepts the immersion into the unconscious, experiences it, and then brings that experience into the light of awareness, consciousness, can the *self* come to be. Not to admit the unconscious, not to be Narcissus, is to be a psychic pauper, living only on the surface of personality. Not to admit the deathliness and regenerative powers of the unconscious, not to be Dionysos, is to be eventually overwhelmed by them, as was Kurtz. But to participate, experience and to *understand*, to become Orpheus, is to become the whole personality, the *self* in Jung's sense of that word. This is true deliverance, deliverance from the constrained ego itself (to go beyond the point, line or border) and deliverance from the ego-destructive unconscious: "the disharmony with himself is precisely the neurotic and intolerable condition from which [man] seeks to be delivered, and deliverance from this condition will come only when he can be and act as he feels is conformable with his true self."[24]

After being so opaque, so unresponsive to signals from the unconscious, Ed does finally enter into that unconscious and repairs the divorce between his narrow ego and his whole self—he experiences both the joy and the terror, eros and death, the involvement of himself and the full earth. His final knowledge is summed up in his words about the ultimate horror circling him: "I finished, and I was withdrawn from." He speaks as both man and woman following erotic exchange; he is now man and woman, *animus* and *anima*, the conscious and the unconscious, a whole. He has been in the mysterious places, they are part of him, and yet he is different from them. When all the loose ends are cared for—all the bodies disposed of, the trip ended, the police questions satisfied—Ed concludes his account of September 16, "I lay awake all night in brilliant sleep." (p. 240) From sleep had come his dreams, and from dreams had come the first tugs toward his dark journey; now it is a brilliant sleep, light-flooded awareness; now he is awake, he knows. As Orpheus he has come back, with the lost treasure. Nor is it an ephemeral awareness. Before he leaves for home, Ed stoops and drinks from the river (p. 267), ingesting the symbol of his new wisdom, taking it into himself. From being so obtuse in the course of the novel, Ed progresses to great perception of what has happened:

> The river and everything I remembered about it became a possession to me, a personal, private possession, as nothing else in my life ever had. Now it ran nowhere but in my head, but there it ran as though immortally. I could feel it—I can feel it—on different places on my body. It pleases me in some curious way that the river does not exist, and that I have it. In me it still is, and will be until I die, green, rocky, deep, fast, slow, and beautiful beyond reality. I had a friend there who in a way had died for me, and my enemy was there. (p. 275)

There is an ambiguity in his words that reflects Ed's new complex awareness: the friend who died there is not only Drew, but also the man he had killed, their minds locked, the agency of Ed's realization of at-one-ness. The enemy who was there is not only the mountain man but Ed's own earlier foreshortened self, the truncated man who would not be and who would not understand. That is the deliverance.

To my mind, there is no question but that James Dickey's *Deliverance* is a wonderfully precise reenactment of the Orpheus myth, and a thoroughly perceptive dramatization of a psychoanalytic truth. But this is by no means to say that *Deliverance* is simply an allegory, a fiction that exists only to hang a doctrine upon. The action is real, the men are real. The myth inheres in them, they do not exist for the myth. Human experience is not granite, impervious to penetration. Human experience is porous, spongy, and concepts and themes can invade the tissue of that experience and live there like benign organisms that come from the outside but become part of the living creature. So too with this novel, which is not an allegory but a symbol: a symbol of the fact that the myth lives within the very structure of the real and the human.

# NOTES

1. Carl Jung, *The Archetypes and the Collective Unconscious, Works,* IX, part 1, 288.

2. Jung, *The Structure and Dynamics of the Psyche, Works,* VIII, 73.

3. Joseph Campbell, *The Hero With a Thousand Faces* (Princeton, Princeton University Press, 1968), pp. 245–6.

4. Carlos Castenada described his own confrontation, the fright and the eventual sense of expanded consciousness that followed his own quest, and admitted that when he first began his apprenticeship with Don Juan he had moments when he was profoundly, even suicidally, depressed. But after exploring the shadow land of his mind he was struck by a sense of absolute wonder and serenity. See *Psychology Today,* December, 1972.

5. As Conrad's *Heart of Darkness* is a recreation of the Dionysos myth, his *Secret Sharer* is a new quickening of the Orpheus myth. The finest discussion I know of *The Secret Sharer* is in Albert Guerard's *Conrad the Novelist* (Cambridge, Mass., Harvard University Press, 1958), which pays due attention to the Jungian mode of analysis.

6. Jung, *Two Essays on Analytical Psychology, Works,* VII, 169–70. See also *Structure and Dynamics of the Psyche,* 212; and *Symbols of Tranformation,* p. 205.

7. Herbert Marcuse, in *Eros and Civilization,* considers Orpheus the prime symbol of the poet as liberator and creator, the pacification of man and nature through art rather than force. See pp. 154–5.

8. Jung, *Two Essays on Analytical Psychology,* p. 152; *The Archetypes and the Collective Unconscious,* p. 289.

9. Erich Neumann, in *Origins and History of Consciousness,* discusses symbols as the bridge between a freedom-bent consciousness and the unconscious; and sees art, myth, and religion as the ways of keeping the two realms from falling apart. See p. 365.

10. Neumann, *Art and the Creative Unconscious,* pp. 17 and 90.

11. The ensuing discussion will focus entirely on the novel. However, I would recommend that the film version of *Deliverance* be kept in mind as a valuable supplement to the novel and not as a simple redaction of the novel. While the film lacks (too) much of the exposition of the book, certain of its visual images have a superlative force and value of their own. Case in point: when the four men pass under a trestle-bridge at the start of their trip, the boy with the banjo stands on the bridge, slowly swinging his banjo back and forth. Visually, the action resembles a railroad semaphore signal, shunting a train from one track to another. The four men, unknowingly, are entering a new life-path; and the cinematic image announces that fact.

12. James Dickey, *Deliverance* (Copyright © 1967 by James Dickey), p. 4. Reprinted by permission of Houghton Mifflin Company, and by Hamish Hamilton, London.

13. M. Esther Harding, *Woman's Mysteries* (New York, G. B. Putnam's Sons, 1973), p. 42.

14. *Ibid.,* p. 38.

15. Jung, *The Archetypes and the Collective Unconscious,* pp. 304, 305.

16. *The Structure and Dynamics of the Psyche,* p. 219; *Two Essays on Analytical Psychology,* pp. 72 ff.; *The Archetypes and the Collective Unconscious,* pp. 215, 229.

17. Northrop Frye distinguishes between "apocalyptic imagery" and "demonic imagery," and discusses several examples of enantiodromatic symbols in *Anatomy of Criticism* (Princeton, Princeton University Press, 1957), pp. 131–150, and also in *Fables of Identity.*

18. "In dreams, it is always the father-figure from whom the decisive convictions, prohibitions, and wise counsels emanate. . . . Mostly, therefore, it is the figure of a 'wise old man' who symbolizes the spiritual factor. . . . He can be positive, in which case he signifies the 'higher' personality, the self or *Filius regius* as conceived by the alchemists. But he can also be negative, and then he signifies the infantile shadow" (Jung, *The Archetypes and the Collective Unconscious,* p. 215).

19. For instance, the Church has been imaged as both the Bride of Christ and the Whore of Babylon; the Hindu goddess Kali is both the Great Mother and Destroyer of Men. Jung was fond of, and frequently cited, the ambivalent character *She* in Rider Haggard's novel; see especially *The Archetypes and the Collective Unconscious,* pp. 28, 200.

20. Jung, *Two Essays on Analytical Psychology,* p. 73.

21. Jung, *Ibid.*

22. Laurel, it might be noted, was the leaf used to crown the victors in the Olympic contests. The setting here conspires with Lewis's conception of life as combat.

23. Campbell, *The Hero With a Thousand Faces,* p. 259.

24. Jung, *Two Essays on Analytical Psychology,* p. 225.

25. Lewis, too, seems to be experiencing a deliverance as the novel ends, deliverance from his own narrow ethic of attack and domination. Largely recovered from his accident on the river, Lewis returns to archery, and he remarks to Ed, "I think my release is passing over into Zen. . . . Those gooks are right. You shouldn't fight it. Better to cooperate with it. Then it'll take you there; take the arrow there." (p. 278) In Zen archery there is no sense of mind-weapon-target, warrior-subject-object. Instead, there is a unity, a nondifferentiation, of archer, instrument, goal. The tables have turned completely: now Ed is the guide (a true one), and Lewis begins to learn Ed's creed.

# THIRD INTERLUDE:
## RECOVERY AND RETURN

We must be still and still moving
Into another intensity
For a further union, a deeper communion
Through the dark cold and the empty desolation,
The wave cry, the wind cry, the vast waters
Of the petrel and the porpoise. In my end is my beginning.

*T. S. Eliot*, East Coker*

# The Secret Sharer

*Joseph Conrad*

## I

On my right hand there were lines of fishing stakes resembling a mysterious system of half-submerged bamboo fences, incomprehensible in its division of the domain of tropical fishes, and crazy of aspect as if abandoned forever by some nomad tribe of fishermen now gone to the other end of the ocean; for there was no sign of human habitation as far as the eye could reach. To the left a group of barren islets, suggesting ruins of stone walls, towers, and blockhouses, had its foundations set in a blue sea that itself looked solid, so still and stable did it lie below my feet; even the track of light from the westering sun shone smoothly, without that animated glitter which tells of an imperceptible ripple. And when I turned my head to take a parting glance at the tug which had just left us anchored outside the bar, I saw the straight line of the flat shore joined to the stable sea, edge to edge, with a perfect and unmarked closeness, in one leveled floor half brown, half

*From "East Coker," in Four Quartets, copyright 1943, by T. S. Eliot, copyright 1971, by Esme Valerie Eliot. Reprinted by permission of Harcourt Brace Jovanovich, Inc., and Faber and Faber, Ltd.

blue under the enormous dome of the sky. Corresponding in their insignificance to the islets of the sea, two small clumps of trees, one on each side of the only fault in the impeccable joint, marked the mouth of the river Meinam we had just left on the first preparatory stage of our homeward journey; and, far back on the inland level, a larger and loftier mass, the grove surrounding the great Paknam pagoda, was the only thing on which the eye could rest from the vain task of exploring the monotonous sweep of the horizon. Here and there gleams as of a few scattered pieces of silver marked the windings of the great river; and on the nearest of them, just within the bar, the tug steaming right into the land became lost to my sight, hull and funnel and masts, as though the impassive earth had swallowed her up without an effort, without a tremor. My eye followed the light cloud of her smoke, now here, now there, above the plain, according to the devious curves of the stream, but always fainter and farther away, till I lost it at last behind the miter-shaped hill of the great pagoda. And then I was left alone with my ship, anchored at the head of the Gulf of Siam.

She floated at the starting point of a long journey, very still in an immense stillness, the shadows of her spars flung far to the eastward by the setting sun. At that moment I was alone on her decks. There was not a sound in her—and around us nothing moved, nothing lived, not a canoe on the water, not a bird in the air, not a cloud in the sky. In this breathless pause at the threshold of a long passage we seemed to be measuring our fitness for a long and arduous enterprise, the appointed task of both our existences to be carried out, far from all human eyes, with only sky and sea for spectators and for judges.

There must have been some glare in the air to interfere with one's sight, because it was only just before the sun left us that my roaming eyes made out beyond the highest ridges of the principal islet of the group something which did away with the solemnity of perfect solitude. The tide of darkness flowed on swiftly; and with tropical suddenness a swarm of stars came out above the shadowy earth, while I lingered yet, my hand resting lightly on my ship's rail as if on the shoulder of a trusted friend. But, with all that multitude of celestial bodies staring down at one, the comfort of quiet communion with her was gone for good. And there were also disturbing sounds by this time—

voices, footsteps forward; the steward flitted along the main-deck, a busily ministering spirit; a hand bell tinkled urgently under the poop deck. . . .

I found my two officers waiting for me near the supper table, in the lighted cuddy. We sat down at once, and as I helped the chief mate, I said:

"Are you aware that there is a ship anchored inside the islands? I saw her mastheads above the ridge as the sun went down."

He raised sharply his simple face, overcharged by a terrible growth of whisker, and emitted his usual ejaculations: "Bless my soul, sir! You don't say so!"

My second mate was a round-cheeked, silent young man, grave beyond his years, I thought; but as our eyes happened to meet I detected a slight quiver on his lips. I looked down at once. It was not my part to encourage sneering on board my ship. It must be said, too, that I knew very little of my officers. In consequence of certain events of no particular significance, except to myself, I had been appointed to the command only a fortnight before. Neither did I know much of the hands forward. All of these people had been together for eighteen months or so, and my position was that of the only stranger on board. I mention this because it has some bearing on what is to follow. But what I felt most was my being a stranger to the ship; and if all the truth must be told, I was somewhat of a stranger to myself. The youngest man on board (barring the second mate), and untried as yet by a position of the fullest responsibility, I was willing to take the adequacy of the others for granted. They had simply to be equal to their tasks; but I wondered how far I should turn out faithful to that ideal conception of one's own personality every man sets up for himself secretly.

Meantime the chief mate, with an almost visible effect of collaboration on the part of his round eyes and frightful whiskers, was trying to evolve a theory of the anchored ship. His dominant trait was to take all things into earnest consideration. He was of a painstaking turn of mind. As he used to say, he "liked to account to himself' for practically everything that came in his way, down to a miserable scorpion he had found in his cabin a week before. The why and the wherefore of that scorpion—how it got on board and came to select his room rather than the pantry (which was a dark place and more what a scorpion would be partial to), and how on earth it managed to drown itself in the inkwell of his writing desk—had exercised him infinitely. The ship within the islands was much more easily accounted for; and just as we were about to rise from table he made his pronouncement. She was, he doubted not, a ship from home lately arrived. Probably she drew too much water to cross the bar except at the top of spring tides. Therefore she went into that natural harbor to wait for a few days in preference to remaining in an open roadstead.

"That's so," confirmed the second mate, suddenly, in his slightly hoarse voice. "She draws over twenty feet. She's the Liverpool ship *Sephora* with a cargo of coal. Hundred and twenty-three days from Cardiff."

We looked at him in surprise.

"The tugboat skipper told me when he came on board for your letters, sir," explained the young man. "He expects to take her up the river the day after tomorrow."

After thus overwhelming us with the extent of his information he slipped out of the cabin. The mate observed regretfully that he "could not account for that young fellow's whims." What prevented him telling us all about it at once, he wanted to know.

I detained him as he was making a move. For the last two days the crew had had plenty of hard work, and the night before they had very little sleep. I felt painfully that I—a stranger—was doing something unusual when I directed him to let all hands turn in without setting an anchor watch. I proposed to keep on deck myself till one o'clock or thereabouts. I would get the second mate to relieve me at that hour.

"He will turn out the cook and steward at four," I concluded, "and then give you a call. Of course at the slightest sign of any sort of wind we'll have the hands up and make a start at once."

He concealed his astonishment. "Very well, sir." Outside the cuddy he put his head in the second mate's door to inform him of my unheard-of caprice to take a five hours' anchor watch on myself. I heard the other raise his voice incredulously—"What? The Captain himself?" Then a few more murmurs, a door closed, then another. A few moments later I went on deck.

My strangeness, which had made me sleepless, had prompt-ed that unconventional arrangement, as if I had expected in those solitary hours of the night to get on terms with the ship of which I knew nothing, manned by men of whom I knew very little more. Fast alongside a wharf, littered like any ship in port with a tangle of unrelated things, invaded by unrelated shore people, I had hardly seen her yet properly. Now, as she lay cleared for sea, the stretch of her main-deck seemed to me very fine under the stars. Very fine, very roomy for her size, and very inviting. I descended the poop and paced the waist, my mind picturing to myself the coming passage through the Malay Archipelago, down the Indian Ocean, and up the Atlantic. All its phases were familiar enough to me, every characteristic, all the alternatives which were likely to face me on the high seas— everything! . . . except the novel responsibility of command. But I took heart from the reasonable thought that the ship was like other ships, the men like other men, and that the sea was not likely to keep any special surprises expressly for my discomfi-ture.

Arrived at that comforting conclusion, I bethought myself of a cigar and went below to get it. All was still down there. Everybody at the after end of the ship was sleeping profoundly. I came out again on the quarter-deck, agreeably at ease in my sleeping suit on that warm breathless night, barefooted, a glowing cigar in my teeth, and, going forward, I was met by the profound silence of the fore end of the ship. Only as I passed the door of the forecastle I heard a deep, quiet, trustful sigh of some sleeper inside. And suddenly I rejoiced in the great security of the sea as compared with the unrest of the land, in my choice of that untempted life presenting no disquieting problems, invested with an elementary moral beauty by the absolute straight-forwardness of its appeal and by the singleness of its purpose.

The riding light in the forerigging burned with a clear, untroubled, as if symbolic, flame, confident and bright in the mysterious shades of the night. Passing on my way aft along the other side of the ship, I observed that the rope side ladder, put over, no doubt, for the master of the tug when he came to fetch away our letters, had not been hauled in as it should have been. I became annoyed at this, for exactitude in some small matters is the very soul of discipline. Then I reflected that I had myself peremptorily dismissed my officers from duty, and by my own act had prevented the anchor watch being formally set and things properly attended to. I asked myself whether it was wise ever to interfere with the established routine of duties even from the kindest of motives. My action might have made me appear eccentric. Goodness only knew how that absurdly whiskered mate would "account" for my conduct, and what the whole ship thought of that informality of their new captain. I was vexed with myself.

Not from compunction certainly, but, as it were mechanically, I proceeded to get the ladder in myself. Now a side ladder of that sort is a light affair and comes in easily, yet my vigorous tug, which should have brought it flying on board, merely recoiled upon my body in a totally unexpected jerk. What the devil! . . . I was so astounded by the immovableness of that ladder that I remained stockstill, trying to account for it to myself like that imbecile mate of mine. In the end, of course, I put my head over the rail.

The side of the ship made an opaque belt of shadow on the darkling glassy shimmer of the sea. But I saw at once something elongated and pale floating very close to the ladder. Before I could form a guess a faint flash of phosphorescent light, which seemed to issue suddenly from the naked body of a man, flickered in the sleeping water with the elusive, silent play of summer lightning in a night sky. With a gasp I saw revealed to my stare a pair of feet, the long legs, a broad livid back immersed right up to the neck in a greenish cadaverous glow. One hand, awash, clutched the bottom rung of the ladder. He was complete but for the head. A headless corpse! The cigar dropped out of my gaping mouth with a tiny plop and a short hiss quite audible in the absolute stillness of all things under heaven. At that I suppose he raised up his face, a dimly pale oval in the shadow of the ship's side. But even then I could only barely make out down there the shape of his black-haired head. However, it was enough for the horrid, frostbound sensation which had gripped me about the chest to pass off. The moment of vain exclamations was past, too. I only climbed on the spare spar and leaned over the rail as far as I could, to bring my eyes nearer to that mystery floating alongside.

As he hung by the ladder, like a resting swimmer, the sea lightning played about his limbs at every stir; and he appeared in it ghastly, silvery, fishlike. He remained as mute as a fish, too. He made no motion to get out of the water, either. It was inconceivable that he should not attempt to come on board, and strangely troubling to suspect that perhaps he did not want to. And my first words were prompted by just that troubled incertitude.

"What's the matter?" I asked in my ordinary tone, speaking down to the face upturned exactly under mine.

"Cramp," it answered, no louder. Then slightly anxious, "I say, no need to call anyone."

"I was not going to," I said.

"Are you alone on deck?"

"Yes."

I had somehow the impression that he was on the point of letting go the ladder to swim away beyond my ken—mysterious as he came. But, for the moment, this being appearing as if he had risen from the bottom of the sea (it was certainly the nearest land to the ship) wanted only to know the time. I told him. And he, down there, tentatively:

"I suppose your captain's turned in?"

"I am sure he isn't," I said.

He seemed to struggle with himself, for I heard something like the low, bitter murmur of doubt. "What's the good?" His next words came out with a hesitating effort.

"Look here, my man. Could you call him out quietly?"

I thought the time had come to declare myself.

"I am the captain."

I heard a "By Jove!" whispered at the level of the water. The phosphorescence flashed in the swirl of the water all about his limbs, his other hand seized the ladder.

"My name's Leggatt."

The voice was calm and resolute. A good voice. The self-possession of that man had somehow induced a corresponding state in myself. It was very quietly that I remarked:

"You must be a good swimmer."

"Yes. I've been in the water practically since nine o'clock. The question for me now is whether I am to let go this ladder and go on swimming till I sink from exhaustion, or—to come on board here."

I felt this was no mere formula of desperate speech, but a real alternative in the view of a strong soul. I should have gathered from this that he was young; indeed, it is only the young who are ever confronted by such clear issues. But at the time it was pure intuition on my part. A mysterious communication was established already between us two—in the face of that silent, darkened tropical sea. I was young, too; young enough to make no comment. The man in the water began suddenly to climb up the ladder, and I hastened away from the rail to fetch some clothes.

Before entering the cabin I stood still, listening in the lobby at the foot of the stairs. A faint snore came through the closed door of the chief mate's room. The second mate's door was on the hook, but the darkness in there was absolutely soundless. He, too, was young and could sleep like a stone. Remained the steward, but he was not likely to wake up before he was called. I got a sleeping suit out of my room and, coming back on deck, saw the naked man from the sea sitting on the main hatch, glimmering white in the darkness, his elbows on his knees and his head in his hands. In a moment he had concealed his damp body in a sleeping suit of the same gray-stripe pattern as the one I was wearing and followed me like my double on the poop. Together we moved right aft, barefooted, silent.

"What is it?" I asked in a deadened voice, taking the lighted lamp out of the binnacle, and raising it to his face.

"An ugly business."

He had rather regular features; a good mouth; light eyes under somewhat heavy, dark eyebrows; a smooth, square forehead; no growth on his cheeks; a small, brown mustache, and a well-shaped, round chin. His expression was concentrated, meditative, under the inspecting light of the lamp I held up to his face; such as a man thinking hard in solitude might wear. My sleeping suit was just right for his size. A well-knit young fellow of twenty-five at most. He caught his lower lip with the edge of white, even teeth.

"Yes," I said, replacing the lamp in the binnacle. The warm, heavy tropical night closed upon his head again.

"There's a ship over there," he murmured.

"Yes, I know. The *Sephora*. Did you know of us?"

"Hadn't the slightest idea. I am the mate of her—" He paused and corrected himself. "I should say I *was*."

"Aha! Something wrong?"

"Yes. Very wrong indeed. I've killed a man."

"What do you mean? Just now?"

"No, on the passage. Weeks ago. Thirty nine south. When I say a man—"

"Fit of temper," I suggested, confidently.

The shadowy, dark head, like mine, seemed to nod imperceptibly above the ghostly gray of my sleeping suit. It was in the night, as though I had been faced by my own reflection in the depths of a somber and immense mirror.

"A pretty thing to have to own up to for a Conway boy," murmured my double, distinctly.

"You're a Conway boy?"

"I am," he said, as if startled. Then, slowly . . . "Perhaps you too—"

It was so; but being a couple of years older I had left before he joined. After a quick interchange of dates a silence fell; and I thought suddenly of my absurd mate with his terrific whiskers and the "Bless my soul—you don't say so" type of intellect. My double gave me an inkling of his thoughts by saying: "My father's a parson in Norfolk. Do you see me before a judge and jury on that charge? For myself I can't see the necessity. There are fellows that an angel from heaven—And I am not that. He was one of those creatures that are just simmering all the time with a silly sort of wickedness. Miserable devils that have no business to live at all. He wouldn't do his duty and wouldn't let anybody else do theirs. But what's the good of talking! You know well enough the sort of ill-conditioned snarling cur—."

He appealed to me as if our experiences had been as identical as our clothes. And I knew well enough the pestiferous danger of such a character where there are no means of legal repression. And I knew well enough also that my double there was no homicidal ruffian. I did not think of asking him for details, and he told me the story roughly in brusque, disconnected sentences. I needed no more. I saw it all going on as though I were myself inside that other sleeping suit.

"It happened while we were setting a reefed foresail, at dusk. Reefed foresail! You understand the sort of weather. The only sail we had left to keep the ship running; so you may guess what it had

been like for days. Anxious sort of job, that. He gave me some of
his cursed insolence at the sheet. I tell you I was overdone with
this terrific weather that seemed to have no end to it. Terrific, I
tell you—and a deep ship. I believe the fellow himself was half
crazed with funk. It was no time for gentlemanly reproof, so I
turned round and felled him like an ox. He up and at me. We
closed just as an awful sea made for the ship. All hands saw it
coming and took to the rigging, but I had him by the throat, and
went on shaking him like a rat, the men above us yelling, 'Look out!
look out!' Then a crash as if the sky had fallen on my head. They
say that for over ten minutes hardly anything was to be seen of
the ship—just the three masts and a bit of the forecastle head and
of the poop all awash driving along in a smother of foam. It was a
miracle that they found us, jammed together behind the forebitts.
It's clear that I meant business, because I was holding him by the
throat still when they picked us up. He was black in the face. It
was too much for them. It seems they rushed us aft together,
gripped as we were, screaming 'Murder!' like a lot of lunatics,
and broke into the cuddy. And the ship running for her life,
touch and go all the time, any minute her last in a sea fit to turn
your hair gray only a-looking at it. I understand that the skipper,
too, started raving like the rest of them. The man had been
deprived of sleep for more than a week, and to have this sprung
on him at the height of a furious gale nearly drove him out of his
mind. I wonder they didn't fling me overboard after getting the
carcass of their precious shipmate out of my fingers. They had
rather a job to separate us, I've been told. A sufficiently fierce
story to make an old judge and a respectable jury sit up a bit. The
first thing I heard when I came to myself was the maddening
howling of that endless gale, and on that the voice of the old
man. He was hanging on to my bunk, staring into my face out of his
sou'wester.

"'Mr. Leggatt, you have killed a man. You can act no
longer as chief mate of this ship.'"

His care to subdue his voice made it sound monotonous.
He rested a hand on the end of the skylight to steady himself
with, and all that time did not stir a limb, so far as I could see.
"Nice little tale for a quiet tea party," he concluded in the same
tone.

One of my hands, too, rested on the end of the skylight; neither did I stir a limb, so far as I knew. We stood less than a foot from each other. It occurred to me that if old "Bless my soul—you don't say so" were to put his head up the companion and catch sight of us, he would think he was seeing double, or imagine himself come upon a scene of weird witchcraft; the strange captain having a quiet confabulation by the wheel with his own gray ghost. I became very much concerned to prevent anything of the sort. I heard the other's soothing undertone.

"My father's a parson in Norfolk," it said. Evidently he had forgotten he had told me this important fact before. Truly a nice little tale.

"You had better slip down into my stateroom now," I said, moving off stealthily. My double followed my movements; our bare feet made no sound; I let him in, closed the door with care, and, after giving a call to the second mate, returned on deck for my relief.

"Not much sign of any wind yet," I remarked when he approached.

"No, sir. Not much," he assented, sleepily, in his hoarse voice, with just enough deference, no more, and barely suppressing a yawn.

"Well, that's all you have to look out for. You have got your orders."

"Yes, sir."

I paced a turn or two on the poop and saw him take up his position face forward with his elbow in the ratlines of the mizzen rigging before I went below. The mate's faint snoring was still going on peacefully. The cuddy lamp was burning over the table on which stood a vase with flowers, a polite attention from the ship's provision merchant—the last flowers we should see for the next three months at the very least. Two bunches of bananas hung from the beam symmetrically, one on each side of the rudder casing. Everything was as before in the ship—except that two of her captain's sleeping suits were simultaneously in use, one motionless in the cuddy, the other keeping very still in the captain's stateroom.

It must be explained here that my cabin had the form of the capital letter L, the door being within the angle and opening into the short part of the letter. A couch was to the left, the bed place to the right; my writing desk and the chronometers' table faced the door. But anyone opening it, unless he stepped right inside, had no view of what I call the long (or vertical) part of the letter. It contained some lockers surmounted by a bookcase; and a few clothes, a thick jacket or two, caps, oilskin coat, and such like, hung on hooks. There was at the bottom of that part a door opening into my bathroom, which could be entered also directly from the saloon. But that way was never used.

The mysterious arrival had discovered the advantage of this particular shape. Entering my room, lighted strongly by a big bulkhead lamp swung on gimbals above my writing desk, I did not see him anywhere till he stepped out quietly from behind the coats in the recessed part.

"I heard somebody moving about, and went in there at once," he whispered.

I, too, spoke under my breath.

"Nobody is likely to come in here without knocking and getting permission."

He nodded. His face was thin and the sunburn faded, as though he had been ill. And no wonder. He had been, I heard presently, kept under arrest in his cabin for nearly seven weeks. But there was nothing sickly in his eyes or in his expression. He was not a bit like me, really; yet, as we stood leaning over my bed place, whispering side by side, with our dark heads together and our backs to the door, anybody bold enough to open it stealthily would have been treated to the uncanny sight of a double captain busy talking in whispers with his other self.

"But all this doesn't tell me how you came to hang on to our side ladder," I inquired, in the hardly audible murmurs we used, after he had told me something more of the proceedings on board the *Sephora* once the bad weather was over.

"When we sighted Java Head I had had time to think all those matters out several times over. I had six weeks of doing nothing else, and with only an hour or so every evening for a tramp on the quarter-deck."

He whispered, his arms folded on the side of my bed place, staring through the open port. And I could imagine perfectly the manner of this thinking out—a stubborn if not a steadfast operation; something of which I should have been perfectly incapable.

"I reckoned it would be dark before we closed with the

land," he continued, so low that I had to strain my hearing near as we were to each other, shoulder touching shoulder almost. "So I asked to speak to the old man. He always seemed very sick when he came to see me—as if he could not look me in the face. You know, that foresail saved the ship. She was too deep to have run long under bare poles. And it was I that managed to set it for him. Anyway, he came. When I had him in my cabin—he stood by the door looking at me as if I had the halter round my neck already—I asked him right away to leave my cabin door unlocked at night while the ship was going through Sunda Straits. There would be the Java coast within two or three miles, off Angier Point. I wanted nothing more. I've had a prize for swimming my second year in the Conway."

"I can believe it," I breathed out.

"God only knows why they locked me in every night. To see some of their faces you'd have thought they were afraid I'd go about at night strangling people. Am I a murdering brute? Do I look it? By Jove! if I had been he wouldn't have trusted himself like that into my room. You'll say I might have chucked him aside and bolted out, there and then—it was dark already. Well, no. And for the same reason I wouldn't think of trying to smash the door. There would have been a rush to stop me at the noise, and I did not mean to get into a confounded scrimmage. Some-body else might have got killed—for I would not have broken out only to get chucked back, and I did not want any more of that work. He refused, looking more sick than ever. He was afraid of the men, and also of that old second mate of his who had been sailing with him for years—a gray-headed old humbug; and his steward, too, had been with him devil knows how long—seventeen years or more—a dogmatic sort of loafer who hated me like poison, just because I was the chief mate. No chief mate ever made more than one voyage in the *Sephora*, you know. Those two old chaps ran the ship. Devil only knows what the skipper wasn't afraid of (all his nerve went to pieces altogether in the hellish spell of bad weather we had)—of what the law would do to him—of his wife, perhaps. Oh, yes! she's on board. Though I don't think she would have meddled. She would have been only too glad to have me out of the ship in any way. The 'brand of Cain' business, don't you see. That's all right. I was ready enough to go off wandering on the face of the earth—and that was price enough to pay for an Abel of that sort. Anyhow, he wouldn't listen to me. 'This thing must take its course. I represent the law here.' He was shaking like a leaf. 'So you won't?' 'No!' 'Then I hope you will be able to sleep on that,' I said and turned my back on him. 'I wonder that *you* can,' cries he and locks the door.

"Well after that, I couldn't. Not very well. That was three weeks ago. We have had a slow passage through the Java Sea; drifted about Carimata for ten days. When we anchored here they thought, I suppose, it was all right. The nearest land (and that's five miles) is the ship's destination; the consul would soon set about catching me; and there would have been no object in bolting to these islets there. I don't suppose there's a drop of water on them. I don't know how it was, but tonight that steward, after bringing me my supper, went out to let me eat it, and left the door unlocked. And I ate it—all there was, too. After I had finished I strolled out on the quarter-deck. I don't know that I meant to do anything. A breath of fresh air was all I wanted, I believe. Then a sudden temptation came over me. I kicked off my slippers and was in the water before I had made up my mind fairly. Somebody heard the splash and they raised an awful hullabaloo. 'He's gone! Lower the boats! He's committed suicide! No, he's swimming.' Certainly I was swimming. It's not so easy for a swimmer like me to commit suicide by drowning. I landed on the nearest islet before the boat left the ship's side. I heard them pulling about in the dark, hailing, and so on, but after a bit they gave up. Everything quieted down and the anchorage became as still as death. I sat down on a stone and began to think. I felt certain they would start searching for me at daylight. There was no place to hide on those stony things—and if there had been, what would have been the good? But now I was clear of that ship, I was not going back. So after a while I took off all my clothes, tied them up in a bundle with a stone inside, and dropped them in the deep water on the outer side of that islet. That was suicide enough for me. Let them think what they liked, but I didn't mean to drown myself. I meant to swim till I sank—but that's not the same thing. I struck out for another of these little islands, and it was from that one that I first saw your riding light. Something to swim for. I went on easily, and on the way I came upon a flat rock a foot or two above water. In the daytime, I dare say, you might make it out with a glass from your poop. I scrambled up on it and rested myself for a bit. Then I made another start. That last spell must have been over a mile."

His whisper was getting fainter and fainter, and all the time he stared straight out through the porthole, in which there was not even a star to be seen. I had not interrupted him. There was something that made comment impossible in his narrative, or perhaps in himself; a sort of feeling, a quality, which I can't find a name for. And when he ceased, all I found was a futile whisper: "So you swam for our light?"

"Yes—straight for it. It was something to swim for. I couldn't see any stars low down because the coast was in the way, and I couldn't see the land, either. The water was like glass. One might have been swimming in a confounded thousand-feet deep cistern with no place for scrambling out anywhere; but what I didn't like was the notion of swimming round and round like a crazed bullock before I gave out; and as I didn't mean to go back . . . No. Do you see me being hauled back, stark naked, off one of these little islands by the scruff of the neck and fighting like a wild beast? Somebody would have got killed for certain, and I did not want any of that. So I went on. Then your ladder—"

"Why didn't you hail the ship?" I asked a little louder.

He touched my shoulder lightly. Lazy footsteps came right over our heads and stopped. The second mate had crossed from the other side of the poop and might have been hanging over the rail for all we knew.

"He couldn't hear us talking—could he?" My double breathed into my very ear, anxiously.

His anxiety was in answer, a sufficient answer, to the question I had put to him. An answer containing all the difficulty of that situation. I closed the porthole quietly, to make sure. A louder word might have been overheard.

"Who's that?" he whispered then.

"My second mate. But I don't know much more of the fellow than you do."

And I told him a little about myself. I had been appointed to take charge while I least expected anything of the sort, not quite a fortnight ago. I didn't know either the ship or the people.

Hadn't had the time in port to look about me or size anybody up. And as to the crew, all they knew was that I was appointed to take the ship home. For the rest, I was almost as much of a stranger on board as himself, I said. And at the moment I felt it most acutely. I felt that it would take very little to make me a suspect person in the eyes of the ship's company.

He had turned about meantime; and we, the two strangers in the ship, faced each other in identical attitudes.

"Your ladder—" he murmured, after a silence. "Who'd have thought of finding a ladder hanging over at night in a ship anchored out here! I felt just then a very unpleasant faintness. After the life I've been leading for nine weeks, anybody would have got out of condition. I wasn't capable of swimming round as far as your rudder chains. And, lo and behold! there was a ladder to get hold of. After I gripped it I said to myself, 'What's the good?' When I saw a man's head looking over I thought I would swim away presently and leave him shouting—in whatever language it was. I didn't mind being looked at. I—I liked it. And then you speaking to me so quietly—as if you had expected me—made me hold on a little longer. It had been a confounded lonely time—I don't mean while swimming. I was glad to talk a little to somebody that didn't belong to the *Sephora*. As to asking for the captain, that was a mere impulse. It could have been no use, with all the ship knowing about me and the other people pretty certain to be round here in the morning. I don't know—I wanted to be seen, to talk with somebody, before I went on. I don't know what I would have said. . . . 'Fine night, isn't it?' or something of the sort."

"Do you think they will be round here presently?" I asked with some incredulity.

"Quite likely," he said, faintly.

He looked extremely haggard all of a sudden. His head rolled on his shoulders.

"H'm. We shall see then. Meantime get into that bed," I whispered. "Want help? There."

It was a rather high bed place with a set of drawers underneath. This amazing swimmer really needed the lift I gave him by seizing his leg. He tumbled in, rolled over on his back, and flung one arm across his eyes. And then, with his face nearly hidden, he must have looked exactly as I used to look in that bed. I gazed upon my other self for a while before drawing across carefully the two green serge curtains which ran on a brass rod. I thought for a moment of pinning them together for greater safety, but I sat down on the couch, and once there I felt unwilling to rise and hunt for a pin. I would do it in a moment. I was extremely tired, in a peculiarly intimate way, by the strain of stealthiness, by the effort of whispering and the general secrecy of this excitement. It was three o'clock by now and I had been on my feet since nine, but I was not sleepy; I could not have gone to sleep. I sat there, fagged out, looking at the curtains, trying to clear my mind of the confused sensation of being in two places at once, and greatly bothered by an exasperating knocking in my head. It was a relief to discover suddenly that it was not in my head at all, but on the outside of the door. Before I could collect myself the words "Come in" were out of my mouth, and the steward entered with a tray, bringing in my morning coffee. I had slept, after all, and I was so frightened that I shouted, "This way! I am here, steward," as though he had been miles away. He put down the tray on the table next to the couch and only then said, very quietly, "I can see you are here, sir." I felt him give me a keen look, but I dared not meet his eyes just then. He must have wondered why I had drawn the curtains of my bed before going to sleep on the couch. He went out, hooking the door open as usual.

I heard the crew washing decks above me. I knew I would have been told at once if there had been any wind. Calm, I thought, and I was doubly vexed. Indeed, I felt dual more than ever. The steward reappeared suddenly in the doorway. I jumped up from the couch so quickly that he gave a start.

"What do you want here?"

"Close your port, sir—they are washing decks."

"It is closed," I said, reddening.

"Very well, sir." But he did not move from the doorway and returned my stare in an extraordinary, equivocal manner for a time. Then his eyes wavered, all his expression changed, and in a voice unusually gentle, almost coaxingly:

"May I come in to take the empty cup away, sir?"

"Of course!" I turned my back on him while he popped in and out. Then I unhooked and closed the door and even pushed the bolt. This sort of thing could not go on very long. The cabin was as hot as an oven, too. I took a peep at my double, and discovered that he had not moved, his arm was still over his eyes; but his chest heaved; his hair was wet; his chin glistened with perspiration. I reached over him and opened the port.

"I must show myself on deck," I reflected.

Of course, theoretically, I could do what I liked, with no one to say nay to me within the whole circle of the horizon; but to lock my cabin door and take the key away I did not dare. Directly I put my head out of the companion I saw the group of my two officers, the second mate barefooted, the chief mate in long India-rubber boots, near the break of the poop, and the steward halfway down the poop ladder talking to them eagerly. He happened to catch sight of me and dived, the second ran down on the main-deck shouting some order or other, and the chief mate came to meet me, touching his cap.

There was a sort of curiosity in his eye that I did not like. I don't know whether the steward had told them that I was "queer" only, or downright drunk, but I know the man meant to have a good look at me. I watched him coming with a smile which, as he got into point-blank range, took effect and froze his very whiskers. I did not give him time to open his lips.

"Square the yards by lifts and braces before the hands go to breakfast."

It was the first particular order I had given on board that ship; and I stayed on deck to see it executed, too. I had felt the need of asserting myself without loss of time. That sneering young cub got taken down a peg or two on that occasion, and I also seized the opportunity of having a good look at the face of every foremast man as they filed past me to go to the after braces. At breakfast time, eating nothing myself, I presided with such frigid dignity that the two mates were only too glad to escape from the cabin as soon as decency permitted; and all the time the dual working of my mind distracted me almost to the point of insanity. I was constantly watching myself, my secret self, as dependent on my actions as my own personality, sleeping in that bed, behind that door which faced me as I sat at the head of the table. It was very much like being mad, only it was worse because one was aware of it.

I had to shake him for a solid minute, but when at last he opened his eyes it was in the full possession of his senses, with an inquiring look.

"All's well so far," I whispered. "Now you must vanish into the bathroom."

He did so, as noiseless as a ghost, and then I rang for the steward, and facing him boldly, directed him to tidy up my stateroom while I was having my bath—"and be quick about it." As my tone admitted of no excuses, he said, "Yes, sir," and ran off to fetch his dustpan and brushes. I took a bath and did most of my dressing, splashing and whistling softly for the steward's edification, while the secret sharer of my life stood drawn up bolt upright in that little space, his face looking very sunken in daylight, his eyelids lowered under the stern, dark line of his eyebrows drawn together by a slight frown.

When I left him there to go back to my room the steward was finishing dusting. I sent for the mate and engaged him in some insignificant conversation. It was, as it were, trifling with the terrific character of his whiskers; but my object was to give him an opportunity for a good look at my cabin. And then I could at last shut, with a clear conscience, the door of my stateroom and get my double back into the recessed part. There was nothing else for it. He had to sit still on a small folding stool, half smothered by the heavy coats hanging there. We listened to the steward going into the bathroom out of the saloon, filling the water bottles there, scrubbing the bath, setting things to rights, whisk, bang, clatter—out again into the saloon—turn the key—click. Such was my scheme for keeping my second self invisible. Nothing better could be contrived under the circumstances. And there we sat; I at my writing desk ready to appear busy with some papers, he behind me out of sight of the door. It would not have been prudent to talk in daytime; and I could not have stood the excitement of that queer sense of whispering to myself. Now and then, glancing over my shoulder, I saw him far back there, sitting rigidly on the low stool, his bare feet close together, his arms folded, his head hanging on his breast—and perfectly still. Anybody would have taken him for me.

I was fascinated by it myself. Every moment I had to glance over my shoulder. I was looking at him when a voice outside the door said:

"Beg pardon, sir."

"Well!" . . . I kept my eyes on him, and so when the voice outside the door announced, "There's a ship's boat coming our way, sir," I saw him give a start—the first movement he had made for hours. But he did not raise his bowed head.

"All right. Get the ladder over."

I hesitated. Should I whisper something to him? But what? His immobility seemed to have been never disturbed. What could I tell him he did not know already? . . . Finally I went on deck.

## II

The skipper of the *Sephora* had a thin red whisker all round his face, and the sort of complexion that goes with hair of that color; also the particular, rather smeary shade of blue in the eyes. He was not exactly a showy figure; his shoulders were high, his stature but middling—one leg slightly more bandy than the other. He shook hands, looking vaguely around. A spiritless tenacity was his main characteristic, I judged. I behaved with a politeness which seemed to disconcert him. Perhaps he was shy. He mumbled to me as if he were ashamed of what he was saying; gave his name (it was something like Archbold—but at this distance of years I hardly am sure), his ship's name, and a few other particulars of that sort, in the manner of a criminal making a reluctant and doleful confession. He had had terrible weather on the passage out—terrible—terrible—wife aboard, too.

By this time we were seated in the cabin and the steward brought in a tray with a bottle and glasses. "Thanks! No." Never took liquor. Would have some water, though. He drank two tumblerfuls. Terrible thirsty work. Ever since daylight had been exploring the islands round his ship.

"What was that for—fun?" I asked, with an appearance of polite interest.

"No!" He sighed. "Painful duty."

As he persisted in his mumbling and I wanted my double to hear every word, I hit upon the notion of informing him that I regretted to say I was hard of hearing.

"Such a young man, too!" he nodded, keeping his smeary blue, unintelligent eyes fastened upon me. "What was the cause of it—some disease?" he inquired, without the least sympathy and as if he thought that, if so, I'd got no more than I deserved.

"Yes; disease," I admitted in a cheerful tone which seemed to shock him. But my point was gained, because he had to raise his voice to give me his tale. It is not worth while to record that version. It was just over two months since all this had happened, and he had thought so much about it that he seemed completely muddled as to its bearings, but still immensely impressed.

"What would you think of such a thing happening on board your own ship? I've had the *Sephora* for these fifteen years. I am a well-known shipmaster."

He was densely distressed—and perhaps I should have sympathized with him if I had been able to detach my mental vision from the unsuspected sharer of my cabin as though he were my second self. There he was on the other side of the bulkhead, four or five feet from us, no more, as we sat in the saloon. I looked politely at Captain Archbold (if that was his name), but it was the other I saw, in a gray sleeping suit, seated on a low stool, his bare feet close together, his arms folded, and every word said between us falling into the ears of his dark head bowed on his chest.

"I have been at sea now, man and boy, for seven-and-thirty years, and I've never heard of such a thing happening in an English ship. And that it should be my ship. Wife on board, too."

I was hardly listening to him.

"Don't you think," I said, "that the heavy sea which, you told me, came aboard just then might have killed the man? I have seen the sheer weight of a sea kill a man very neatly, by simply breaking his neck."

"Good God!" he uttered, impressively, fixing his smeary blue eyes on me. "The sea! No man killed by the sea ever looked like that." He seemed positively scandalized at my suggestion. And as I gazed at him certainly not prepared for anything original on his part, he advanced his head close to mine and thrust his tongue out at me so suddenly that I couldn't help starting back.

After scoring over my calmness in this graphic way he nodded wisely. If I had seen the sight, he assured me, I would never forget it as long as I lived. The weather was too bad to give the corpse a proper sea burial. So next day at dawn they took it up on the poop, covering its face with a bit of bunting; he read a short prayer, and then, just as it was, in its oilskins and long boots, they launched it amongst those mountainous seas that seemed ready every moment to swallow up the ship herself and the terrified lives on board of her.

"That reefed foresail saved you," I threw in.

"Under God—it did," he exclaimed fervently. "It was by a special mercy, I firmly believe, that it stood some of those hurricane squalls."

"It was the setting of that sail which—" I began.

"God's own hand in it," he interrupted me. "Nothing less could have done it. I don't mind telling you that I hardly dared give the order. It seemed impossible that we could touch anything without losing it, and then our last hope would have been gone."

The terror of that gale was on him yet. I let him go on for a bit, then said, casually—as if returning to a minor subject:

"You were very anxious to give up your mate to the shore people, I believe?"

He was. To the law. His obscure tenacity on that point had in it something incomprehensible and a little awful; something, as it were, mystical, quite apart from his anxiety that he should not be suspected of "countenancing any doings of that sort." Seven-and-thirty virtuous years at sea, of which over twenty of immaculate command, and the last fifteen in the *Sephora*, seemed to have laid him under some pitiless obligation.

"And you know," he went on, groping shame-facedly amongst his feelings, "I did not engage that young fellow. His people had some interest with my owners. I was in a way forced to take him on. He looked very smart, very gentlemanly, and all that. But do you know—I never liked him, somehow. I am a plain man. You see, he wasn't exactly the sort for the chief mate of a ship like the *Sephora*."

I had become so connected in thoughts and impressions with the secret sharer of my cabin that I felt as if I, personally, were being given to understand that I, too, was not the sort that would have done for the chief mate of a ship like the *Sephora*. I had no doubt of it in my mind.

"Not at all the style of man. You understand," he insisted, superfluously, looking hard at me.

I smiled urbanely. He seemed at a loss for a while.

"I suppose I must report a suicide."

"Beg pardon?"

"Sui-cide! That's what I'll have to write to my owners directly I get in."

"Unless you manage to recover him before tomorrow," I assented, dispassionately . . . . "I mean, alive."

He mumbled something which I really did not catch, and I turned my ear to him in a puzzled manner. He fairly bawled:

"The land—I say, the mainland is at least seven miles off my anchorage."

"About that."

My lack of excitement, of curiosity, of surprise, of any sort of pronounced interest, began to arouse his distrust. But except for the felicitous pretense of deafness I had not tried to pretend anything. I had felt utterly incapable of playing the part of ignorance properly, and therefore was afraid to try. It is also certain that he had brought some ready-made suspicions with him, and that he viewed my politeness as a strange and unnatural phenomenon. And yet how else could I have received him? Not heartily! That was impossible for psychological reasons, which I need not state here. My only object was to keep off his inquiries. Surlily? Yes, but surliness might have provoked a pointblank question. From its novelty to him and from its nature, punctilious courtesy was the manner best calculated to restrain the man. But there was the danger of his breaking through my defense bluntly. I could not, I think, have met him by a direct lie, also for psychological (not moral) reasons. If he had only known how afraid I was of his putting my feeling of identity with the other to the test! But, strangely enough—(I thought of it only afterwards)—I believe that he was not a little disconcerted by the reverse side of that weird situation, by something in me that reminded him of the man he was seeking—suggested a mysterious similitude to the young fellow he had distrusted and disliked from the first.

However that might have been, the silence was not very prolonged. He took another oblique step.

"I reckon I had no more than a two-mile pull to your ship. Not a bit more."

"And quite enough, too, in this awful heat," I said.

Another pause full of mistrust followed. Necessity, they say, is mother of invention, but fear, too, is not barren of ingenious suggestions. And I was afraid he would ask me point-blank for news of my other self.

"Nice little saloon, isn't it?" I remarked, as if noticing for the first time the way his eyes roamed from one closed door to the other. "And very well fitted out, too. Here, for instance," I continued, reaching over the back of my seat negligently and flinging the door open, "is my bathroom."

He made an eager movement, but hardly gave it a glance. I got up, shut the door of the bathroom, and invited him to have a look round, as if I were very proud of my accommodation. He had to rise and be shown round, but he went through the business without any raptures whatever.

"And now we'll have a look at my stateroom," I declared, in a voice as loud as I dared to make it, crossing the cabin to the starboard side with purposely heavy steps.

He followed me in and gazed around. My intelligent double had vanished. I played my part.

"Very convenient—isn't it?"

"Very nice. Very comf . . ." He didn't finish and went out brusquely as if to escape from some unrighteous wiles of mine. But it was not to be. I had been too frightened not to feel vengeful; I felt I had him on the run, and I meant to keep him on the run. My polite insistence must have had something menacing in it, because he gave in suddenly. And I did not let him off a single item; mate's room, pantry, storerooms, the very sail locker which was also under the poop—he had to look into them all. When at last I showed him out on the quarter-deck he drew a long, spiritless sigh, and mumbled dismally that he must really be going back to his ship now. I desired my mate, who had joined us, to see to the captain's boat.

The man of whiskers gave a blast on the whistle which he used to wear hanging round his neck, and yelled, "*Sephora's* away!" My double down there in my cabin must have heard, and certainly could not feel more relieved than I. Four fellows came running out from somewhere forward and went over the side, while my own men, appearing on deck too, lined the rail. I escorted my visitor to the gangway ceremoniously, and nearly overdid it. He was a tenacious beast. On the very ladder he lingered, and in that unique, guiltily conscientious manner of sticking to the point:

"I say . . . you . . . you don't think that—"

I covered his voice loudly:

"Certainly not . . . . I am delighted. Good-by."

I had an idea of what he meant to say, and just saved myself by the privilege of defective hearing. He was too shaken generally to insist, but my mate, close witness of that parting, looked mystified and his face took on a thoughtful cast. As I did not want to appear as if I wished to avoid all communication with my officers, he had the opportunity to address me.

"Seems a very nice man. His boat's crew told our chaps a very extraordinary story, if what I am told by the steward is true. I suppose you had it from the captain, sir?"

"Yes. I had a story from the captain."

"A very horrible affair—isn't it, sir?"

"It is."

"Beats all these tales we hear about murders in Yankee ships."

"I don't think it beats them. I don't think it resembles them in the least."

"Bless my soul—you don't say so! But of course I've no acquaintance whatever with American ships, not I, so I couldn't go against your knowledge. It's horrible enough for me . . . . But the queerest part is that those fellows seemed to have some idea the man was hidden aboard here. They had really. Did you ever hear of such a thing?"

"Preposterous—isn't it?"

We were walking to and fro athwart the quarter-deck. No one of the crew forward could be seen (the day was Sunday), and the mate pursued:

"There was some little dispute about it. Our chaps took offense. 'As if we would harbor a thing like that,' they said. 'Wouldn't you like to look for him in our coalhole?' Quite a tiff. But they made it up in the end. I suppose he did drown himself. Don't you, sir?"

"I don't suppose anything."

"You have no doubt in the matter, sir?"

"None whatever."

I left him suddenly. I felt I was producing a bad impression, but with my double down there it was most trying to be on deck. And it was almost as trying to be below. Altogether a nerve-trying situation. But on the whole I felt less torn in two when I was with him. There was no one in the whole ship whom I dared take into my confidence. Since the hands had got to know his story, it would have been impossible to pass him off for anyone else, and an accidental discovery was to be dreaded now more than ever . . . .

The steward being engaged in laying the table for dinner, we could talk only with our eyes when I first went down. Later in the afternoon we had a cautious try at whispering. The Sunday quietness of the ship was against us; the stillness of air and water around her was against us; the elements, the men were against us—everything was against us in our secret partnership; time itself—for this could not go on forever. The very trust in Providence was, I suppose, denied to his guilt. Shall I confess that this thought cast me down very much? And as to the chapter of accidents which counts for so much in the book of success, I could only hope that it was closed. For what favorable accident could be expected?

"Did you hear everything?" were my first words as soon as we took up our position side by side, leaning over my bed place.

He had. And the proof of it was his earnest whisper, "The man told you he hardly dared to give the order."

I understood the reference to be to that saving foresail.

"Yes. He was afraid of it being lost in the setting."

"I assure you he never gave the order. He may think he did, but he never gave it. He stood there with me on the break of the poop after the main topsail blew away, and whimpered about our last hope—positively whimpered about it and nothing else—and the night coming on! To hear one's skipper go on like that in such weather was enough to drive any fellow out of his mind. It worked me up into a sort of desperation. I just took it into my own hands and went away from him, boiling, and—But what's the use telling you? *You* know! . . . Do you think that if I had not been pretty fierce with them I should have got the men to do anything? Not I! The bo's'n perhaps? Perhaps! It wasn't a heavy

sea—it was a sea gone mad! I suppose the end of the world will be
something like that; and a man may have the heart to see it
coming once and be done with it—but to have to face it day after
day—I don't blame anybody. I was precious little better than the
rest. Only—I was an officer of that old coal wagon, anyhow—"

"I quite understand," I conveyed that sincere assurance
into his ear. He was out of breath with whispering; I could hear
him pant slightly. It was all very simple. The same strung-up
force which had given twenty-four men a chance, at least, for
their lives, had, in a sort of recoil, crushed an unworthy mutinous
existence.

But I had no leisure to weigh the merits of the matter
—footsteps in the saloon, a heavy knock. "There's enough wind
to get under way with, sir." Here was the call of a new claim
upon my thoughts and even upon my feelings.

"Turn the hands up," I cried through the door. "I'll be on
deck directly."

I was going out to make the acquaintance of my ship.
Before I left the cabin our eyes met—the eyes of the only two
strangers on board. I pointed to the recessed part where the little
campstool awaited him and laid my finger on my lips. He made a
gesture—somewhat vague—a little mysterious, accompanied by
a faint smile, as if of regret.

This is not the place to enlarge upon the sensations of a
man who feels for the first time a ship move under his feet to his
own independent word. In my case they were not unalloyed. I
was not wholly alone with my command; for there was that
stranger in my cabin. Or rather, I was not completely and wholly
with her. Part of me was absent. That mental feeling of being in
two places at once affected me physically as if the mood of secrecy
had penetrated my very soul. Before an hour had elapsed since
the ship had begun to move, having occasion to ask the mate (he
stood by my side) to take a compass bearing of the pagoda, I
caught myself reaching up to his ear in whispers. I say I caught
myself, but enough had escaped to startle the man. I can't describe it otherwise than by saying that he shied. A grave, preoc-
cupied manner, as though he were in possession of some perplex-
ing intelligence, did not leave him henceforth. A little later I
moved away from the rail to look at the compass with such a

stealthy gait that the helmsman noticed it—and I could not help noticing the unusual roundness of his eyes. These are trifling instances, though it's to no commander's advantage to be suspected of ludicrous eccentricities. But I was also more seriously affected. There are to a seaman certain words, gestures, that should in given conditions come as naturally, as instinctively as the winking of a menaced eye. A certain order should spring on to his lips without thinking; a certain sign should get itself made, so to speak, without reflection. But all unconscious alertness had abandoned me. I had to make an effort of will to recall myself back (from the cabin) to the conditions of the moment. I felt that I was appearing an irresolute commander to those people who were watching me more or less critically.

And, besides, there were the scares. On the second day out, for instance, coming off the deck in the afternoon (I had straw slippers on my bare feet) I stopped at the open pantry door and spoke to the steward. He was doing something there with his back to me. At the sound of my voice he nearly jumped out of his skin, as the saying is, and incidentally broke a cup.

"What on earth's the matter with you?" I asked, astonished.

He was extremely confused. "Beg your pardon, sir. I made sure you were in your cabin."

"You see I wasn't."

"No, sir. I could have sworn I had heard you moving in there not a moment ago. It's most extraordinary . . . very sorry, sir."

I passed on with an inward shudder. I was so identified with my secret double that I did not even mention the fact in those scanty, fearful whispers we exchanged. I suppose he had made some slight noise of some kind or other. It would have been miraculous if he hadn't at one time or another. And yet, haggard as he appeared, he looked always perfectly self-controlled, more than calm—almost invulnerable. On my suggestion he remained almost entirely in the bathroom, which, upon the whole, was the safest place. There could be really no shadow of an excuse for anyone ever wanting to go in there, once the steward had done with it. It was a very tiny place. Sometimes he reclined on the floor, his legs bent, his head sustained on one elbow. At others I would find him on the campstool, sitting in his gray sleeping suit and with his cropped dark hair like a patient, unmoved convict. At night I would smuggle him into my bed place, and we would whisper together, with the regular footfalls of the officer of the watch passing and repassing over our heads. It was an infinitely miserable time. It was lucky that some tins of fine preserves were stowed in a locker in my stateroom; hard bread I could always get hold of; and so he lived on stewed chicken, paté de foie gras, asparagus, cooked oysters, sardines—on all sorts of abominable sham delicacies out of tins. My early-morning coffee he always drank; and it was all I dared do for him in that respect.

Every day there was the horrible maneuvering to go through so that my room and then the bathroom should be done in the usual way. I came to hate the sight of the steward, to abhor the voice of that harmless man. I felt that it was he who would bring on the disaster of discovery. It hung like a sword over our heads.

The fourth day out, I think (we were then working down the east side of the Gulf of Siam, tack for tack, in light winds and smooth water)—the fourth day, I say, of this miserable juggling with the unavoidable, as we sat at our evening meal, that man, whose slightest movement I dreaded, after putting down the dishes ran up on deck busily. This could not be dangerous. Presently he came down again; and then it appeared that he had remembered a coat of mine which I had thrown over a rail to dry after having been wetted in a shower which had passed over the ship in the afternoon. Sitting stolidly at the head of the table I became terrified at the sight of the garment on his arm. Of course he made for my door. There was no time to lose.

"Steward," I thundered. My nerves were so shaken that I could not govern my voice and conceal my agitation. This was the sort of thing that made my terrifically whiskered mate tap his forehead with his forefinger. I had detected him using that gesture while talking on deck with a confidential air to the carpenter. It was too far to hear a word, but I had no doubt that this pantomime could only refer to the strange new captain.

"Yes, sir," the pale-faced steward turned resignedly to me. It was this maddening course of being shouted at, checked without rhyme or reason, arbitrarily chased out of my cabin, suddenly called into it, sent flying out of his pantry on incomprehensible errands, that accounted for the growing wretchedness of his expression.

"Where are you going with that coat?"

"To your room, sir."

"Is there another shower coming?"

"I'm sure I don't know, sir. Shall I go up again and see, sir?"

"No! never mind."

My object was attained, as of course my other self in there would have heard everything that passed. During this interlude my two officers never raised their eyes off their respective plates; but the lip of that confounded cub, the second mate, quivered visibly.

I expected the steward to hook my coat on and come out at once. He was very slow about it; but I dominated my nervousness sufficiently not to shout after him. Suddenly I became aware (it could be heard plainly enough) that the fellow for some reason or other was opening the door of the bathroom. It was the end. The place was literally not big enough to swing a cat in. My voice died in my throat and I went stony all over. I expected to hear a yell of surprise and terror, and made a movement, but had not the strength to get on my legs. Everything remained still. Had my second self taken the poor wretch by the throat? I don't know what I could have done next moment if I had not seen the steward come out of my room, close the door, and then stand quietly by the sideboard.

"Saved," I thought. "But, no! Lost! Gone! He was gone!"

I laid my knife and fork down and leaned back in my chair. My head swam. After a while, when sufficiently recovered to speak in a steady voice, I instructed my mate to put the ship round at eight o'clock himself.

"I won't come on deck," I went on. "I think I'll turn in, and unless the wind shifts I don't want to be disturbed before midnight. I feel a bit seedy."

"You did look middling bad a little while ago," the chief mate remarked without showing any great concern.

They both went out, and I stared at the steward clearing the table. There was nothing to be read on that wretched man's face. But why did he avoid my eyes, I asked myself. Then I thought I should like to hear the sound of his voice.

"Steward!"

"Sir!" Startled as usual.

"Where did you hang up that coat?"

"In the bathroom, sir." The usual anxious tone. "It's not quite dry yet, sir."

For some time longer I sat in the cuddy. Had my double vanished as he had come? But of his coming there was an explanation, whereas his disappearance would be inexplicable . . . . I went slowly into my dark room, shut the door, lighted the lamp, and for a time dared not turn round. When at last I did I saw him standing bolt-upright in the narrow recessed part. It would not be true to say I had a shock, but an irresistible doubt of his bodily existence flitted through my mind. Can it be, I asked myself, that he is not visible to other eyes than mine? It was like being haunted. Motionless, with a grave face, he raised his hands slightly at me in a gesture which meant clearly, "Heavens! what a narrow escape!" Narrow indeed. I think I had come creeping quietly as near insanity as any man who has not actually gone over the border. That gesture restrained me, so to speak.

The mate with the terrific whiskers was now putting the ship on the other tack. In the moment of profound silence which follows upon the hands going to their stations I heard on the poop his raised voice: "Hard alee!" and the distant shout of the order repeated on the main-deck. The sails, in that light breeze, made but a faint fluttering noise. It ceased. The ship was coming round slowly; I held my breath in the renewed stillness of expectation; one wouldn't have thought that there was a single living soul on her decks. A sudden brisk shout, "Mainsail haul!" broke the spell, and in the noisy cries and rush overhead of the men running away with the main brace we two, down in my cabin, came together in our usual position by the bed place.

He did not wait for my question. "I heard him fumbling here and just managed to squat myself down in the bath," he whispered to me. "The fellow only opened the door and put his arm in to hang the coat up. All the same—"

"I never thought of that," I whispered back, even more appalled than before at the closeness of the shave, and marveling at that something unyielding in his character which was carrying

him through so finely. There was no agitation in his whisper.
Whoever was being driven distracted, it was not he. He was sane.
And the proof of his sanity was continued when he took up the
whispering again.

"It would never do for me to come to life again."

It was something that a ghost might have said. But what
he was alluding to was his old captain's reluctant admission of the
theory of suicide. It would obviously serve his turn—if I had
understood at all the view which seemed to govern the unaltera-
ble purpose of his action.

"You must maroon me as soon as ever you can get amongst
these islands off the Cambodge shore," he went on.

"Maroon you! We are not living in a boy's adventure tale,"
I protested. His scornful whispering took me up.

"We aren't indeed! There's nothing of a boy's tale in this.
But there's nothing else for it. I want no more. You don't suppose
I am afraid of what can be done to me? Prison or gallows or
whatever they may please. But you don't see me coming back to
explain such things to an old fellow in a wig and twelve respectable tradesmen, do you? What can they know whether I am guilty
or not—or of *what* I am guilty, either? That's my affair. What
does the Bible say? 'Driven off the face of the earth.' Very well, I
am off the face of the earth now. As I came at night so I shall go."

"Impossible!" I murmured. "You can't."

"Can't? . . . Not naked like a soul on the Day of Judgment. I shall freeze on to this sleeping suit. The Last Day is not
yet—and . . . you have understood thoroughly. Didn't you?"

I felt suddenly ashamed of myself. I may say truly that I
understood—and my hesitation in letting that man swim away
from my ship's side had been a mere sham sentiment, a sort of
cowardice.

"It can't be done now till next night," I breathed out. "The
ship is on the off-shore tack and the wind may fail us."

"As long as I know that you understand," he whispered.
"But of course you do. It's a great satisfaction to have got somebody to understand. You seem to have been there on purpose."
And in the same whisper, as if we two whenever we talked had to
say things to each other which were not fit for the world to hear,
he added, "It's very wonderful."

We remained side by side talking in our secret way—but

sometimes silent or just exchanging a whispered word or two at long intervals. And as usual he stared through the port. A breath of wind came now and again into our faces. The ship might have been moored in dock, so gently and on an even keel she slipped through the water, that did not murmur even at our passage, shadowy and silent like a phantom sea.

At midnight I went on deck, and to my mate's great surprise put the ship round on the other tack. His terrible whiskers flitted round me in silent criticism. I certainly should not have done it if it had been only a question of getting out of that sleepy gulf as quickly as possible. I believe he told the second mate, who relieved him, that it was a great want of judgment. The other only yawned. That intolerable cub shuffled about so sleepily and lolled against the rails in such a slack, improper fashion that I came down on him sharply.

"Aren't you properly awake yet?"

"Yes, sir! I am awake."

"Well, then, be good enough to hold yourself as if you were. And keep a lookout. If there's any current we'll be closing with some islands before daylight."

The east side of the gulf is fringed with islands, some solitary, others in groups. On the blue background of the high coast they seem to float on silvery patches of calm water, arid and gray, or dark green and rounded like clumps of evergreen bushes, with the larger ones, a mile or two long, showing the outlines of ridges, ribs of gray rock under the dank mantle of matted leafage. Unknown to trade, to travel, almost to geography, the manner of life they harbor is an unsolved secret. There must be villages —settlements of fishermen at least—on the largest of them, and some communication with the world is probably kept up by native craft. But all that forenoon, as we headed for them, fanned along by the faintest of breezes, I saw no sign of man or canoe in the field of the telescope I kept on pointing at the scattered group.

At noon I gave no orders for a change of course, and the mate's whiskers became much concerned and seemed to be offering themselves unduly to my notice. At last I said:

"I am going to stand right in. Quite in—as far as I can take her."

The stare of extreme surprise imparted an air of ferocity also to his eyes, and he looked truly terrific for a moment.

"We're not doing well in the middle of the gulf," I continued, casually. "I am going to look for the land breezes tonight."

"Bless my soul! Do you mean, sir, in the dark amongst the lot of all them islands and reefs and shoals?"

"Well—if there are any regular land breezes at all on this coast one must get close inshore to find them, mustn't one?"

"Bless my soul!" he exclaimed again under his breath. All that afternoon he wore a dreamy, contemplative appearance which in him was a mark of perplexity. After dinner I went into my stateroom as if I meant to take some rest. There we two bent our dark heads over a half-unrolled chart lying on my bed.

"There," I said. "It's got to be Koh-ring. I've been looking at it ever since sunrise. It has got two hills and a low point. It must be inhabited. And on the coast opposite there is what looks like the mouth of a biggish river—with some towns, no doubt, not far up. It's the best chance for you that I can see."

"Anything. Koh-ring let it be."

He looked thoughtfully at the chart as if surveying chances and distances from a lofty height—and following with his eyes his own figure wandering on the blank land of Cochin-China, and then passing off that piece of paper clean out of sight into uncharted regions. And it was as if the ship had two captains to plan her course for her. I had been so worried and restless running up and down that I had not had the patience to dress that day. I had remained in my sleeping suit, with straw slippers and a soft floppy hat. The closeness of the heat in the gulf had been most oppressive, and the crew were used to seeing me wandering in that airy attire.

"She will clear the south point as she heads now," I whispered into his ear. "Goodness only knows when, though, but certainly after dark. I'll edge her in to half a mile, as far as I may be able to judge in the dark—"

"Be careful," he murmured, warningly—and I realized suddenly that all my future, the only future for which I was fit, would perhaps go irretrievably to pieces in any mishap to my first command.

I could not stop a moment longer in the room. I motioned him to get out of sight and made my way on the poop. That unplayful cub had the watch. I walked up and down for a while thinking things out, then beckoned him over.

"Send a couple of hands to open the two quarter-deck ports," I said, mildly.

He actually had the impudence, or else so forgot himself in his wonder at such an incomprehensible order, as to repeat:

"Open the quarter-deck ports! What for, sir?"

"The only reason you need concern yourself about is because I tell you to do so. Have them open wide and fastened properly."

He reddened and went off, but I believe made some jeering remark to the carpenter as to the sensible practice of ventilating a ship's quarter-deck. I know he popped into the mate's cabin to impart the fact to him because the whiskers came on deck, as it were by chance, and stole glances at me from below—for signs of lunacy or drunkenness, I suppose.

A little before supper, feeling more restless than ever, I rejoined, for a moment, my second self. And to find him sitting so quietly was surprising, like something against nature, inhuman.

I developed my plan in a hurried whisper.

"I shall stand in as close as I dare and then put her round. I will presently find means to smuggle you out of here into the sail locker, which communicates with the lobby. But there is an opening, a sort of square for hauling the sails out, which gives straight on the quarter-deck and which is never closed in fine weather, so as to give air to the sails. When the ship's way is deadened in stays and all the hands are aft at the main braces you will have a clear road to slip out and get overboard through the open quarter-deck port. I've had them both fastened up. Use a rope's end to lower yourself into the water so as to avoid a splash—you know. It could be heard and cause some beastly complication."

He kept silent for a while, then whispered, "I understand."

"I won't be there to see you go," I began with an effort. "The rest . . . I only hope I have understood, too."

"You have. From first to last"—and for the first time there

seemed to be a faltering, something strained in his whisper. He caught hold of my arm, but the ringing of the supper bell made me start. He didn't though; he only released his grip.

After supper I didn't come below again till well past eight o'clock. The faint, steady breeze was loaded with dew; and the wet, darkened sails held all there was of propelling power in it. The night, clear and starry, sparkled darkly, and the opaque, lightless patches shifting slowly against the low stars were the drifting islets. On the port bow there was a big one more distant and shadowily imposing by the great space of sky it eclipsed.

On opening the door I had a back view of my very own self looking at a chart. He had come out of the recess and was standing near the table.

"Quite dark enough," I whispered.

He stepped back and leaned against my bed with a level, quiet glance. I sat on the couch. We had nothing to say to each other. Over our heads the officer of the watch moved here and there. Then I heard him move quickly. I knew what that meant. He was making for the companion; and presently his voice was outside my door.

"We are drawing in pretty fast, sir. Land looks rather close."

"Very well," I answered. "I am coming on deck directly."

I waited till he was gone out of the cuddy, then rose. My double moved too. The time had come to exchange our last whispers, for neither of us was ever to hear each other's natural voice.

"Look here!" I opened a drawer and took out three sovereigns. "Take this anyhow. I've got six and I'd give you the lot, only I must keep a little money to buy some fruit and vegetables for the crew from native boats as we go through Sunda Straits."

He shook his head.

"Take it," I urged him, whispering desperately. "No one can tell what—"

He smiled and slapped meaningly the only pocket of the sleeping jacket. It was not safe, certainly. But I produced a large old silk handkerchief of mine, and tying the three pieces of gold in a corner, pressed it on him. He was touched, I suppose, because he took it at last and tied it quickly round his waist under the jacket, on his bare skin.

Our eyes met; several seconds elapsed, till, our glances still mingled, I extended my hand and turned the lamp out. Then I passed through the cuddy, leaving the door of my room wide open . . . . "Steward!"

He was still lingering in the pantry in the greatness of his zeal, giving a rub-up to a plated cruet stand the last thing before going to bed. Being careful not to wake up the mate, whose room was opposite, I spoke in an undertone.

He looked round anxiously. "Sir!"

"Can you get me a little hot water from the galley?"

"I am afraid, sir, the galley fire's been out for some time now."

"Go and see."

He flew up the stairs.

"Now," I whispered, loudly, into the saloon—too loudly, perhaps, but I was afraid I couldn't make a sound. He was by my side in an instant—the double captain slipped past the stairs— through a tiny dark passage . . . a sliding door. We were in the sail locker, scrambling on our knees over the sails. A sudden thought struck me. I saw myself wandering barefooted, bareheaded, the sun beating on my dark poll. I snatched off my floppy hat and tried hurriedly in the dark to ram it on my other self. He dodged and fended off silently. I wonder what he thought had come to me before he understood and suddenly desisted. Our hands met gropingly, lingered united in a steady, motionless clasp for a second . . . . No word was breathed by either of us when they separated.

I was standing quietly by the pantry door when the steward returned.

"Sorry, sir. Kettle barely warm. Shall I light the spirit lamp?"

"Never mind."

I came out on deck slowly. It was now a matter of con- science to shave the land as close as possible—for now he must go overboard whenever the ship was put in stays. Must! There could be no going back for him. After a moment I walked over to leeward and my heart flew into my mouth at the nearness of the land on the bow. Under any other circumstances I would not have held on a minute longer. The second mate had followed me anxiously.

I looked on till I felt I could command my voice.

"She will weather," I said then in a quiet tone.

"Are you going to try that, sir?" he stammered out incredulously.

I took no notice of him and raised my tone just enough to be heard by the helmsman.

"Keep her good full."

"Good full, sir."

The wind fanned my cheek, the sails slept, the world was silent. The strain of watching the dark loom of the land grow bigger and denser was too much for me. I had shut my eyes— because the ship must go closer. She must! The stillness was intolerable. Were we standing still?

When I opened my eyes the second view started my heart with a thump. The black southern hill of Koh-ring seemed to hang right over the ship like a towering fragment of the everlasting night. On that enormous mass of blackness there was not a gleam to be seen, not a sound to be heard. It was gliding irresistibly towards us and yet seemed already within reach of the hand. I saw the vague figures of the watch grouped in the waist, gazing in awed silence.

"Are you going on, sir?" inquired an unsteady voice at my elbow.

I ignored it. I had to go on.

"Keep her full. Don't check her way. That won't do now," I said, warningly.

"I can't see the sails very well," the helmsman answered me, in strange, quavering tones.

Was she close enough? Already she was, I won't say in the shadow of the land, but in the very blackness of it, already swallowed up as it were, gone too close to be recalled, gone from me altogether.

"Give the mate a call," I said to the young man who stood at my elbow as still as death. "And turn all hands up."

My tone had a borrowed loudness reverberated from the height of the land. Several voices cried out together: "We are all on deck, sir."

Then stillness again, with the great shadow gliding closer, towering higher, without a light, without a sound. Such a hush had fallen on the ship that she might have been a bark of the dead floating in slowly under the very gate of Erebus.

"My God! Where are we?"

It was the mate moaning at my elbow. He was thunderstruck, and as it were deprived of the moral support of his whiskers. He clapped his hands and absolutely cried out, "Lost!"

"Be quiet," I said, sternly.

He lowered his tone, but I saw the shadowy gesture of his despair. "What are we doing here?"

"Looking for the land wind."

He made as if to tear his hair, and addressed me recklessly.

"She will never get out. You have done it, sir. I knew it'd end in something like this. She will never weather, and you are too close now to stay. She'll drift ashore before she's round. O my God!"

I caught his arm as he was raising it to batter his poor devoted head, and shook it violently.

"She's ashore already," he wailed, trying to tear himself away.

"Is she? . . . Keep good full there!"

"Good full, sir," cried the helmsman in a frightened, thin, childlike voice.

I hadn't let go the mate's arm and went on shaking it. "Ready about, do you hear? You go forward"—shake—"and stop there"—shake—"and hold your noise"—shake—"and see these head-sheets properly overhauled"—shake, shake—shake.

And all the time I dared not look towards the land lest my heart should fail me. I released my grip at last and he ran forward as if fleeing for dear life.

I wondered what my double there in the sail locker thought of the commotion. He was able to hear everything—and perhaps he was able to understand why, on my conscience, it had to be thus close—no less. My first order "Hard alee!" re-echoed ominously under the towering shadow of Koh-ring as if I had shouted in a mountain gorge. And then I watched the land intently. In that smooth water and light wind it was impossible to feel the ship coming-to. No! I could not feel her. And my second self was making now ready to ship out and lower himself overboard. Perhaps he was gone already . . . ?

The great black mass brooding over our very mastheads began to pivot away from the ship's side silently. And now I forgot the secret stranger ready to depart, and remembered only that I was a total stranger to the ship. I did not know her. Would she do it? How was she to be handled?

I swung the mainyard and waited helplessly. She was perhaps stopped, and her very fate hung in the balance, with the black mass of Koh-ring like the gate of the everlasting night towering over her taffrail. What would she do now? Had she way on her yet? I stepped to the side swiftly, and on the shadowy water I could see nothing except a faint phosphorescent flash revealing the glassy smoothness of the sleeping surface. It was impossible to tell—and I had not learned yet the feel of my ship. Was she moving? What I needed was something easily seen, a piece of paper, which I could throw overboard and watch. I had nothing on me. To run down for it I didn't dare. There was no time. All at once my strained, yearning stare distinguished a white object floating within a yard of the ship's side. White on the black water. A phosphorescent flash passed under it. What was that thing? . . . I recognized my own floppy hat. It must have fallen off his head . . . and he didn't bother. Now I had what I wanted—the saving mark for my eyes. But I hardly thought of my other self, now gone from the ship, to be hidden forever from all friendly faces, to be a fugitive and a vagabond on the earth, with no brand of the curse on his sane forehead to stay a slaying hand . . . too proud to explain.

And I watched the hat—the expression of my sudden pity for his mere flesh. It had been meant to save his homeless head from the dangers of the sun. And now—behold—it was saving the ship, by serving me for a mark to help out the ignorance of my strangeness. Ha! It was drifting forward, warning me just in time that the ship had gathered sternway.

"Shift the helm," I said in a low voice to the seaman standing still like a statue.

The man's eyes glistened wildly in the binnacle light as he jumped round to the other side and spun round the wheel.

I walked to the break of the poop. On the overshadowed deck all hands stood by the forebraces waiting for my order. The stars ahead seemed to be gliding from right to left. And all was so still in the world that I heard the quiet remark, "She's round," passed in a tone of intense relief between two seamen.

"Let go and haul."

The foreyards ran round with a great noise, amidst cheery cries. And now the frightful whiskers made themselves heard giving various orders. Already the ship was drawing ahead. And I was alone with her. Nothing! no one in the world should stand now between us, throwing a shadow on the way of silent knowledge and mute affection, the perfect communion of a seaman with his first command.

Walking to the taffrail, I was in time to make out, on the very edge of a darkness thrown by a towering black mass like the very gateway of Erebus—yes, I was in time to catch an evanescent glimpse of my white hat left behind to mark the spot where the secret sharer of my cabin and of my thoughts, as though he were my second self, had lowered himself into the water to take his punishment: a free man, a proud swimmer striking out for a new destiny.

# 4

# The

# CHRIST

# Myth

"The Christ myth"—it could be a phrase out of a fundamentalist nightmare or a testimonial from a rationalist nonbeliever, shock or contempt. But it is neither, and to speak of the mythic qualities of the gospel of Matthew is not a denial or diminishment of its value. For myth is not a delusion but an insight, not a confusion but a perception, not a childishness but the memory of a reality. The patterns and images through which myth speaks may be as naturalistic or fantastic as their narrators choose, but the validity of a genuine myth will not be disturbed. Orpheus descending to Hades may seem to us less "real" than Ed taking a canoe trip, but the truth of the myth is the same in each instance. Orpheus may or may not have been a priest of Dionysos who tried to mollify and tame some of the wilder practices of that cult; but the significance of the Orphic myth depends not a whit on the literal existence or non-existence of a priest called Orpheus. The proposition is two-edged: (a) a "mythic" event is not necessarily historic, and (b) a "mythic" event is not necessarily nonhistoric. To recognize *myth* in any event will neither confer upon nor take away the "reality" of the event. Hence, when we consider Matthew's narrative of the life of Christ as *myth*, we in no way make a prejudgment of it as a historical account. The *fact* that there literally was an itinerant preacher from Nazareth who announced a reformed religion is a matter of historical record. If we speak of the "mythicness" of the gospel's account of this same preacher, we do not thereby deny the evidence of history. Myth sees one thing, history sees another. The myth must speak for itself.

Keeping this in mind, then, we can remark on the following:

1. Matthew's account of Jesus extends and completes the matter of the myths of Narcissus, Dionysos, and Orpheus. The story of Jesus is mythic in the sense that it participates in an archetypal situation that it shares with those other myths.

2. This account of Jesus depends on the language of myth, its primary vehicle of expression is image and symbol. The story is mythic in the sense that it communicates to us in the distinctive mode of myth, dream, and poetry.

3. The archetype being fulfilled and the symbols being activated are such that they require the element of historicity. "Realness" *is* essen-

tial to this particular myth, and this myth itself makes that point through its own strategies and professions. The *fact* of Christ does not dispel the *myth* of Christ in this gospel. Quite the contrary. The myth absorbs the fact, and turns factualness to mythic use.

In considering the other myths, we have observed the stadial unfolding of a pattern. Narcissus is the annihilation of autonomous personality, a severance with the supposedly self-sufficient ego and a turning back to the communal roots of humankind. Dionysos is the image of those roots, the underlying instinctual and unconscious moorings of human awareness. Orpheus is the assimilation of that unconscious by consciousness, the expansion of awareness. "The force that through the green fuse drives the flower/Drives my green age," wrote Dylan Thomas; the stunted ego by driving deep into the nourishing unconscious explodes into a fuller bloom.

But the pattern, the archetype, is not yet complete. Orpheus leads us back to the bright world of expanded consciousness, but he tells us nothing of the Shakespearean "immortal longings," nothing of the Wordsworthian "intimations of immortality," nothing of Rudolph Otto's "sense of the holy." An apprehension of the transcendent, an intuition that there is real experience beyond the borders of the mundane, is an attested phenomenon. No matter how far secular myths take us, we are sensitive to the fact that we are drawn still further, on beyond Orpheus.

Carl Jung has shown how Jesus responds to the "longings of immortality," how he completes the archetype. "The spontaneous symbols of the self, or of wholeness, cannot in practice be distinguished from a God-image . . . there is an ever-present archetype of wholeness which may easily disappear from the purview of consciousness or may never be perceived at all until a consciousness illuminated by conversion recognizes it in the figure of Christ."[1]

By "conversion," Jung obviously does not mean anything like a prayer meeting "declaration for Christ," he is not dealing with any form of sectarianism. He is speaking of a renascense, a reawakening of the entire range of consciousness, an awareness beyond the ego-centered and the pragmatic. It is the sense of "conversion" as Fr. John S. Dunne describes it in his study *A Search for God in Time and*

*Memory.* [2] Dunne proposes that there are four major turning points, conversions, in any man's life. The first is an inward experiencing of the spirit; the second is living in accord with that experience; the third is facing the prospect of death; and the fourth is dying. These are not denominational or confessional matters, they are details of the human condition. The life of Jesus exemplifies and dramatizes these universal turning-points, the gospel narrative gives a palpability and a shape to the abstractions. The first kind of conversion is demonstrated when Jesus is baptized by John; the second, when Jesus takes up the ministry of the imprisoned John; the third, when Jesus resolves to die, as did John, for his teaching; the fourth, when Jesus is killed. Jesus thus becomes an exemplar of the multiply converted man, every man. The achievement of selfhood is a sequence, not a stasis. Mind tenses and flexes, then leaps forward from where it stands to a fuller place; that greater mind gathers itself and leaps again; and again. A *lived* life is a progress of conversions from emptinesses to fullnesses, from potentialities to realities. This is precisely the pattern of the life of Christ. That pattern we can *appropriate* (to use Dunne's term) to ourselves. We can recognize (as Jung meant) that the figure of Christ is the figure of illuminated consciousness.

The realization and release of energies that lie within is the archetypal meaning of the gospel; and as in all myth that meaning is transmitted through image and symbol. St. Matthew's narrative is considerably more rich in symbolic statement than any of the other myths we have looked at, but the *mode* of revelation in the gospel is the same as in the other myths. Within a linear narrative that moves through time, there are columns of images that are synchronous with one another, image clusters that contain the central elements of the myth. *Water* and *women*, for instance, occur randomly throughout the Dionysos narrative; but though water episodes and women episodes are separate from each other in the telling, we must view them as coexisting simultaneously if we are to receive their symbolic value. Narrative speaks in segments, symbols speak in wholes. [3]

The gospel narrative of Matthew is replete with image-clusters, recurrent icons that manifest the archetype of unfolding consciousness: the hidden seed, [4] the fulfilled prophecy and dream, [5] emergence from solitary places,[6] miraculous appearance of unsuspected powers,[7] the symbolic child,[8] the promise of immediate redemption,[9] and the divine ancestry of Jesus.[10] All these episodes, spaced apart in the narrative, have at the same time a simultaneous existence; they function as a single revelation of the central myth, many voices united in one statement—the power to be transformed lies hidden within.

The strongest encouragement to seek out the symbolic and mythic sense of these recurrent motifs can be found in the great emphasis Jesus put on parables. The value of the parabolic method for preaching and teaching seems obvious: the graphicness, the vividness, the physicalness of the parables make them effective vehicles for conveying abstract spiritual insights. And yet the disciples themselves were puzzled: "Why do you speak to them in parables?" Jesus' reply is at first even more puzzling. He did *not* say, I speak to them in parables so that they might see and so that they might understand. Instead, he responds, "This is why I speak to them in parables, because seeing they do not see, and hearing they do not hear, nor do they understand." (13.13) In other words, the parables are not exercises in illumination, but demonstrations of darkness. The parables are a rebuke to the listeners that they see only the physical husk of the tales, and fail to penetrate into the hidden secret. The people relive the cause of Isaiah's anger, with their dull hearts, closed ears and dim eyes, failing to seek out the truth embedded within the literal details of the parables. The disciples are blessed for they see and hear (13.16), and so cooperate with Jesus in his mission to fulfill the prophet Isaiah, "I will open my mouth in parables, I will utter what has been hidden since the foundation of the world." (13.35)

The great subtlety of Jesus' use of parables lies in this: that the dramatic details are not clarifying vehicles but metaphors of reality. As Jesus uses them, the literal details of the parables are not expendable items, there only to visually present an invisible truth; the details are analogous to the very stuff of the world within which reposes a wisdom. The parables are microcosms of existence itself, physical realities that shelter an in-dwelling secret. The parables are linguistic models of the Incarnation, the Word hidden since the foundation of the world but always enfleshed within the world.

They are at the same time the central model of all the image-clusters of the Matthean narrative. Seeds, children, dreams, deserts, miracles, divine ancestry are replications of the parable-symbolism. The seed lies hidden in the loam until in the fullness of time it breaks forth, not denying the earth, but nourished even as it was hidden by the earth. The child symbolizes potential wholeness, a promise to be kept; "[the child] represents the strongest, the most ineluctable urge in every being, namely the urge to realize itself."[11] Christ withdrew into the desert before his ministry, then again after the death of John the Baptist, and yet again at Gethsemane; and each time emerged with a fuller awareness of his mission. Seed, child and Jesus' actions are all versions of the parable-symbol, the hidden potency.

Further: the gospel narrative of Matthew has the constant refrain, "This was done to fulfill the prophecy." The birth of Jesus, Herod's slaughter of the innocents, John the Baptist's ministry, Jesus' miraculous cures, his entry into Jerusalem, Judas' burial, "all this took place to fulfill what the Lord had spoken by the prophet." The vision of history implied is strongly agrarian. Time is a great field; and lying within that earth of time is a promise that will be manifest in the life of Jesus. So too the relationship between Jesus and God, Son and Father, has slept through all the generations, until the moment of its revelation has come. History holds the truth hidden and then history relinquishes the truth in act. History too is parable and seed and child.

Or consider the miracles recorded by Matthew. Those episodes show material objects behaving as if they were history, revealing potencies that were hidden but are now revealed. *Things* behave like *Time* in this gospel. For instance, the words of Isaiah, "A voice was heard in Ramah, wailing and loud lamentation, Rachel weeping for her children," were not fulfilled, not completed, until the murder of the children. Nor was the prophecy of the voice crying in the wilderness fulfilled until the appearance of John the Baptist in history. Nor were Jeremiah's words "And they took thirty pieces of silver" comprehensible until Judas' betrayal. Nor was it imagined that there was wholeness in the body of the leper (8.1-3), in the body of the centurion's servant (8.5-13), in the silence of the mute (9.32-33), in the eyes of the blind men (10.27-30); nor that there was a sufficiency in the five loaves and three fishes (14.16-21), nor a solidity in the sea (14.26). An unsuspected power lies within things, as unfulfilled prophecies lie within history.

Consider a modern version of the unsuspected potencies within natural objects, the great surprises in ordinary matter revealed by modern physics. Recall Sir Arthur Eddington's description of the simple act of walking through a door:

> I am standing on the threshold about to enter a room. It is a complicated business. In the first place I must shove against an atmosphere pressing with a force of fourteen pounds on every square inch of my body. I must make sure of landing on a plank travelling at twenty miles a second round the sun—a fraction of a second too early or too late, the plank would be miles away. I must do this whilst hanging from a round planet head outward into space, and with a wind of aether blowing at no one knows how many miles a second through every interstice of my body. The plank has no solidity of substance. To step on it is like stepping on a swarm of flies [the sparsely scattered electric charges that constitute the fundament of "matter"]. Shall I not slip through? No, if I make the venture one of the flies hits me and gives a boost up again; I fall again and am knocked upwards by another fly; and so on. I may hope that the net result will be that I remain about steady; but if unfortunately I should slip through the floor or be boosted too violently up to the ceiling, the occurrence would be, not a violation of the laws of Nature, but a rare coincidence. These are some of the minor difficulties. I ought really to look at the problem four-dimensionally as concerning the intersection of my world-line with that of the plank. Then again it is necessary to determine in which direction the entropy of the world is increasing in order to make sure that my passage over the threshold is an entrance, not an exit.[12]

The physical world too is a parable.

With so many parable-configurations, it is small wonder that Jesus could say that the kingdom is at hand. The possibilities of transformation are everywhere, within language, within history, within events, within things, seed-like in the soil of existence. When the tax-collectors had to be paid, Jesus instructed Peter to "go to the sea and cast a hook, and take the first fish that comes up, and when you open its mouth you will find a shekel; take that and give it to them for me and for yourself" (17.27). There is sufficiency within.

"In the world of Christian ideas Christ undoubtedly represents the self,"[13] wrote Carl Jung. By *self*, Jung meant the whole, the total, the fully-realized, a selfhood achieved with nothing left out. He expressed this idea in a cruciform diagram:

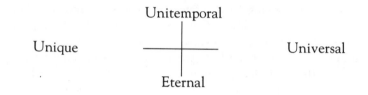

This formula expresses not only the psychological self but also the dogmatic figure of Christ. As an historical personage Christ is unitemporal and unique; as God, universal and eternal. Likewise the self: as the essence of individuality it is unitemporal and unique; as an archetypal symbol it is God-image and therefore universal and eternal.[14]

A divided self is a crippled self. A personality that is ignorant of or denying of parts of itself is an unfinished personality. A demi-psyche is a monster. The achieved self recognizes all the dualities it is heir to—the angelic and the demonic, the spiritual and the material, the unconscious and the conscious—and achieves an integration of them. The crucified Jesus hung between earth and sky, speaking first to the thieves and then to the Father, crying out first in despair and then in consummation, is an entire emblem of the integrated self.

All the symbolism of the gospel supports the integration of matter and spirit, Jesus as Man and Jesus as Idea. The seed needs the agency of earth, the prophecies need the agency of history, the man requires the child. The entire symbolic texture of the gospel, with all its motifs in-folding upon one another, dramatizes the *In-Carnation*, the in-flesh-edness, of the transfiguring power. To undervalue or to set aside as "problematic" the historicity of Jesus is to rip the fabric of the gospel and to misjudge the totality of the narrator's symbolism. Narcissus is expendable, Orpheus is expendable, for what they represent mythically does not require their existence historically. But Jesus is required, for his myth is total transformation within total existence. Nothing can be left out, including his own temporality.

Nor are we exempt from the totality, the inclusivity, of the gospel. As all the elements of the narrative converge to the single point of transformation, so the observer (or reader) of the narrative is expected to be transformed. First, a transformation from observer into participant. Moving into the gospel is analogous to the seed falling into the earth, the mind moving into history, Jesus walking into the desert. We become, willy-nilly, by the act of reading, doers of the event of the gospel, one of the penetrators. From the fecund wholeness of the gospel, it is intended, then, that we come forth reborn. Jesus made terrible demands of his followers: "If any man would come after me, let him deny himself and take up his cross and follow me" (16.24); his great instruction (the Sermon on the Mount) is a radical ethic, requiring total commitment. Not a pietistic nor even a conventionally "religious" commitment, but a total self-transformation: that is the gospel's demand.

No recent author has better understood that demand than Flannery O'Connor. Her great comic novel, the Southern-grotesque *Wise Blood*, [15] and its central figure of the God-tormented Hazel Motes, takes a firm hold on the Christ who will not be accommodating, will make no compromises, will settle for nothing less than everything. The Christ of St. Matthew is voracious, as this myth of inclusivity requires; and *Wise Blood* is about a man who expends himself entirely, in accordance with the myth.

As a child terrified by his Bible-thumping preacher grandfather (who was accustomed to point to his grandson at revival meetings and pronounce him *redeemed,* therefore inescapably in Jesus' clutches), Haze found early that "There was already a deep black wordless conviction in him that the way to avoid Jesus was to avoid sin. He knew by the time he was twelve years old that he was going to be a preacher. Later he saw Jesus move from tree to tree in the back of his mind, a

wild ragged figure motioning him to turn around and come off into the
dark where he was not sure of his footing, where he might be walking
on the water and not know it and then suddenly know it and drown."
(p. 22) Now, years later, after a four year hitch in the Army, Haze
does indeed become a preacher:

> I preach the Church Without Christ. I'm member and preach-
> er to that church where the blind don't see and the lame don't walk
> and what's dead stays that way. Ask me about that church and I'll
> tell you it's the church that the blood of Jesus don't fool with
> redemption. . . . I'm going to preach there was no Fall because
> there was nothing to fall from and no Redemption because there
> was no Fall and no Judgement because there wasn't the first two.
> Nothing matters but that Jesus was a liar. (p. 105)

Haze's fast running away from Jesus is not an easeful and comforting
dereliction of an old responsibility. It scorches him, fills him with a
terrible resolve, and makes him a stranger in his own land where
empty religiosity and fatuousness prevail. Preaching antiChrist, he
finds that the enemy is not a rockhard commitment to Christ but a
lardlike bogus Christianity, so soft and unaware that it cannot distinguish itself from its attacker. (When Haze tells his landlady that he's
the preacher of the Church Without Christ, she inquires "Protestant
. . . or something foreign?" (p. 106) On finding that it's homegrown,
she's content.) Such a mushy pseudo-faith gives Haze no handhold,
and in his angry frustration against his God-mouthing compatriots he
comes more and more to resemble, paradoxically, an Old Testament
prophet blasting the faithless or Jesus reiterating "Woe unto you,
scribes and Pharisees, hypocrites!" The most devastating (and hugely
comic) clash between Haze's Jeremiac intensity and slovenly faith
occurs one night while Haze is preaching his new creed. A hustler by
the name of Onnie Jay Holy, seeing that Haze's intensity can attract a
crowd, co-opts the preaching, sensing a chance to turn a fast dollar. It's
a head-to-head contest between honesty and fraud.

'I met this Prophet here . . . two months ago, folks, [and] I heard how he was out to help me, how he was preaching the Church of Christ Without Christ, the church that was going to get a new Jesus to help me bring my sweet nature into the open where ever'body could enjoy it. That was two months ago, friends, and now you wouldn't know me for the same man. I love ever' one of you people and I want you to listen to him and me and join our church, the Holy Church of Christ Without Christ, the new church with the new Jesus, and then you'll all be helped like me!'

Haze leaned forward. 'This man is not true,' he said. 'I never saw him before tonight. I wasn't preaching this church two months ago and the name of it ain't the Holy Church of Christ Without Christ!'

The man ignored this and so did the people. There were ten or twelve gathered around. 'Friends,' Onnie Jay Holy said, 'I'm mighty glad you're seeing me now instead of two months ago because then I couldn't have testified to this new church and this Prophet here. If I had my gittarr with me, I could say all this better but I'll just have to do the best I can by myself.' He had a winning smile and it was evident that he didn't think he was any better than anybody else even though he was.

'Now I just want to give you folks a few reasons why you can trust this church,' he said. 'In the first place, friends, you can rely on it that it's nothing foreign connected with it. You don't have to believe nothing you don't understand and approve of. If you don't understand it, it ain't true, and that's all there is to it. No jokers in the deck, friends.'

Haze leaned forward. 'Blasphemy is the way to the truth,' he said, 'and there's no other way whether you understand it or not!'

'Now, friends,' Onnie Jay said, 'I want to tell you a second reason why you can absolutely trust this church—it's based on the Bible. Yes sir! It's based on your own personal interpitation of the Bible, friends. You can sit at home and interpit your own Bible however you feel in your heart it ought to be interpited. That's right,' he said, 'just the way Jesus would have done it. Gee, I wish I had my gittarr here,' he complained.

'This man is a liar,' Haze said. 'I never saw him before tonight. I never . . .'

'That ought to be enough reasons, friends,' Onnie Jay Holy said, 'but I'm going to tell you one more, just to show I can. This church is up-to-date! When you're in this church you can know that there's nothing or nobody ahead of you, nobody knows nothing you don't know, all the cards are on the table, friends, and tha's a fack!'. (pp. 151–3)

Haze's response to this inane, irresponsible harangue is total. He mashes Onnie Jay Holy's (whose name even is a fraud—his real name, he tells Haze, is Hoover Shoats) hand in his car door and departs; and when he later discovers that Onnie Jay—Hoover Shoats—has hired another Prophet and dressed him to look like Haze, Haze backs his car over the false prophet, mashing *him* dead. Haze's muttered "you ain't true" punctuates his violence like a litany.

When Haze had first begun preaching his gospel of antiChrist, he had met Asa Hawks, a blind (or so he says) preacher, who evidently had in his calling the same intensity, whole commitment and fervor that Haze had in his countercalling. With his young daughter, Sabbath, Asa Hawks in his mendicant ministry thundered out damnation and repentance with as much energy as Haze himself could muster on the opposite side. Hawks had (he said) blinded himself with quicklime at a revival service, to show how thoroughly committed he was to Christ; and with his dark glasses, scarred cheeks, and fierce intensity he became a real adversary to Haze, entirely different from the porcinely pious Onnie Jay Holy. Haze so thoroughly recognizes that Asa Hawks is a formidable enemy, that he resolves to seduce Sabbath. "He thought that when the blind preacher saw his daughter ruined, he would realize that he was in earnest when he said he preached The Church Without Christ." (p. 110)

It is immediately after killing the false prophet, Onnie Jay Holy's fellow con-man, that Haze goes to Asa Hawks' boarding house, creeps into his room, so he can stare at those eyes ruined for Christ. It is an act of affirmation, a need to find some evidence of someone having done something thoroughly. But as he strikes a match to see such evidence, Asa Hawks looks back at him, with two good eyes. He has not blinded himself; he had wavered; he was as much a fraud as Onnie Jay. The very next night Sabbath, the intended child-victim of Haze's anger, seduces Haze, expertly. Preacher and child both, "you ain't true."

While Haze is fleeing that ragged figure moving from tree to tree in the back of his mind, and finding in the process that there is no truth or fullness in those who profess Christ, he is exactly counterbalanced by Enoch Emery. It is Enoch, a befuddled child who had attached himself to Haze at the beginning of Haze's crusade against Christ, who explains the title of the novel. When Haze tries to detach himself from the pesty Enoch, who follows him unwanted, Enoch snaps at him, "You act like you think you got wiser blood than anybody else," he said, "but you ain't! I'm the one has it. Not you. *Me!*" (p. 59). The operation of Enoch's wise blood is in this, that he dumbly and instinctively knows that there is a dimension of reality beyond the material, that there is a sacred center toward which creation ought to be moving. As Haze tries to move away from that center, Enoch's wise blood draws him to it. Unfortunately, his blood can't instruct him how to reach that center, and Enoch gets entangled in easy rituals, false formulas, God-searches that do not involve his real self. He has Haze's passion (but in the opposite direction, toward rather than away from a sense of the sacred), but he is afflicted with the allure of the easy and the partial.

The first time they are together, Haze and Enoch both witness a street-hawker demonstrating a potato peeler:

> The man had on a small canvas hat and a shirt patterned with bunches of upside-down pheasants and quails and bronze turkeys. He was pitching his voice under the street noises so that it reached every ear distinctly as if in a private conversation. A few people gathered around. There were two buckets on the card table, one empty and the other full of potatoes. Between the two buckets there was a pyramid of green cardboard boxes and, on top of the stack, one peeler was open for demonstration. The man stood in front of this altar, pointing over it at various people.

'How about you?' he said, pointing at a damp-haired pimpled boy. 'You ain't gonna let one of these go by?' He stuck a brown potato in one side of the open machine. The machine was a square tin box with a red handle, the potato went into the box and then in a second, backed out the other side, white. 'You ain't gonna let one of these go by!' he said. ( p. 38)

This hawker with his peeler is a variation on Onnie Jay, the hustler with his new church. The potato goes into the machine, the handle turns, the potato comes out white. The sinful soul goes into the redemption machine, a crank turns, the soul comes out white. No effort, no strain. Just the quick promise of easy salvation. Enoch is entranced, he wants one of those machines, but can't afford one. (Haze buys one and, with contempt, gives it to Sabbath and Asa Hawks, a wordless commentary on what he thinks of their crusade for souls.)

Enoch is employed at the city park, and he has found there something even more enchanting than the redemption machine. At the very center of the park is a grove with a mysterious building in the center; and within that building is an even greater mystery, to which Enoch's wise blood draws him. For reasons he can't explain, Enoch must always approach that mystery by a formulated, ritualistic route: every day he must first circle the zoo section of the park, then stop at the refreshment stand, and only then approach the holy place. One day he brings Haze with him:

[Enoch] knew something was going to happen to him. His blood stopped beating. All the time it had been beating like a drum noise and now it had stopped. They started down the hill. It was a steep hill, full of trees painted white from the ground up four feet. They looked as if they had on ankle socks. He gripped Hazel Motes's arm. 'It gets damp as you go down,' he said, looking around vaguely. Hazel Motes shook him off. In a second, Enoch gripped his arm again and stopped him. He pointed down through the trees. 'Muvseevum,' he said. The strange word made him shiver. That was the first time he had ever said it aloud. A

> piece of gray building was showing where he pointed. It grew
> larger as they went down the hill, then as they came to the end of
> the wood and stepped out on the gravel driveway, it seemed to
> shrink suddenly. It was round and soot-colored. There were col-
> umns at the front of it and in between each column there was an
> eyeless stone woman holding a pot on her head. A concrete band
> was over the columns and the letters, MVSEVM, were cut into
> it. Enoch was afraid to pronounce the word again. (p. 96)

Poor Enoch has enacted a parody of ceremonial religion: the required ritual, the sense of a consecrated temple, the awe before an
incomprehensible and ineffable deity, the unpronounceable One, the
Tetragrammaton. Inside is the real object of his veneration: a three-
foot long mummy, locked in a glass case. This has been his great
discovery, that "something, in the center of the park. . . . It was a
mystery, although it was right there in a glass case for everybody to see
and there was a typewritten card over it telling all about it. But there
was something the card couldn't say and what it couldn't say was
inside him, a terrible knowledge without any words to it, a terrible
knowledge like a big nerve growing inside him." (p. 81)

Enoch has an exact plan for this awesome object. Back in his room
he has converted an old washstand into a tabernacle. Suspecting that
the mummy might be the new Jesus, he plans to steal it from the
museum and install it in that homemade tabernacle and then, something would happen, "he didn't know what." (p. 174) And nothing
happens. After all his plans, the theft, the installation in the tabernacle, nothing. In disgust, Enoch waits for his wise blood to tell him
what to do next. He has followed a formula, pronounced the mysterious word, built his little temple, sat before the idol, and no white
potato came out the other side of the redemption machine. He is just
as he was before the whole episode. So there must be another way.

The other way presents itself in "GONGA! Giant Jungle Monarch
and a Great Star! Here in Person!!!", a man dressed in a gorilla suit,
touting the new movie in town. (p. 177) Once again, as he was by the
potato peeler and the mummified new Jesus, Enoch is enthralled.
Here, surely, is a way to be transformed. He hides in the truck that
carries Gonga from theater to theater. As the truck drives off,

There came from the van certain thumping noises, not those of the normal gorilla, but they were drowned out by the drone of the motor and the steady sound of wheels against the road. The night was pale and quiet, with nothing to stir it but an occasional complaint from a hoot owl and the distant muted jarring of a freight train. The truck sped on until it slowed for a crossing, and as the van rattled over the tracks, a figure slipped from the door and almost fell, and then limped hurriedly off towards the woods . . . . Burning with the intensest kind of happiness [Enoch] dug rapidly until he had made a trench about a foot long and a foot deep. Then he placed the stack of clothes in it and stood aside to rest a second. Burying his clothes was not a symbol to him of burying his former self; he only knew he wouldn't need them any more. . . . No gorilla in existence, whether in the jungles of Africa or California, or in New York City in the finest apartment in the world, was happier at that moment than this one, whose god had finally rewarded it. (p. 195–8)

In his transformed condition, Enoch moves to reach out to the world:

A man and woman sitting close together on a rock just off the highway were looking across an open stretch of valley at a view of the city in the distance and they didn't see the shaggy figure approaching. The smokestacks and square tops of buildings made a black uneven wall against the lighter sky and here and there a steeple cut a sharp wedge out of a cloud. The young man turned his neck just in time to see the gorilla standing a few feet away, hideous and black, with its hand extended. He eased his arm from around the woman and disappeared silently into the woods. She, as soon as she turned her eyes, fled screaming down the highway. The gorilla stood as though surprised and presently its arm fell to its side. It sat down on the rock where they had been sitting and stared over the valley at the uneven skyline of the city. (p. 198)

In the book of Genesis it is recounted that Isaac had two sons, Jacob and Esau. Jacob was a smooth man, and Esau was a hairy man. Their mother Rebekah loved Jacob the better, but Isaac loved Esau. When it came time for the dying Isaac to bestow his blessing on his most-loved son, Rebekah clothed Jacob in rough skins. The blind Isaac, feeling the rough skin, mistook Jacob for Esau, and gave his blessing to the wrong son. And so Jacob came into his inheritance not in his own skin, but in another's. (Genesis, 27.1–38) Metaphorically, Enoch in the Gonga suit is Jacob, courting the blessing of redemption not in his own skin. His mummy-ritual, practicing a strange worship alien to himself, is also Jacob in Esau-skin. Onnie Jay Holy and Asa Hawks, all Jacobs in Esau-skins, all determined to have their inheritance but not in their own skins, not at the expense of their own involvement. They all avoid penetration into themselves, into the dark places, they all sidestep around the totality of the gospel myth. All but Hazel Motes.

While Enoch is living out an Old Testament episode, Haze lives out a New Testament event. In his old beatup car, he takes to the roads, preaching against Christ to whomever will listen. "[I've got] to preach the truth. The Church Without Christ! And I got a car to get there in." (p. 189) It's a car that "a lightning bolt couldn't stop." (p. 207) But the lightning bolt comes in the shape of a policeman who, bemused by the incredibly ramshackle condition of Haze's automobile, clears it from the highway: "The patrolman got behind the Essex and pushed it over the embankment and the cow stumbled up and galloped across the field and into the woods; the buzzard flapped off to a tree at the edge of the clearing. The car landed on its top, with the three wheels that stayed on spinning. The motor bounced out and rolled some distance away and various odd pieces scattered this way and that." (p. 209) Haze considers this for a while, then goes and buys some quicklime, takes it to his room at Mrs. Flood's boardinghouse, rubs it into his eyes, and blinds himself.

As Enoch is from Genesis, Haze is from the Acts of the Apostles. He is Saul of Tarsus, preacher against the Lord, struck down and blinded on the road to Damascus, and identified by the Lord as a chosen vessel who must suffer great things for the Lord's sake. (Acts, 9.3–19)

Haze does nothing halfway or partially. Having had his Pauline experience, he subjects himself to terrible mortifications: he fills his shoes with broken glass, he wraps his body in barbed wire. He had been running from that image in the back of his mind, the "wild ragged figure motioning him to tirn around and come off into the dark where he was not sure of his footing, where he might be walking on the water and not know it and then suddenly know it and drown." (p. 22) Now, finally, he turns and faces that dread: he sets off one night, stumbling in his blindness, into a driving icy rain. He is discovered crawling in a ditch by two policemen, one of whom cracks him on the head with his billyclub so that Haze will give them no trouble. He dies in the squad car but, unnoticing, the policemen deliver him back to his boardinghouse. There, his landlady Mrs. Flood converses with him.

> She had [the policemen] put him on her bed and when she had pushed them out the door, she locked it behind them and drew up a straight chair and sat down close to his face where she could talk to him. 'Well, Mr. Motes,' she said, 'I see you've come home!'
>
> His face was stern and tranquil. 'I knew you'd come back,' she said. 'And I've been waiting for you. And you needn't to pay any more rent but have it free here, any way you like, upstairs or down. Just however you want it and with me to wait on you, or if you want to go on somewhere, we'll both go.'
>
> She had never observed his face more composed and she grabbed his hand and held it to her heart. It was resistless and dry. The outline of a skull was plain under his skin and the deep burned eye sockets seemed to lead into the dark tunnel where he had disappeared. She leaned closer and closer to his face, looking deep into them, trying to see how she had been cheated or what had cheated her, but she couldn't see anything. She shut her eyes and saw the pin point of light but so far away that she could not hold it steady in her mind. She felt as if she were blocked at the entrance of something. She sat staring with her eyes shut, into his eyes, and felt as if she had finally got to the beginning of

something she couldn't begin, and she saw him moving farther
and farther away, farther and farther into the darkness until he
was the pin point of light. (pp. 231–2)

All through the novel, people slide along the surface of things,
acting without passion, without wholeness. They speak to one
another on trains, they curse, they throw cars over cliffs, they beat
blind men in ditches, all without heat or feeling or intensity. None of
them go into that dark tunnel where Haze had disappeared or into the
darkness where he became a point of light. Haze gives himself up, uses
himself up, loses himself, and so finds that figure in the back of his
mind. " 'Well, Mr. Motes, I see you've come home.' "

In her note to the second edition of *Wise Blood,* Flannery O'Connor
wrote that for her, Hazel Motes' integrity lay in his not being able to
get rid of the ragged figure who moves from tree to tree in the back of
his mind. *Integrity, wholeness* leads necessarily to that figure, for the
"symbols of the self, or of wholeness, cannot in practice be distinguished from a God-image . . . there is an ever-present archetype of
wholeness which may easily disappear from the purview of consciousness or may never be perceived at all until a consciousness illuminated
by conversion recognizes it in the figure of Christ."[16] Flannery
O'Connor's regional, contemporary, comic novel reiterates a universal, timeless, serious insight that belongs to both theology and
psychology and above all to myth.

# NOTES

1. Carl Jung, "Christ, A Symbol of the Self," *Aion: Researches into the Phenomenology of the
   Self* (Copyright © 1959 and 1968 by BollingenFoundation) p. 40. Reprinted by permission
   of Princeton University Press.

2. *A Search For God in Time and Memory* (New York, Macmillan Co., 1969), especially chapter VI.

3. The Swiss linguist Ferdinand de Saussure, upon whose work much of modern language theory is based, often used the game of chess to describe how symbolic statement works. If we approach a chess match already in progress and observe the position of all the pieces on the board, we can see the entire game situation, we do not need to know the sequence of moves that occurred before we arrived on the scene. The route or the narrative of the game before the instant of our arrival is irrelevant. (*Course in General Linguistics*, tr. W. Baskin, New York, Philosophical Library, 1966, p. 89) Following a road-map is a *diachronous* experience, a moving from point to point to a destination. Each settled point of a chess game is a *synchronous* experience, with all pieces coexisting in a single instant to create a whole situation independent of any antecedent situation.

4. Chapter 7, verses 17–20; 12.33; 13.1–9, 18–33; 21.18–22.

5. 2.1–6, 12–19, 22; 3.3; 4.14–16; 5.17–18; 8.17; 11.13–14; 12.17–18, 39–41; 13.14; 21.4–5; 27.9, 35.

6. 4.11; 14.23; 26.36–44.

7. 4.23–24; 8.2–3, 5–16, 23–27; 9.2, 18–29, 32–33; 12.22; 14.15–21, 35–36; 15.22–38; 17.14–18; 20.30–34; 21.14.

8. 18.1–6; 19.13–14.

9. 10.7; 11.3–6; 16.28; 24.1–51.

10. 1.18–25; 3.16–17; 10.32–33; 12.48–50; 14.33; 16.13–16; 17.1–5; 18.10; 20.23.

11. Carl Jung, "The Psychology of the Child Archetype," *Essays on a Science of Mythology*, p. 89.

12. Sir Arthur Eddington, *The Nature of the Physical World* (Ann Arbor, University of Michigan Press, 1958), p. 342.

13. Jung, "Christ, A Symbol of the Self," p. 62.

14. *Ibid.*, p. 63.

15. Flannery O'Connor, *Wise Blood* (Copyright © 1949, 1952, 1962 by Flannery O'Connor). Excerpts reprinted with the permission of Farrar, Straus and Giroux, Inc.

16. Jung, "Christ, A Symbol of the Self," p. 40.

# FOURTH INTERLUDE:
## CONSUMED IS CONSUMMATED

There is a seal or sepulcher to be
broken, a rock to be broke open, to dis-
close the living water; an eruption.
Begin then with a fracture, a cesura, a
rent; opening a crack in this fallen
world, a shaft of light . . . Stretch
yourself, to the breaking point. It
is not true unless it hurts; the evidence
is martyrdom. 'All truths are bloody
truths for me.' We do not know the truth
because we repress it; and we repress it
because it is painful.

*Norman O. Brown*, Love's Body

# Greenleaf

## *Flannery O'Connor*

Mrs. May's bedroom window was low and faced on the east
and the bull, silvered in the moonlight, stood under it, his head
raised as if he listened—like some patient god come down to woo
her—for a stir inside the room. The window was dark and the
sound of her breathing too light to be carried outside. Clouds
crossing the moon blackened him and in the dark he began to
tear at the hedge. Presently they passed and he appeared again in
the same spot, chewing steadily, with a hedge-wreath that he had
ripped loose for himself caught in the tips of his horns. When the

moon drifted into retirement again, there was nothing to mark his place but the sound of steady chewing. Then abruptly a pink glow filled the window. Bars of light slid across him as the venetian blind was slit. He took a step backward and lowered his head as if to show the wreath across his horns.

For almost a minute there was no sound from inside, then as he raised his crowned head again, a woman's voice, guttural as if addressed to a dog, said, "Get away from here, Sir!" and in a second muttered, "Some nigger's scrub bull."

The animal pawed the ground and Mrs. May, standing bent forward behind the blind, closed it quickly lest the light make him charge into the shrubbery. For a second she waited, still bent forward, her nightgown hanging loosely from her narrow shoulders. Green rubber curlers sprouted neatly over her forehead and her face beneath them was smooth as concrete with an egg-white paste that drew the wrinkles out while she slept.

She had been conscious in her sleep of a steady rhythmic chewing as if something were eating one wall of the house. She had been aware that whatever it was had been eating as long as she had had the place and had eaten everything from the beginning of her fence line up to the house and now was eating the house and calmly with the same steady rhythm would continue through the house, eating her and the boys, and then on, eating everything but the Greenleafs, on and on, eating everything until nothing was left but the Greenleafs on a little island all their own in the middle of what had been her place. When the munching reached her elbow, she jumped up and found herself, fully awake, standing in the middle of her room. She identified the sound at once: a cow was tearing at the shrubbery under her window. Mr. Greenleaf had left the lane gate open and she didn't doubt that the entire herd was on her lawn. She turned on the dim pink table lamp and then went to the window and slit the blind. The bull, gaunt and long-legged, was standing about four feet from her, chewing calmly like an uncouth country suitor.

For fifteen years, she thought as she squinted at him fiercely, she had been having shiftless people's hogs root up her oats, their mules wallow on her lawn, their scrub bulls breed her cows. If this one was not put up now, he would be over the fence, ruining her herd before morning—and Mr. Greenleaf was soundly sleeping a half mile down the road in the tenant house. There was no way to get him unless she dressed and got in her car and rode down there and woke him up. He would come but his expression, his whole figure, his every pause, would say: "Hit looks to me like one or both of them boys would not make their maw ride out in the middle of the night thisaway. If hit was my boys, they would have got thet bull up theirself."

The bull lowered his head and shook it and the wreath slipped down to the base of his horns where it looked like a menacing prickly crown. She had closed the blind then; in a few seconds she heard him move off heavily.

Mr. Greenleaf would say, "If hit was my boys they would never have allowed their maw to go after hired help in the middle of the night. They would have did it theirself."

Weighing it, she decided not to bother Mr. Greenleaf. She returned to bed thinking that if the Greenleaf boys had risen in the world it was because she had given their father employment when no one else would have him. She had had Mr. Greenleaf fifteen years but no one else would have had him five minutes. Just the way he approached an object was enough to tell anybody with eyes what kind of a worker he was. He walked with a high-shouldered creep and he never appeared to come directly forward. He walked on the perimeter of some invisible circle and if you wanted to look him in the face, you had to move and get in front of him. She had not fired him because she had always doubted she could do better. He was too shiftless to go out and look for another job; he didn't have the initiative to steal, and after she had told him three or four times to do a thing, he did it; but he never told her about a sick cow until it was too late to call the veterinarian and if her barn had caught on fire, he would have called his wife to see the flames before he began to put them out. And of the wife, she didn't even like to think. Beside the wife, Mr. Greenleaf was an aristocrat.

"If it had been my boys," he would have said, "they would have cut off their right arm before they would have allowed their maw to . . ."

"If your boys had any pride, Mr. Greenleaf," she would like to say to him some day, "there are many things that they would not *allow* their mother to do."

The next morning as soon as Mr. Greenleaf came to the back door, she told him there was a stray bull on the place and that she wanted him penned up at once.

"Done already been here three days," he said, addressing his right foot which he held forward, turned slightly as if he were trying to look at the sole. He was standing at the bottom of the three back steps while she leaned out the kitchen door, a small woman with pale near-sighted eyes and grey hair that rose on top like the crest of some disturbed bird.

"Three days!" she said in the restrained screech that had become habitual with her.

Mr. Greenleaf, looking into the distance over the near pasture, removed a package of cigarets from his shirt pocket and let one fall into his hand. He put the package back and stood for a while looking at the cigaret. "I put him in the bull pen but he torn out of there," he said presently. "I didn't see him none after that." He bent over the cigaret and lit it and then turned his head briefly in her direction. The upper part of his face sloped gradually into the lower which was long and narrow, shaped like a rough chalice. He had deep-set fox-colored eyes shadowed under a grey felt hat that he wore slanted forward following the line of his nose. His build was insignificant.

"Mr. Greenleaf," she said, "get that bull up this morning before you do anything else. You know he'll ruin the breeding schedule. Get him up and keep him up and the next time there's a stray bull on this place, tell me at once. Do you understand?"

"Where you want him put at?" Mr. Greenleaf asked.

"I don't care where you put him," she said. "You are supposed to have some sense. Put him where he can't get out. Whose bull is he?"

For a moment Mr. Greenleaf seemed to hesitate between silence and speech. He studied the air to the left of him. "He must be somebody's bull," he said after a while.

"Yes, he must!" she said and shut the door with a precise little slam.

She went into the dining room where the two boys were eating breakfast and sat down on the edge of her chair at the head of the table. She never ate breakfast but she sat with them to see that they had what they wanted. "Honestly!" she said, and began

to tell about the bull, aping Mr. Greenleaf saying, "It must be
*somebody's* bull."

Wesley continued to read the newspaper folded beside his
plate but Scofield interrupted his eating from time to time to look
at her and laugh. The two boys never had the same reaction to
anything. They were as different, she said, as night and day. The
only thing they did have in common, was that neither of them
cared what happened on the place. Scofield was a business type
and Wesley was an intellectual.

Wesley, the younger child, had had rheumatic fever when
he was seven and Mrs. May thought that this was what had
caused him to be an intellectual. Scofield, who had never had a
day's sickness in his life, was an insurance salesman. She would
not have minded his selling insurance if he had sold a nicer kind
but he sold the kind that only Negroes buy. He was what Negroes
call a "policy man." He said there was more money in nigger-
insurance than any other kind, and before company, he was very
loud about it. He would shout, "Mamma don't like to hear me say it
but I'm the best nigger-insurance salesman in this country."

Scofield was thirty-six and he had a broad pleasant smiling
face but he was not married. "Yes," Mrs. May would say, "and if
you sold decent insurance, some *nice* girl would be willing to
marry you. What nice girl wants to marry a nigger-insurance
man? You'll wake up some day and it'll be too late."

And at this Scofield would yodel and say, "Why, Mamma,
I'm not going to marry until you're dead and gone and then I'm
going to marry some nice fat farm girl that can take over this
place!" And once he had added, "—some nice lady like Mrs.
Greenleaf." When he had said this, Mrs. May had risen from her
chair, her back stiff as a rake handle, and had gone to her room.
There she had sat down on the edge of her bed for some time with
her small face drawn. Finally she had whispered, "I work and
slave, I struggle and sweat to keep this place for them and soon as
I'm dead, they'll marry trash and bring it in here and ruin everything. They'll marry trash and ruin everything I've done," and
she had made up her mind at that moment to change her will.
The next day she had gone to her lawyer and had had the property entailed so that if they married, they could not leave it to
their wives.

The idea that one of them might marry a woman even remotely like Mrs. Greenleaf was enough to make her ill. She had put up with Mr. Greenleaf for fifteen years, but the only way she had endured his wife had been by keeping entirely out of her sight. Mrs. Greenleaf was large and loose. The yard around her house looked like a dump and her five girls were always filthy; even the youngest one dipped snuff. Instead of making a garden or washing their clothes, her preoccupation was what she called "prayer healing."

Every day she cut all the morbid stories out of the newspaper—the accounts of women who had been raped and criminals who had escaped and children who had been burned and of train wrecks and plane crashes and the divorces of movie stars. She took these to the woods and dug a hole and buried them and then she fell on the ground over them and mumbled and groaned for an hour or so, moving her huge arms back and forth under her and out again and finally just lying down flat and, Mrs. May suspected, going to sleep in the dirt.

She had not found out about this until the Greenleafs had been with her a few months. One morning she had been out to inspect a field that she had wanted planted in rye but that had come up in clover because Mr. Greenleaf had used the wrong seeds in the grain drill. She was returning through a wooded path that separated two pastures, muttering to herself and hitting the ground methodically with a long stick she carried in case she saw a snake. "Mr. Greenleaf," she was saying in a low voice, "I cannot afford to pay for your mistakes. I am a poor woman and this place is all I have. I have two boys to educate. I cannot . . . ."

Out of nowhere a guttural agonized voice groaned, "Jesus! Jesus!" In a second it came again with a terrible urgency. "Jesus! Jesus!"

Mrs. May stopped still, one hand lifted to her throat. The sound was so piercing that she felt as if some violent unleashed force had broken out of the ground and was charging toward her. Her second thought was more reasonable: somebody had been hurt on the place and would sue her for everything she had. She had no insurance. She rushed forward and turning a bend in the path, she saw Mrs. Greenleaf sprawled on her hands and knees off the side of the road, her head down.

"Mrs. Greenleaf!" she shrilled, "what's happened?"

Mrs. Greenleaf raised her head. Her face was a patchwork of dirt and tears and her small eyes, the color of two field peas, were red-rimmed and swollen, but her expression was as composed as a bulldog's. She swayed back and forth on her hands and knees and groaned, "Jesus, Jesus."

Mrs. May winced. She thought the word, Jesus, should be kept inside the church building like other words inside the bedroom. She was a good Christian woman with a large respect for religion, though she did not, of course, believe any of it was true. "What is the matter with you?" she asked sharply.

"You broken my healing," Mrs. Greenleaf said, waving her aside. "I can't talk to you until I finish."

Mrs. May stood, bent forward, her mouth open and her stick raised off the ground as if she were not sure what she wanted to strike with it.

"Oh Jesus, stab me in the heart!" Mrs. Greenleaf shrieked. "Jesus, stab me in the heart!" and she fell back flat in the dirt, a huge human mound, her legs and arms spread out as if she were trying to wrap them around the earth.

Mrs. May felt as furious and helpless as if she had been insulted by a child. "Jesus," she said, drawing herself back, "would be *ashamed* of you. He would tell you to get up from there this instant and go wash your children's clothes!" and she had turned and walked off as fast as she could.

Whenever she thought of how the Greenleaf boys had advanced in the world, she had only to think of Mrs. Greenleaf sprawled obscenely on the ground, and say to herself, "Well, no matter how far they *go*, they *came* from that."

She would like to have been able to put in her will that when she died, Wesley and Scofield were not to continue to employ Mr. Greenleaf. She was capable of handling Mr. Greenleaf; they were not. Mr. Greenleaf had pointed out to her once that her boys didn't know hay from silage. She had pointed out to him that they had other talents, that Scofield was a successful business man and Wesley a successful intellectual. Mr. Greenleaf did not comment, but he never lost an opportunity of letting her see, by his expression or some simple gesture, that he held the two of them in infinite contempt. As scrub-human as the Greenleafs were, he never hesitated to let her know that in any like circumstance in which his own boys might have been involved, they—O. T. and E. T. Greenleaf—would have acted to better advantage.

The Greenleaf boys were two or three years younger than the May boys. They were twins and you never knew when you spoke to one of them whether you were speaking to O. T. or E. T., and they never had the politeness to enlighten you. They were long-legged and raw-boned and red-skinned, with bright grasping fox-colored eyes like their father's. Mr. Greenleaf's pride in them began with the fact that they were twins. He acted, Mrs. May said, as if this were something smart they had thought of themselves. They were energetic and hard working and she would admit to anyone that they had come a long way—and that the Second World War was responsible for it.

They had both joined the service and, disguised in their uniforms, they could not be told from other people's children. You could tell, of course, when they opened their mouths but they did that seldom. The smartest thing they had done was to get sent overseas and there to marry French wives. They hadn't married French trash either. They had married nice girls who naturally couldn't tell that they murdered the king's English or that the Greenleafs were who they were.

Wesley's heart condition had not permitted him to serve his country but Scofield had been in the army for two years. He had not cared for it and at the end of his military service, he was only a Private First Class. The Greenleaf boys were both some kind of sergeants, and Mr. Greenleaf, in those days, had never lost an opportunity of referring to them by their rank. They had both managed to get wounded and now they both had pensions. Further, as soon as they were released from the army, they took advantage of all the benefits and went to the school of agriculture at the university—the taxpayers meanwhile supporting their French wives. The two of them were living now about two miles down the highway on a piece of land that the government had helped them to buy and in a brick duplex bungalow that the government had helped to build and pay for. If the war had made anyone, Mrs. May said, it had made the Greenleaf boys. They each had three little children apiece, who spoke Greenleaf English and French, and who, on account of their mothers' background, would be sent to the convent school and brought up with manners. "And in twenty years," Mrs. May asked Scofield and Wesley, "do you know what those people will be?"

"*Society*," she said blackly.

She had spent fifteen years coping with Mr. Greenleaf and, by now, handling him had become second nature with her. His disposition on any particular day was as much a factor in what she could and couldn't do as the weather was, and she had learned to read his face the way real country people read the sunrise and sunset.

She was a country woman only by persuasion. The late Mr. May, a business man, had bought the place when land was down, and when he died it was all he had to leave her. The boys had not been happy to move to the country to a broken-down farm, but there was nothing else for her to do. She had the timber on the place cut and with the proceeds had set herself up in the dairy business after Mr. Greenleaf had answered her ad. "i seen yor ad and i will come have 2 boys," was all his letter said, but he arrived the next day in a pieced-together truck, his wife and five daughters sitting on the floor in back, himself and the two boys in the cab.

Over the years they had been on her place, Mr. and Mrs. Greenleaf had aged hardly at all. They had no worries, no responsibilities. They lived like the lilies of the field, off the fat that she struggled to put into the land. When she was dead and gone from overwork and worry, the Greenleafs, healthy and thriving, would be just ready to begin draining Scofield and Wesley.

Wesley said the reason Mrs. Greenleaf had not aged was because she released all her emotions in prayer healing. "You ought to start praying, Sweetheart," he had said in the voice that, poor boy, he could not help making deliberately nasty.

Scofield only exasperated her beyond endurance but Wesley caused her real anxiety. He was thin and nervous and bald and being an intellectual was a terrible strain on his disposition. She doubted if he would marry until she died but she was certain that then the wrong woman would get him. Nice girls didn't like Scofield but Wesley didn't like nice girls. He didn't like anything. He drove twenty miles every day to the university where he taught and twenty miles back every night, but he said he hated the twenty-mile drive and he hated the second-rate university and he hated the morons who attended it. He hated the country and he hated the life he lived; he hated living with his mother and his idiot brother and he hated hearing about the damn dairy and the damn help and the damn broken machinery. But in spite of all he said, he never made any move to leave. He talked about Paris and Rome but he never went even to Atlanta.

"You'd go to those places and you'd get sick," Mrs. May would say. "Who in Paris is going to see that you get a salt-free diet? And do you think if you married one of those odd numbers you take out that *she* would cook a salt-free diet for you? No, indeed, she would not!" When she took this line Wesley would turn himself roughly around in his chair and ignore her. Once when she had kept it up too long, he had snarled, "Well, why don't you do something practical, Woman? Why don't you pray for me like Mrs. Greenleaf would?"

"I don't like to hear you boys make jokes about religion," she had said. "If you would go to church, you would meet some nice girls."

But it was impossible to tell them anything. When she looked at the two of them now, sitting on either side of the table, neither one caring the least if a stray bull ruined her herd—which was their herd, their future—when she looked at the two of them, one hunched over a paper and the other teetering back in his chair, grinning at her like an idiot, she wanted to jump up and beat her fist on the table and shout, "You'll find out one of these days, you'll find out what *Reality* is when it's too late!"

"Mamma," Scofield said, "don't you get excited now but I'll tell you whose bull that is." He was looking at her wickedly. He let his chair drop forward and he got up. Then with his shoulders bent and his hands held up to cover his head, he tiptoed to the door. He backed into the hall and pulled the door almost to so that it hid all of him but his face. "You want to know, Sugarpie?" he asked.

Mrs. May sat looking at him coldly.

"That's O. T. and E. T.'s bull," he said. "I collected from their nigger yesterday and he told me they were missing it," and he showed her an exaggerated expanse of teeth and disappeared silently.

Wesley looked up and laughed.

Mrs. May turned her head forward again, her expression unaltered. "I am the only *adult* on this place," she said. She leaned across the table and pulled the paper from the side of his plate. "Do you see how it's going to be when I die and you boys have to handle him?" she began. "Do you see why he didn't know whose bull that was? Because it was theirs. Do you see what I have to put up with? Do you see that if I hadn't kept my foot on his neck all these years, you boys might be milking cows every morning at four o'clock?"

Wesley pulled the paper back toward his plate and staring at her full in the face, he murmured, "I wouldn't milk a cow to save your soul from hell."

"I know you wouldn't," she said in a brittle voice. She sat back and began rapidly turning her knife over at the side of her plate. "O. T. and E. T. are fine boys," she said. "They ought to have been my sons." The thought of this was so horrible that her vision of Wesley was blurred at once by a wall of tears. All she saw was his dark shape, rising quickly from the table. "And you two," she cried, "you two should have belonged to that woman!"

He was heading for the door.

"When I die," she said in a thin voice, "I don't know what's going to become of you."

"You're always yapping about when-you-die," he growled as he rushed out, "but you look pretty healthy to me."

For some time she sat where she was, looking straight ahead through the window across the room into a scene of indistinct greys and greens. She stretched her face and her neck muscles and drew in a long breath but the scene in front of her flowed together anyway into a watery grey mass. "They needn't think I'm going to die any time soon," she muttered, and some more defiant voice in her added: I'll die when I get good and ready.

She wiped her eyes with the table napkin and got up and went to the window and gazed at the scene in front of her. The cows were grazing on two pale green pastures across the road and behind them, fencing them in, was a black wall of trees with a sharp sawtooth edge that held off the indifferent sky. The pastures were enough to calm her. When she looked out any window in her house, she saw the reflection of her own character. Her city friends said she was the most remarkable woman they knew, to go, practically penniless and with no experience, out to a rundown farm and make a success of it. "Everything is against you," she would say, "the weather is against you and the dirt is against you and the help is against you. They're all in a league against you. There's nothing for it but an iron hand!"

"Look at Mamma's iron hand!" Scofield would yell and grab her arm and hold it up so that her delicate blue-veined little hand would dangle from her wrist like the head of a broken lily. The company always laughed.

The sun, moving over the black and white grazing cows, was just a little brighter than the rest of the sky. Looking down, she saw a darker shape that might have been its shadow cast at an angle, moving among them. She uttered a sharp cry and turned and marched out of the house.

Mr. Greenleaf was in the trench silo, filling a wheelbarrow. She stood on the edge and looked down at him. "I told you to get up that bull. Now he's in with the milk herd."

"You can't do two thangs at oncet," Mr. Greenleaf remarked.

"I told you to do that first."

He wheeled the barrow out of the open end of the trench toward the barn and she followed close behind him. "And you needn't think, Mr. Greenleaf," she said, "that I don't know exactly whose bull that is or why you haven't been in any hurry to notify me he was here. I might as well feed O. T. and E. T.'s bull as long as I'm going to have him here ruining my herd."

Mr. Greenleaf paused with the wheelbarrow and looked behind him. "Is that them boys' bull?" he asked in an incredulous tone.

She did not say a word. She merely looked away with her mouth taut.

"They told me their bull was out but I never known that was him," he said.

"I want that bull put up now," she said, "and I'm going to drive over to O. T. and E. T.'s and tell them they'll have to come get him today. I ought to charge for the time he's been here—then it wouldn't happen again."

"They didn't pay but seventy-five dollars for him," Mr. Greenleaf offered.

"I wouldn't have had him as a gift," she said.

"They was just going to beef him," Mr. Greenleaf went on, "but he got loose and run his head into their pickup truck. He don't like cars and trucks. They had a time getting his horn out the fender and when they finally got him loose, he took off and they was too tired to run after him—but I never known that was him there."

"It wouldn't have paid you to know, Mr. Greenleaf," she said. "But you know now. Get a horse and get him."

In a half hour, from her front window she saw the bull, squirrel-colored, with jutting hips and long light horns, ambling down the dirt road that ran in front of the house. Mr. Greenleaf was behind him on the horse. "That's a Greenleaf bull if I ever saw one," she muttered. She went out on the porch and called, "Put him where he can't get out."

"He likes to bust loose," Mr. Greenleaf said, looking with approval at the bull's rump. "This gentleman is a sport."

"If those boys don't come for him, he's going to be a dead sport," she said. "I'm just warning you."

He heard her but he didn't answer.

"That's the awfullest looking bull I ever saw," she called but he was too far down the road to hear.

It was mid-morning when she turned into O. T. and E. T.'s driveway. The house, a new red-brick, low-to-the-ground building that looked like a warehouse with windows, was on top of a treeless hill. The sun was beating down directly on the white roof of it. It was the kind of house that everybody built now and nothing marked it as belonging to Greenleafs except three dogs, part hound and part spitz, that rushed out from behind it as soon as she stopped her car. She reminded herself that you could always tell the class of people by the class of dog, and honked her horn. While she sat waiting for someone to come, she continued to study the house. All the windows were down and she wondered if the government could have air-conditioned the thing. No one came and she honked again. Presently a door opened and several children appeared in it and stood looking at her, making no move to come forward. She recognized this as a true Greenleaf trait—they could hang in a door, looking at you for hours.

"Can't one of you children come here?" she called.

After a minute they all began to move forward, slowly. They had on overalls and were barefooted but they were not as dirty as she might have expected. There were two or three that looked distinctly like Greenleafs; the others not so much so. The smallest child was a girl with untidy black hair. They stopped about six feet from the automobile and stood looking at her.

"You're mighty pretty," Mrs. May said, addressing herself to the smallest girl.

There was no answer. They appeared to share one dispassionate expression between them.

"Where's your Mamma?" she asked.

There was no answer to this for some time. Then one of them said something in French. Mrs. May did not speak French.

"Where's your daddy?" she asked.

After a while, one of the boys said, "He ain't hyar neither."

"Ahhhh," Mrs. May said as if something had been proven. "Where's the colored man?"

She waited and decided no one was going to answer. "The cat has six little tongues," she said "How would you like to come home with me and let me teach you how to talk?" She laughed and her laugh died on the silent air. She felt as if she were on trial for her life, facing a jury of Greenleafs. "I'll go down and see if I can find the colored man," she said.

"You can go if you want to," one of the boys said.

"Well, thank you," she murmured and drove off.

The barn was down the lane from the house. She had not seen it before but Mr. Greenleaf had described it in detail for it had been built according to the latest specifications. It was a milking parlor arrangement where cows are milked from below. The milk ran in pipes from the machines to the milk house and was never carried in no bucket, Mr. Greenleaf said, by no human hand. "When you gonter get you one?" he had asked.

"Mr. Greenleaf," she had said, "I have to do for myself. I am not assisted hand and foot by the government. It would cost me $20,000 to install a milking parlor. I barely make ends meet as it is."

"My boys done it," Mr. Greenleaf had murmured, and then—"but all boys ain't alike"

"No indeed!" she had said. "I thank God for that!"

"I thank Gawd for ever-thang," Mr. Greenleaf had drawled.

You might as well, she had thought in the fierce silence that followed; you've never done anything for yourself.

She stopped by the side of the barn and honked but no one appeared. For several minutes she sat in the car, observing the various machines parked around, wondering how many of them were paid for. They had a forage harvester and a rotary hay baler. She had those too. She decided that since no one was here, she would get out and have a look at the milking parlor and see if they kept it clean.

She opened the milking room door and stuck her head in and for the first second she felt as if she were going to lose her breath. The spotless white concrete room was filled with sunlight that came from a row of windows head-high along both walls. The metal stanchions gleamed ferociously and she had to squint to be able to look at all. She drew her head out the room quickly and closed the door and leaned against it, frowning. The light outside was not so bright but she was conscious that the sun was directly on top of her head, like a silver bullet ready to drop into her brain.

A Negro carrying a yellow calf-feed bucket appeared from around the corner of the machine shed and came toward her. He was a light yellow boy dressed in the cast-off army clothes of the Greenleaf twins. He stopped at a respectable distance and set the bucket on the ground.

"Where's Mr. O. T. and Mr. E. T.?" she asked.

"Mist O. T. he in town, Mist E. T. he off yonder in the field," the Negro said, pointing first to the left and then to the right as if he were naming the position of two planets.

"Can you remember a message?" she asked, looking as if she thought this doubtful.

"I'll remember it if I don't forget it," he said with a touch of sullenness.

"Well, I'll write it down then," she said. She got in her car and took a stub of pencil from her pocketbook and began to write on the back of an empty envelope. The Negro came and stood at the window. "I'm Mrs. May," she said as she wrote. "Their bull is on my place and I want him off *today*. You can tell them I'm furious about it."

"That bull lef here Sareday," the Negro said, "and none of us ain't seen him sence. We ain't knowed where he was."

"Well, you know now," she said, "and you can tell Mr. O. T. and Mr. E. T. that if they don't come get him today, I'm going to have their daddy shoot him the first thing in the morning. I can't have that bull ruining my herd." She handed him the note.

"If I knows Mist O. T. and Mist E. T.," he said, taking it, "they goin to say you go ahead on and shoot him. He done busted up one of our trucks already and we be glad to see the last of him."

She pulled her head back and gave him a look from slightly bleared eyes. "Do they expect me to take my time and my worker to shoot their bull?" she asked. "They don't want him so they just let him loose and expect somebody else to kill him? He's eating my oats and ruining my herd and I'm expected to shoot him too?"

"I speck you is," he said softly. "He done busted up . . . "

She gave him a very sharp look and said, "Well, I'm not surprised. That's just the way some people are," and after a second she asked, "Which is boss, Mr. O. T. or Mr. E. T.?" She had always suspected that they fought between themselves secretly.

"They never quarls," the boy said. "They like one man in two skins."

"Hmp. I expect you just never heard them quarrel."

"Nor nobody else heard them neither," he said, looking away as if this insolence were addressed to some one else.

"Well," she said, "I haven't put up with their father for fifteen years not to know a few things about Greenleafs."

The Negro looked at her suddenly with a gleam of recognition. "Is you my policy man's mother?" he asked.

"I don't know who your policy man is," she said sharply. "You give them that note and tell them if they don't come for that bull today, they'll be making their father shoot it tomorrow," and she drove off.

She stayed at home all after afternoon waiting for the Greenleaf twins to come for the bull. They did not come. I might as well be working for them, she thought furiously. They are simply going to use me to the limit. At the supper table, she went over it again for the boys' benefit because she wanted them to see exactly what O. T. and E. T. would do. "They don't want that bull" she said, "—pass the butter—so they simply turn him loose and let somebody else worry about getting rid of him for them. How do you like that? I'm the victim. I've always been the victim."

"Pass the butter to the victim." Wesley said. He was in a worse humor than usual because he had had a flat tire on the way home from the university.

Scofield handed her the butter and said, "Why Mamma, ain't you ashamed to shoot an old bull that ain't done nothing but give you a little scrub strain in your herd? I declare," he said, "with the Mamma I got it's a wonder I turned out to be such a nice boy!"

"You ain't her boy, Son," Wesley said.

She eased back in her chair, her fingertips on the edge of the table.

"All I know is," Scofield said, "I done mighty well to be as nice as I am seeing what I come from."

When they teased her they spoke Greenleaf English but Wesley made his own particular tone come through it like a knife edge. "Well lemme tell you one thang, Brother," he said, leaning over the table, "that if you had half a mind you would already know."

"What's that, Brother?" Scofield asked, his broad face grinning into the thin constricted one across from him.

"That is," Wesley said, "that neither you nor me is her boy . . .," but he stopped abruptly as she gave a kind of hoarse wheeze like an old horse lashed unexpectedly. She reared up and ran from the room.

"Oh, for God's sake," Wesley growled, "what did you start her off for?"

"I never started her off," Scofield said. "You started her off."

"Hah."

"She's not as young as she used to be and she can't take it."

"She can only give it out," Wesley said. "I'm the one that takes it."

His brother's pleasant face had changed so that an ugly family resemblance showed between them. "Nobody feels sorry for a lousy bastard like you," he said and grabbed across the table for the other's shirtfront.

From her room she heard a crash of dishes and she rushed back through the kitchen into the dining room. The hall door was open and Scofield was going out of it. Wesley was lying like a large bug on his back with the edge of the over-turned table cutting him across the middle and broken dishes scattered on top of him. She pulled the table off him and caught his arm to help him rise but he scrambled up and pushed her off with a furious charge of energy and flung himself out of the door after his brother.

She would have collapsed but a knock on the back door stiffened her and she swung around. Across the kitchen and back porch, she could see Mr. Greenleaf peering eagerly through the screenwire. All her resources returned in full strength as if she had only needed to be challenged by the devil himself to regain them. "I heard a thump," he called, "and I thought the plastering might have fell on you."

If he had been wanted someone would have had to go on a horse to find him. She crossed the kitchen and the porch and stood inside the screen and said, "No, nothing happened but the table turned over. One of the legs was weak," and without pausing, "the boys didn't come for the bull so tomorrow you'll have to shoot him."

The sky was crossed with thin red and purple bars and behind them the sun was moving down slowly as if it were descending a ladder. Mr. Greenleaf squatted down on the step, his back to her, the top of his hat on a level with her feet. "Tomorrow I'll drive him home for you," he said.

"Oh no, Mr. Greenleaf," she said in a mocking voice, "you drive him home tomorrow and next week he'll be back here. I know better than that." Then in a mournful tone, she said, "I'm surprised at O. T. and E. T. to treat me this way. I thought they'd have more gratitude. Those boys spent some mighty happy days on this place, didn't they, Mr. Greenleaf?"

Mr. Greenleaf didn't say anything.

"I think they did," she said. "I think they did. But they've forgotten all the nice little things I did for them now. If I recall, they wore my boys' old clothes and played with my boys' old toys and hunted with my boys' old guns. They swam in my pond and shot my birds and fished in my stream and I never forgot their birthday and Christmas seemed to roll around very often if I remember it right. And do they think of any of those things now?" she asked. "NOOOOO," she said.

For a few seconds she looked at the disappearing sun and Mr. Greenleaf examined the palms of his hands. Presently as if it had just occurred to her, she asked, "Do you know the real reason they didn't come for that bull?"

"Naw I don't," Mr. Greenleaf said in a surly voice.

"They didn't come because I'm a woman," she said. "You can get away with anything when you're dealing with a woman. If there were a man running this place . . . "

Quick as a snake striking Mr. Greenleaf said, "You got two boys. They know you got two men on the place."

The sun had disappeared behind the tree line. She looked down at the dark crafty face, upturned now, and at the wary eyes, bright under the shadow of the hatbrim. She waited long enough for him to see that she was hurt and then she said, "Some people learn gratitude too late, Mr. Greenleaf, and some never learn it at all," and she turned and left him sitting on the steps.

Half the night in her sleep she heard a sound as if some large stone were grinding a hole on the outside wall of her brain. She was walking on the inside, over a succession of beautiful rolling hills, planting her stick in front of each step. She became aware after a time that the noise was the sun trying to burn through the tree line and she stopped to watch, safe in the knowledge that it couldn't, that it had to sink the way it always did outside of her property. When she first stopped it was a swollen red ball, but as she stood watching it began to narrow and pale until it looked like a bullet. Then suddenly it burst through the tree line and raced down the hill toward her. She woke up with her hand over her mouth and the same noise, diminished but distinct, in her ear. It was the bull munching under her window. Mr. Greenleaf had let him out.

She got up and made her way to the window in the dark and looked out through the slit blind, but the bull had moved away from the hedge and at first she didn't see him. Then she saw a heavy form some distance away, paused as if observing her. This is the last night I am going to put up with this, she said, and watched until the iron shadow moved away in the darkness.

The next morning she waited until exactly eleven o'clock. Then she got in her car and drove to the barn. Mr. Greenleaf was cleaning milk cans. He had seven of them standing up outside the milk room to get the sun. She had been telling him to do this for two weeks. "All right, Mr. Greenleaf," she said, "go get your gun. We're going to shoot that bull."

"I thought you wanted theseyer cans . . ."

"Go get your gun, Mr. Greenleaf," she said. Her voice and face were expressionless.

"That gentleman torn out of there last night," he murmured in a tone of regret and bent again to the can he had his arm in.

"Go get your gun, Mr. Greenleaf," she said in the same triumphant toneless voice. "The bull is in the pasture with the dry cows. I saw him from my upstairs window. I'm going to drive you up to the field and you can run him into the empty pasture and shoot him there."

He detached himself from the can slowly. "Ain't nobody ever ast me to shoot my boys' own bull!" he said in a high rasping voice. He removed a rag from his back pocket and began to wipe his hands violently, then his nose.

She turned as if she had not heard this and said, "I'll wait for you in the car. Go get your gun."

She sat in the car and watched him stalk off toward the harness room where he kept a gun. After he had entered the room, there was a crash as if he had kicked something out of his way. Presently he emerged again with the gun, circled behind the car, opened the door violently and threw himself onto the seat beside her. He held the gun between his knees and looked straight ahead. He'd like to shoot me instead of the bull, she thought, and turned her face away so that he could not see her smile.

The morning was dry and clear. She drove through the woods for a quarter of a mile and then out into the open where there were fields on either side of the narrow road. The exhilaration of carrying her point had sharpened her senses. Birds were screaming everywhere, the grass was almost too bright to look at, the sky was an even piercing blue. "Spring is here!" she said gaily. Mr. Greenleaf lifted one muscle somewhere near his mouth as if he found this the most asinine remark ever made. When she stopped at the second pasture gate, he flung himself out of the car door and slammed it behind him. Then he opened the gate and she drove through. He closed it and flung himself back in, silently, and she drove around the rim of the pasture until she spotted the bull, almost in the center of it, grazing peacefully among the cows.

"The gentleman is waiting on you," she said and gave Mr. Greenleaf's furious profile a sly look. "Run him into that next pasture and when you get him in, I'll drive in behind you and shut the gate myself."

He flung himself out again, this time deliberately leaving the car door open so that she had to lean across the seat and close it. She sat smiling as she watched him make his way across the pasture toward the opposite gate. He seemed to throw himself forward at each step and then pull back as if he were calling on some power to witness that he was being forced. "Well," she said aloud as if he were still in the car, "it's your own boys who are making you do this, Mr. Greenleaf." O. T. and E. T. were probably splitting their sides laughing at him now. She could hear their identical nasal voices saying, "Made Daddy shoot our bull for us. Daddy don't know no better than to think that's a fine bull he's shooting. Gonna kill Daddy to shoot that bull!"

"If those boys cared a thing about you, Mr. Greenleaf," she said, "they would have come for that bull. I'm surprised at them."

He was circling around to open the gate first. The bull, dark among the spotted cows, had not moved. He kept his head down, eating constantly. Mr. Greenleaf opened the gate and then began circling back to approach him from the rear. When he was about ten feet behind him, he flapped his arms at his sides. The bull lifted his head indolently and then lowered it again and continued to eat. Mr. Greenleaf stooped again and picked up something and threw it at him with a vicious swing. She decided it was a sharp rock for the bull leapt and then began to gallop until he disappeared over the rim of the hill. Mr. Greenleaf followed at his leisure.

"You needn't think you're going to lose him!" she cried and started the car straight across the pasture. She had to drive slowly over the terraces and when she reached the gate, Mr. Greenleaf and the bull were nowhere in sight. This pasture was smaller than the last, a green arena, encircled almost entirely by woods. She got out and closed the gate and stood looking for some sign of Mr. Greenleaf but he had disappeared completely. She knew at once that his plan was to lose the bull in the woods. Eventually, she would see him emerge somewhere from the circle of trees and come limping toward her and when he finally reached her, he would say, "If you can find that gentleman in them woods, you're better than me."

She was going to say, "Mr. Greenleaf, if I have to walk into those woods with you and stay all afternoon, we are going to find that bull and shoot him. You are going to shoot him if I have to pull the trigger for you." When he saw she meant business he would return and shoot the bull quickly himself.

She got back into the car and drove to the center of the pasture where he would not have so far to walk to reach her when he came out of the woods. At this moment she could picture him sitting on a stump, marking the lines in the ground with a stick. She decided she would wait exactly ten minutes by her watch. Then she would begin to honk. She got out of the car and walked around a little and then sat down on the front bumper to wait and rest. She was very tired and she lay her head back against the hood and closed her eyes. She did not understand why she should be so tired when it was only mid-morning. Through her closed eyes, she could feel the sun, red-hot overhead. She opened her eyes slightly but the white light forced her to close them again.

For some time she lay back against the hood, wondering drowsily why she was so tired. With her eyes closed, she didn't think of time as divided into days and nights but into past and future. She decided she was tired because she had been working continuously for fifteen years. She decided she had every right to be tired, and to rest for a few minutes before she began working again. Before any kind of judgement seat, she would be able to say: I've worked, I have not wallowed. At this very instant while she was recalling a lifetime of work, Mr. Greenleaf was loitering in the woods and Mrs. Greenleaf was probably flat on the ground, asleep over her holeful of clippings. The woman had got worse over the years and Mrs. May believed that now she was actually demented. "I'm afraid your wife has let religion warp her," she said once tactfully to Mr. Greenleaf. "Everything in moderation, you know."

"She cured a man oncet that half his gut was eat out with worms," Mr. Greenleaf said, and she had turned away, half sickened. Poor souls, she thought now, so simple. For a few seconds she dozed.

When she sat up and looked at her watch, more than ten minutes had passed. She had not heard any shot. A new thought occurred to her: suppose Mr. Greenleaf had aroused the bull chunking stones at him and the animal had turned on him and run him up against a tree and gored him? The irony of it deepened: O. T. and E. T. would then get a shyster laywer and sue her. It would be the fitting end to her fifteen years with the Greenleafs. She thought of it almost with pleasure as if she had hit on the perfect ending for a story she was telling her friends. Then she dropped it, for Mr. Greenleaf had a gun with him and she had insurance.

She decided to honk. She got up and reached inside the car window and gave three sustained honks and two or three shorter ones to let him know she was getting impatient. Then she went back and sat down on the bumper again.

In a few minutes something emerged from the tree line, a black heavy shadow that tossed its head several times and then bounded forward. After a second she saw it was the bull. He was crossing the pasture toward her at a slow gallop, a gay almost rocking gait as if he were overjoyed to find her again. She looked beyond him to see if Mr. Greenleaf was coming out of the woods too but he was not. "Here he is, Mr. Greenleaf!" she called and looked on the other side of the pasture to see if he could be coming out there but he was not in sight. She looked back and saw that the bull, his head lowered, was racing toward her. She remained perfectly still, not in fright, but in a freezing unbelief. She stared at the violent black streak bounding toward her as if she had no sense of distance, as if she could not decide at once what his intention was, and the bull had buried his head in her lap, like a wild tormented lover, before her expression changed. One of his horns sank until it pierced her heart and the other curved around her side and held her in an unbreakable grip. She continued to stare straight ahead but the entire scene in front of her had changed—the tree line was a dark wound in a world that was nothing but sky—and she had the look of a person whose sight has been suddenly restored but who finds the light unbearable.

Mr. Greenleaf was running toward her from the side with his gun raised and she saw him coming though she was not looking in his direction. She saw him approaching on the outside of some invisible circle, the tree line gaping behind him and nothing under his feet. He shot the bull four times through the eye. She did not hear the shots but she felt the quake in the huge body as it sank, pulling her forward on its head, so that she seemed, when Mr. Greenleaf reached her, to be bent over whispering some last discovery into the animal's ear.

# Epilogue

There is a symmetry in the myths of Narcissus, Dionysos, Orpheus and Christ, a certain rightness is seeing them as parts of a single great commentary on the human psyche. There is a rightness, too, in looking at the myths not in some dessicated paraphrased form, but in living literature; for all myths need to take on new shapes and new words if they are to remain alive. Literature is most particularly suited to giving myths new life, since it shares something of the nature of the four mythic figures discussed here.

Narcissus is the impulse to rediscover the unity of being. The primary language of literature is symbol and metaphor, both of which unite and assemble disparate ideas and themes. Literature associates what is ordinarily and insensitively disassociated. In a sense, literature is Narcissistic.

Dionysos is the daring to leave the security of the commonplace and enter the challenge of the unusual. Literature will not be domesticated, it will pursue differentness, madness, strangeness, the tabooed lands—the Heathcliffs, the Roskalnikofs, the Iagos, the Fausts. In this sense literature is Dionysiac.

Orpheus comes back to the upper world, he bridges the strange and the familiar, the two domains of the mysterious and the lucid. Literature, by affixing words to visions, moods, passions, the whole spectrum of experience, creates passageways between the ineffable and the expressible. In this sense, literature is Orphic.

Christ symbolizes wholeness, the unity of matter and spirit. Literature, revealing universal themes within particular situations, by "seeing the universe in a grain of sand," by recognizing Everyman in every man, by having ideas engrained in quantified, measurable syllables, is itself a kind of incarnation. In a sense, literature is Christlike.

But in the very "mythicness" of literature, there is a snare, a temptation to let the myth swallow the literature. If a fictional hero undertakes a fearsome journey, it is not enough to simply say "Orpheus!" and put the critical imagination to rest. To recognize Dionysos in a contemporary novel or Narcissus in a poem is not enough. The object is not to put the work of literature in a mythological cage. That is not it, that is not it at all. Within a true myth is a theme, an insightful and important theme; but only a theme. And a theme without a lively image, without movement, manners, speech, is dead, conceptual geometry without a soul. Recognizing the myth within a work of literature is only the beginning. How does the author vivify the theme, how does he structure his material to remake the myth? The strength of a Brautigan, a Conrad, a Dickey, an O'Connor is not that they incorporate myths within their work, but that they revive the myths with all their literary craft. Myth criticism is not reductionist, shrinking literature to fit a mythological mode. Rather, such criticism can lead to a more informed awareness of both the myth *and* the literature, each nourishing the other.

The companionship of myth, literature and self-awareness is dynamic—being open to one encourages openness to all. That's just the way it is.

# INDEX